App Inventor
Create Your Own Android Apps

David Wolber, Hal Abelson,
Ellen Spertus & Liz Looney

O'REILLY®

Beijing · Cambridge · Farnham · Köln · Sebastopol · Tokyo

App Inventor
by David Wolber, Hal Abelson, Ellen Spertus & Liz Looney

Published by O'Reilly Media, Inc., 1005 Gravenstein Highway North, Sebastopol, CA 95472.

O'Reilly books may be purchased for educational, business, or sales promotional use. Online editions are also available for most titles (*safari.oreilly.com*). For more information, contact our corporate/institutional sales department: 800-998-9938 or *corporate@oreilly.com*.

Editors: Courtney Nash and Brian Jepson	**Indexer:** Denise Getz
Production Editor: Holly Bauer	**Cover Designer:** Mark Paglietti
Copyeditor: Rachel Monaghan	**Interior Designer:** Ron Bilodeau
Proofreader: Holly Bauer	**Illustrator:** Robert Romano

Printing History:

April 2011: First Edition.

978-1-4493-9748-7

[TI]

For Tomás, who reinvents me every day.

Contents

Part II.   Inventor's Manual

Foreword

Our consumer culture gives us all sorts of opportunities for entertainment, pleasure and sometimes even learning. However, by and large, these are passive activities. That's OK—we all like to kick back sometimes and be entertained—but it shouldn't be the whole picture. In addition to the appeal of consuming, there's the satisfaction of producing—that is, of creating. It's the joy and pride that results when we draw a picture, build a model airplane, or bake some bread.

The high-tech objects (like cell phones, tablet computers, TVs, etc.) that we use today to consume entertainment and information are black boxes to most of us. Their workings are incomprehensible and, while there are capabilities in some of them that enable the user to draw pictures, make videos, etc., they are not, in and of themselves, creative media. In other words, most people can't create the apps that run on these gadgets.

What if we could change that? What if we could take creative control of our everyday gadgets, like cell phones? What if building an app for your cell phone was as easy as drawing a picture or baking a loaf of bread? What if we could close the gap between the objects of our consumer culture and the media of our creative lives?

For one, it could demystify those objects. Rather than being black boxes, impenetrable to our sight, they become objects that can be tinkered with. They become objects capable of our understanding. We gain a less passive and more creative relationship to them, and we get to play with these devices in a much deeper, more significant way when we can actually build things for them.

When Hal Abelson first spoke to me about the idea that became App Inventor, we talked about the unique motivating force that cell phones could have in education. He wondered if we could use that motivating force to help introduce students to concepts in computer science. As we built it and tried it in classes like Dave Wolber's, we started to realize that something even more powerful was happening: App Inventor was starting to turn students from consumers to creators. Students thought it was fun and exhilarating to build apps for their phones! When one of Dave's students built the simple but powerful "No Texting While Driving" app, we really started to imagine what would happen if anybody, not just professional software engineers, could build an app.

So we worked hard to make App Inventor easier and more fun to use. We've worked to make it more powerful (but still simple) as well. And we're continuing this work—App Inventor is still a beta product and we have exciting plans for it.

The authors of this book are truly world-class educators and software engineers. I'd like to personally thank them for their work in building, testing, and documenting the App Inventor for Android product and, of course, for writing this wonderful book.

Now go, unleash your creativity and build an app!

—Mark Friedman
Tech Lead and Manager of the App Inventor for Android project, Google

Preface

You're on your regular running route, just jogging along, and an idea for the next killer mobile app hits you. All the way home, you don't even care what your time is, all you can think about is getting your idea out there. But how exactly do you do that? You're no programmer, and that would take years, and time is money, and…well, someone has probably done it already anyway. Just like that, your idea is dead in the water.

Now imagine a different world, where creating apps doesn't require years of programming experience, where artists, scientists, humanitarians, health-care workers, attorneys, firefighters, marathon runners, football coaches, and people from all walks of life can create apps. Imagine a world where you can transform ideas into prototypes without hiring programmers, where you can make apps that work specifically for you, where you can adapt mobile computing to fit your personal needs.

This is the world of App Inventor, Google's new visual programming tool for building mobile apps. Based on a visual "blocks" programming method that's proven successful even with kids, App Inventor dramatically lowers the barriers to creating apps for Android phones and devices. How about a video game where the characters look like you and your friends? Or a "did you pick up the milk?" app that reminds you if it's after 3 p.m. and you're near the grocery store? Or a quiz app you give your significant other that's in fact a surprise marriage proposal? "Question 4: Will you marry me? Press the button to accept by sending a text message." Someone really created an App Inventor app to propose marriage like this, and she said yes!

A Blocks Language for Mobile Phones

App Inventor is a visual, drag-and-drop tool for building mobile apps on the Android platform. You design the user interface (the visual appearance) of an app using a web-based graphical user interface (GUI) builder, then you specify the app's behavior by piecing together "blocks" as if you were working on a puzzle.

Figure 0-1 shows the blocks for an early version of an app created by Daniel Finnegan, a university student who had never programmed before. Can you tell what the app does?

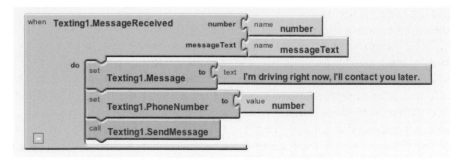

Figure 0-1. App Inventor blocks specify the functionality of your app

The app is a text "answering machine." You launch it when you're driving and it auto-responds to the texts you receive.

Because the blocks are more understandable than traditional programming code, you're immediately drawn in, and the real-world utility gets you asking questions like: Can I make it so the received texts are spoken aloud? Can I make it so the response sent back could be customized? Can I write an app that lets people vote for something by text, like on American Idol? The answer to all these questions is "yes," and in this book, we'll show you how.

What Can You Do with App Inventor?

Play

Creating apps for your phone is fun, and App Inventor promotes exploration and discovery. Just open App Inventor in a web browser, connect your phone, and start putting together blocks like those in Figure 0-1. You can immediately see and interact with the app you're building on the phone. So you're programming, but you're also emailing your friend to send you a text to test your app, or you're controlling a LEGO NXT robot with the app you just built, or you're unplugging the phone and walking outside to see if your app is using the location sensor correctly.

Prototype

Have an idea for an app? Instead of writing it down on a napkin or letting it float off into the ether, build a quick prototype. Prototypes are incomplete and unrefined working models of your idea. Expressing an idea in text is like writing a to a friend or loved one with prose; think of an App Inventor prototype as poetry to a venture capitalist. In this way, App Inventor can serve as an electronic napkin for mobile app development.

Build apps with personal utility

> In the current state of the mobile app world, we're stuck with the apps we're given. Who hasn't complained about an app and wished it could be personalized or adjusted in some way? With App Inventor, you can build an app exactly how you want it. In Chapter 3, you'll build a MoleMash game that lets you score points by touching a randomly moving mole. But instead of using the image of the mole in the tutorial, you can customize it so that you mash a picture of your brother or sister—something that only you might want to do, but who cares? In Chapter 8, you'll write a quiz app that asks questions about US Presidents, but you can easily customize it to ask questions on any topic you want, from your favorite music to your family history.

Develop complete apps

> App Inventor is not just a prototyping system or an interface designer—you can build complete, general-purpose apps. The language provides all the fundamental programming building blocks like loops and conditionals, but in block form.

Teach and learn

> Whether you're at a middle school, high school, or university, App Inventor is a great teaching and learning tool. It's great for computer science, but is also a terrific tool for math, physics, entrepreneurship, and just about any other discipline. The key is that you learn by creating. Instead of memorizing formulas, you build an app to, say, find the closest hospital (or mall!). Instead of writing an essay on Black History, you create a multimedia quiz app with video and speeches from Martin Luther King, Jr., and Malcolm X. We think App Inventor, and this book, can be a great tool in classes throughout the curriculum.

Why App Inventor Works

Most people say that App Inventor is easy to use because of its visual, drag-and-drop interface. But what does this mean? Why is App Inventor so easy to use?

You don't have to remember and type instructions

> One of the biggest sources of frustration for beginning programmers comes from typing in code and having the computer spit back indecipherable error messages. This frustration discourages many beginners from programming before they even get to the more fun, logical problem solving.

You choose from a set of options

> With App Inventor, the components and blocks are organized into drawers that are readily available to you. You program by finding a block—which helps specify the functionality you want to build—and dragging it into the program. You don't have to remember what the instructions are or refer to a programming manual.

Only some blocks plug in to each other

Instead of chastising programmers with cryptic error messages, App Inventor's blocks language restricts you from making many mistakes in the first place. For instance, if a function block expects a number, you can't plug in text. This doesn't eliminate all errors, but it sure helps.

You deal with events directly

Traditional programming languages were designed when programming was like working with recipes, or sets of instructions. But with graphical interfaces, and especially with mobile apps where events can happen at any time (for example, receiving a text message or phone call), most programs are not recipes, but are instead sets of event handlers. An event handler is a way of saying, "When this happens, the app does this." In a traditional language like Java, you have to understand classes, objects, and special objects called listeners to express a simple event. With App Inventor, you can say, "When a user clicks this button..." or "When a text is received..." by dragging out a "When" block.

What Kind of Apps Can You Build?

You can build many different types of apps with App Inventor. Use your imagination, and you can create all kinds of fun, useful apps.

Games

People often begin by building games like MoleMash (Chapter 3) or apps that let you draw funny pictures on your friend's faces (Chapter 2). As you progress, you can build your own versions of more complex games like Pac-Man and Space Invaders. You can even use the phone's sensors and move characters by tilting the phone (Chapter 5).

Educational software

App building is not limited to simple games. You can also build apps that inform and educate. You can create a quiz app (Chapter 8) to help you and your classmates study for a test, or even a create-a-quiz app (Chapter 10) that lets the users of your app create their own quizzes (think of all the parents that would love this one for those long road trips!).

Location-aware apps

Because App Inventor provides access to a GPS-location sensor, you can build apps that know where you are. You can build an app to help you remember where you parked your car (Chapter 7), an app that shows the location of your friends or colleagues at a concert or conference, or your own custom tour app of your school, workplace, or a museum.

High-tech apps

You can create apps that scan bar codes, talk, listen (recognize words), play music, make music (Chapter 9), play video, detect the phone's orientation and acceleration, take pictures, and make phone calls. Smartphones are like Swiss-Army knives for technology, and a group of Google engineers has dedicated themselves to making that technology easy to control through App Inventor.

SMS apps

"No Texting While Driving" (Chapter 4) is just one example of the SMS processing apps you can build. You can also write an app that periodically texts "missing you" to your loved ones, or an app like "Broadcast Hub" (Chapter 11) that helps coordinate large events. Want an app that lets your friends vote for things by texting, like on American Idol? You can build it with App Inventor.

Apps that control robots

Chapter 12 shows how to create an app that acts as a controller for a LEGO robot. You can use the phone as a remote control, or you can program it to be a "brain" that the robot carries around with it. The robot and phone communicate via Bluetooth, and App Inventor's Bluetooth components let you create similar apps that control other Bluetooth devices.

Complex apps

App Inventor dramatically lowers the entrance barrier to programming and lets you build flashy, high-tech apps within hours. But the language also provides loops, conditionals, and other programming and logic constructs necessary to build apps with complex logic. You'll be surprised at how fun such logic problems can be when you're trying to build an app.

Web-enabled apps

App Inventor also provides a way for your apps to communicate with the Web. You can write apps that pull in data from Twitter or an RSS feed, or an Amazon Bookstore Browser that lets you check the online cost of a book by scanning its barcode.

Who Can Build Apps?

App Inventor is freely available for anyone to use. It runs online (instead of directly on your computer) and is accessible from any browser. You don't even need a phone to use it: you can test your apps on an included Android emulator. As of January 2011, there were tens of thousands of active App Inventor users and hundreds of thousands of apps.

Who are these app builders? Were they already programmers when they started? Some of them were, but most were not. One of the most telling experiences has been the courses that coauthor David Wolber taught at the University of San Francisco. At

USF, App Inventor is taught as part of a general education computer science course targeting primarily business and humanities students. Many students take the course because they either hate or are afraid of math, and the course fulfills the dreaded Math Core requirement. The vast majority have never even dreamed of writing a computer program.

Despite their lack of prior experience, the students have been successful in learning App Inventor and building great apps. An English major created the first "No Texting While Driving" app; two communications majors created "Android, Where's My Car?"; and an International Studies major created the "BroadcastHub" app (Chapter 11). When an art major knocked on Wolber's office door one night well after hours, asking how to write a while loop, he knew that App Inventor had dramatically changed the landscape.

The media grasped the significance as well. The *New York Times* called App Inventor "Do-It-Yourself App Creation Software." The *San Francisco Chronicle* reported on the USF students' work in an article, "Google brings app making to the masses." Wired magazine featured Daniel Finnegan, the author of "No Texting While Driving," and wrote that "Finnegan's story illustrates a powerful point: It's time for computer programming to be democratized."

The cat is, as they say, out of the bag (your first app will involve a kitty, by the way). App Inventor is now used in high school courses; in the Technovation Challenge, a San Francisco Bay Area after-school program for high school girls; the Lakeside School in Seattle; and in new introductory courses at several universities. There are now thousands of hobbyists, businesspersons, marriage-proposers, and tinkerers roaming the App Inventor site and forum (*http://appinventor.googlelabs.com/forum/*). Want to get in on the action? No programming experience is required!

Conventions Used in This Book

This book uses the following typographical conventions:

Bold, green text
> Used to refer to program blocks that appear in App Inventor programs.

Italic
> Used to indicate email addresses, URLs, filenames, pathnames, and to emphasize terms when they're first introduced.

`Constant width`
> Indicates Python code and component, property, variable, and function names.

This icon signifies instructions for testing the app being developed.

 This icon indicates a tip, suggestion, or general note.

How to Use This Book

This book can be used as a textbook for middle school, high school, and university courses or as a how-to guide for aspiring app developers. The book is split into two sections: a set of tutorials for building specific apps, and an Inventor's Manual section organized more like a typical programming textbook. The tutorials progress in complexity as you go, from "Hello Purr" in Chapter 1—which lets you click a cat to make it meow—to a web-enabled app that lets you scan a book to view information from the Amazon web service (Chapter 13).

Working through the tutorials in order is advantageous from a conceptual viewpoint, but as you start to feel comfortable with the system, you may want to jump around. The tutorials provide step-by-step instructions and snapshots of the blocks to help, and you'll be referred to chapters in the Inventor's Manual section to help solidify your understanding of the concepts.

One advantage of having a book at hand is that the App Inventor environment takes up most of your computer screen, so there's not really room for an on-screen tutorial window. We envision folks setting the book next to them as they walk through the tutorials and build each app. Then, we hope, people will be so engrossed that they'll use the book away from the computer, to read the more conceptual Inventor's Manual chapters.

For teachers and students, the book can serve as a textbook for an introductory computer science course, or as a resource for any course in which students learn by building. In our experience, a sequence of tutorial→discussion→creativity works best. So you might first assign the task of completing a couple of the apps in the tutorial chapters, with the minimal expectation of the students mechanically building the apps. Then you can assign a chapter from the Inventor's Manual section and slow the process down with some in-class discussion and lecture. The third phase encourages exploration: have the students build some of the suggested variations at the end of each tutorial, without detailed instruction, and then follow this up with a creative assignment in which students come up with their own ideas for apps and then implement them.

You can also download files for each chapter, along with complete code samples, here: *http://examples.oreilly.com/0636920016632/.*

Acknowledgments

The educational perspective that motivates App Inventor holds that computing can be a vehicle for engaging powerful ideas through active learning. As such, App Inventor is part of an ongoing movement in computers and education that began with the work of Seymour Papert and the MIT Logo Group in the 1960s, and whose influence persists today through many activities and programs designed to support computational thinking.

App Inventor's design draws upon prior research in educational computing and upon Google's work with online development environments. The visual programming framework is closely related to the MIT Scratch programming language. The specific implementation here is based on Open Blocks, which is distributed by MIT's Scheller Teacher Education Program and derives from MIT thesis research by Ricarose Roque. We thank Eric Klopfer and Daniel Wendel of the Scheller Program for making Open Blocks available and for their assistance in working with it. The compiler that translates the visual blocks language for implementation on Android uses the Kawa Language Framework and Kawa's dialect of the Scheme programming language, developed by Per Bothner and distributed as part of the GNU Operating System by the Free Software Foundation.

The authors would like to thank Google and the App Inventor team for their support of our work and teaching efforts at USF, Mills College, and MIT. Special thanks go to App Inventor Technical Lead Mark Friedman, Project Manager Karen Parker, and engineers Sharon Perl and Debby Wallach.

We also owe a special thanks to our O'Reilly editors, Courtney Nash and Brian Jepson, as well as Kathy Riutzel, Brian Kernighan, Debby Wallach, and Rafiki Cai for their feedback and insights.

Finally, we'd like to acknowledge the support of our respective spouses: Ellen's husband, Keith Golden; Hal's wife, Lynn Abelson; Liz's husband, Kevin Looney; and David's wife, Minerva Novoa. New mother Ellen is also grateful for the help of nanny Neil Fullagar.

CHAPTER 1

Hello Purr

This chapter gets you started building apps. It presents the key elements of App Inventor—the Component Designer and the Blocks Editor—and leads you through the basic steps of creating your first app, HelloPurr. When you're finished, you'll be ready to build apps on your own.

A typical first program with a new computer system prints the message "Hello World" to show that everything is connected correctly. This tradition goes back to the 1970s and Brian Kernighan's work on the C programming language at Bell Labs (Brian is now a visiting scholar at Google working on the App Inventor team!). With App Inventor, even the simplest apps do more than just show messages: they play sounds and react when you touch the phone. So we're going to get started right away with something more exciting; your first app (as shown in Figure 1-1) will be "HelloPurr," a picture of a cat that meows when you touch it and purrs when you shake it.

Figure 1-1. The HelloPurr app

What You'll Learn

The chapter covers the following topics:

- Building apps by selecting components and then telling them what to do and when to do it.

- Using the Component Designer to select components. Some components are visible on the phone screen and some aren't.

- Adding media (sounds and images) to apps by uploading them from your computer.

- Working in the Blocks Editor to assemble blocks that define the components' behavior.

- Testing apps with App Inventor's *live testing*. This lets you see how apps will look and behave on the phone step by step, even as you're building them.

- Packaging the apps you build and downloading them to a phone.

The App Inventor Environment

You can set up App Inventor using the instructions at *http://appinventor.googlelabs .com/learn/setup/*. App Inventor runs primarily through the browser, but you need to download some software to your computer's desktop and change some settings on your phone. Typically you can get set up in just a few minutes, though sometimes there are issues with setting up device drivers for particular Android phones. If you have any phone issues, we suggest you get started using the Android emulator that comes packaged with the App Inventor download.

The App Inventor programming environment has three key parts, all shown in Figure 1-2:

- The *Component Designer*, shown on the left side of Figure 1-2, runs in your browser window. You use it to select components for your app and specify their properties.

- The *Blocks Editor* runs in a window separate from the Component Designer—it is often easiest to arrange this to the right of the Component Designer on your screen while you are working on your app. You use the Blocks Editor to create behaviors for the components.

- A phone allows you to actually run and test your app as you are developing it. If you don't have an Android phone handy, you can test the apps you build using the Android emulator (shown in the bottom right of Figure 1-2) that comes integrated with the system.

Figure 1-2. The Component Designer, Blocks Editor, and Android emulator

You start App Inventor by browsing to *http://appinventor.googlelabs.com*. If this is the first time you've used App Inventor, you'll see the Projects page, which will be mostly blank because you haven't created any projects yet. To create a project, click New at the top left of the page, enter the project name "HelloPurr" (one word with no spaces), and click OK.

The first window that opens is the Component Designer. When it appears, click Open Blocks Editor in the menu at the top right. The Blocks Editor comes up in a separate window, aided by a tool called Java Web Start. (You don't have to worry about all the Java messages—App Inventor is using Java, which should already be installed on your computer, to help launch the Blocks Editor.) This process usually takes about 30 seconds.

If everything is OK, the Blocks Editor will appear and you'll see two buttons near the top right of the screen, as shown in Figure 1-3.

Figure 1-3. Plug a phone into your computer or click "New emulator"; then, click "Connect to Device"

If you have an Android phone and a USB cable, plug the phone into the computer and select "Connect to Device." If instead you want to test the apps you build using an emulator, click "New emulator" and wait about 30 seconds while the Android emulator loads. When it is fully operational, click "Connect to Device" so that App Inventor will run your app in the emulator.

If all is well, you should see a window for the Component Designer, a window for the Blocks Editor, and the emulator window if you chose that option (your screen should look something like Figure 1-2, shown previously, but with the windows mostly empty). If you're having problems here, review the setup instructions at *http://app inventor.googlelabs.com/learn/setup/*.

Designing the Components

The first tool you'll use is the Component Designer (or just *Designer*). *Components* are the elements you combine to create apps, like ingredients in a recipe. Some components are very simple, like a Label component, which shows text on the screen, or a Button component, which you tap to initiate an action. Other components are more elaborate: a drawing Canvas that can hold still images or animations; an accelerometer, a motion sensor that works like a Wii controller and detects when you move or shake the phone; or components that make or send text messages, play music and video, get information from websites, and so on.

When you open the Designer, it will appear as shown in Figure 1-4.

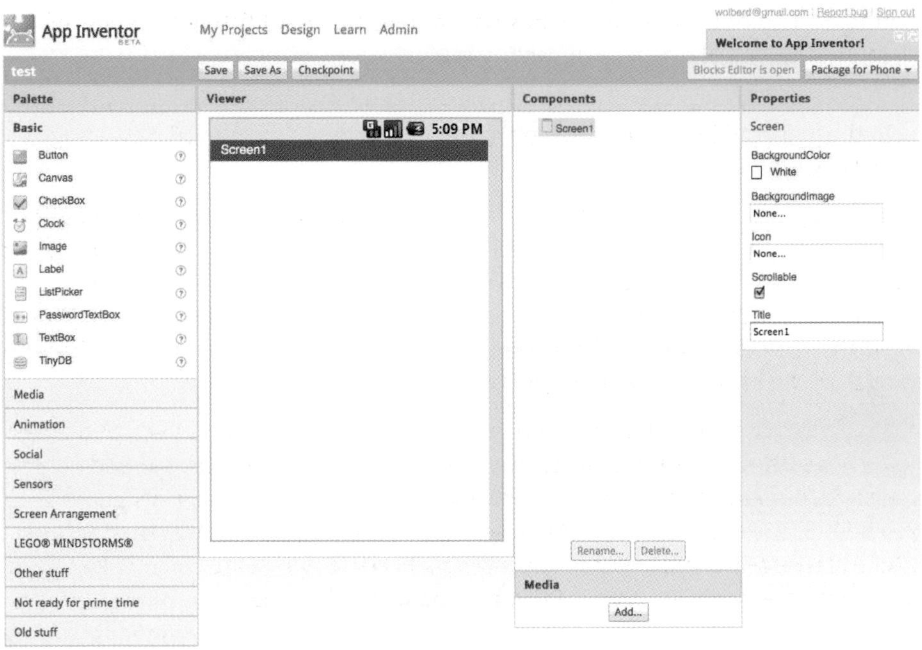

Figure 1-4. The App Inventor Component Designer

The Designer is divided into several areas:

- Toward the center is a white area called the *Viewer*. This is where you place components and arrange them to map out what you want your app to look like. The Viewer shows only a rough indication of how the app will look, so, for example, a line of text might break at a different place in your app than what you see in the Viewer. To see how your app will *really* appear, you'll need to either download the app to your phone (we'll go through how to do this a bit later, in the section "Packaging the App for Downloading") or view it in the emulator that comes with App Inventor.

- To the left of the Viewer is the *Palette*, which is a list of components you can select from. The Palette is divided into sections; at this point, only the Basic components are visible, but you can see components in other sections of the Palette by clicking the headers labeled Media, Animation, and so on.

- To the right of the Viewer is the *Components* list, which lists the components in your project. Any component that you drag into the Viewer will show up in this list. Currently, the project has only one component listed: Screen1, which represents the phone screen itself.

- Under the Components list is an area that shows the *Media* (pictures and sound) in the project. This project doesn't have any media yet, but you'll be adding some soon.

At the far right is a section that shows the *Properties* of components; when you click a component in the Viewer, you'll see its Properties listed here. Properties are details about each component that you can change. (For example, when clicking on a Label component, you might see properties related to color, text, font, and so on.) Right now, it shows the properties of the screen (called Screen1), which include a background color, a background image, and a title.

For the HelloPurr app, you'll need two *visible* components (you can think of these as components you can actually see in the app): the Label component reading "Pet the Kitty" and a Button component with an image of a cat in it. You'll also need a *non-visible* Sound component that knows how to play sounds, such as "meow," and an Accelerometer component for detecting when the phone is being shaken. Don't worry—we'll walk you through each component step by step.

Making a Label

The first component to add is a Label:

1. Go to the Palette, click Label (which appears about five spots down in the list of components), and drag it to the Viewer. You'll see a rectangular shape appear on the Viewer, with the words "Text for Label1."

2. Look at the Properties box on the right side of the Designer. It shows the properties of the label. There's a property called Text about halfway down, with a box for the label's text. Change the text to "Pet the Kitty" and press Return. You'll see the text change in the Viewer.

3. Change the BackgroundColor of the label by clicking the box, which currently reads None, to select a color from the list that appears. Select Blue. Also change the TextColor of the label to Yellow. Finally, change the FontSize to 20.

The Designer should now appear as shown in Figure 1-5.

Figure 1-5. The app now has a label

Be sure you have your phone connected and the Blocks Editor open. You should see the label appear on the phone as you add it in the Designer. In App Inventor, you build the application on the phone as you pick the components in the Designer. That way, you can see right away how your application will look. This is called *live testing*, and it also applies to the behaviors you create for the components in the Blocks Editor, as you'll see shortly.

Adding the Button

The kitty for HelloPurr is implemented as a Button component—you create a normal button, and then change the button image to the kitty. To make the basic button first, go to the Palette in the Designer and click Button (at the top of the list of components). Drag it onto the Viewer, placing it below the label. You'll see a rectangular button appear on the Viewer. After about 10 seconds, the button should appear on the phone. Go ahead and tap the phone button—do you think anything will happen? It won't, because your app hasn't told the button to do anything yet. This is the first important point to understand about App Inventor: for every component you add in the Designer, you have to move over to the Blocks Editor and create the code to make something happen with that component (we'll do that after we finish adding the components we need in the Designer).

Now we've got a button that we'll use to trigger the sound effect when someone clicks it, but we really want it to look like the picture of the kitty, not a plain old rectangle. To make the button look like the kitty:

1. First, you need to download a picture of the kitty and save it on your computer desktop. You can download it from the site for this book at *http://examples .oreilly.com/0636920016632/*. The picture is the file called *kitty.png*. (*.png* is a standard image format similar to *.jpg* and *.gif*; all of these file types will work in App Inventor, as will most standard sound files like *.mpg* or *.mp3*.) You can also download the sound file we need, *meow.mp3*.

2. The Properties box should show the properties of the button. If it doesn't, click the image of the button in the Viewer to expose the button's properties on the right. In the Properties box, click the area under Image (which currently reads None). A box appears with a button marked Add.

3. Click Add and you'll see "Upload file." Click Choose File, browse to select the *kitty.png* file you downloaded to your computer earlier, and click OK.

4. You'll see a yellow message at the top of the screen: "Uploading kitty.png to the AppInventor server." After about 30 seconds, the message and the upload box will disappear, and *kitty.png* should be listed as the image property for the button. You'll also see this listed in the Media area of the Designer window, just below the Components list. And if you look at the phone, you'll see the kitty picture displayed—the button now looks like a kitty.

5. You may have also noticed that the kitty picture on your phone has the words "Text for button 1" displayed on it. You probably don't want that in your app, so go ahead and change the Text property of Button1 to something like "Pet the Kitty," or just delete the text altogether.

Now the Designer should appear as shown in Figure 1-6.

Figure 1-6. The app with a label and a button with an image on it

Adding the Meow Sound

In your app, the kitty will meow when you tap the button. For this, you'll need to add the meow sound and program the button behavior to play that sound when the button is clicked:

1. If you haven't downloaded the *meow.mp3* file to your computer's desktop, do so now at *http://examples.oreilly.com/0636920016632/*.

2. Go to the Palette at the left of the Designer window and click the header marked Media to expand the Media section. Drag out a Sound component and place it in the Viewer. Wherever you drop it, it will appear in the area at the bottom of the Viewer marked "Non-visible components." Non-visible components are objects that do things for the app but don't appear in the visual user interface of the app.

3. Click Sound1 to show its properties. Set its Source to *meow.mp3*. You'll need to follow the same steps to upload this file from your computer as you did for the kitty picture. When you're done, you should see both *kitty.png* and *meow.mp3* listed in the Media section of the Designer.

You should now have the components depicted in Table 1-1.

Table 1-1. The components you've added to the HelloPurr app

Component type	Palette group	Name of component	Purpose
Button	Basic	Button1	Press to make the kitty meow.
Label	Basic	Label1	Shows the text "Pet the Kitty."
Sound	Media	Sound1	Play the meow sound.

Adding Behaviors to the Components

You've just added Button, Label, and Sound components as the building blocks for your first app. Now let's make the kitty meow when you tap the button. You do this with the Blocks Editor. If your Blocks Editor isn't yet open, click "Open the Blocks Editor" in the top right of the Component Designer.

Look at the Blocks Editor window. This is where you tell the components what to do and when to do it. You're going to tell the kitty button to play a sound when the user taps it. If components are ingredients in a recipe, you can think of blocks as the cooking instructions.

Making the Kitty Meow

At the top left of the window, you'll see buttons labeled "Built-In" and "My Blocks." Click My Blocks, and you'll see a column that includes a *drawer* for each component you created in the Designer: Button1, Label1, Screen1, and Sound1. When you click a drawer, you get a bunch of options (*blocks*) for that component you created. (Don't worry about the Built-In column for now—we'll get to that in Chapter 2.) Click the drawer for Button1. The drawer opens, showing a selection of blocks that you can use to tell the button what to do, starting with **Button1.Click** at the top, as shown in Figure 1-7.

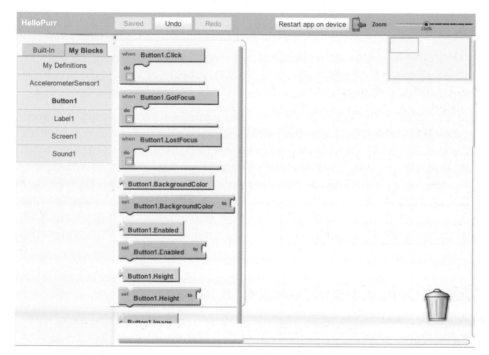

Figure 1-7. Clicking Button1 shows the component's blocks

Click the block labeled **Button1.Click** and drag it into the workspace. When you're looking for the block, you'll notice that the word "when" is smaller than **Button1 .Click**. Blocks including the word "when" are called *event handlers*; they specify what components should do *when* some particular event happens. In this case, the event we're interested in happens when the app user clicks on the kitty (which is really a button), as shown in Figure 1-8. Next, we'll add some blocks to program what will happen in response to that event.

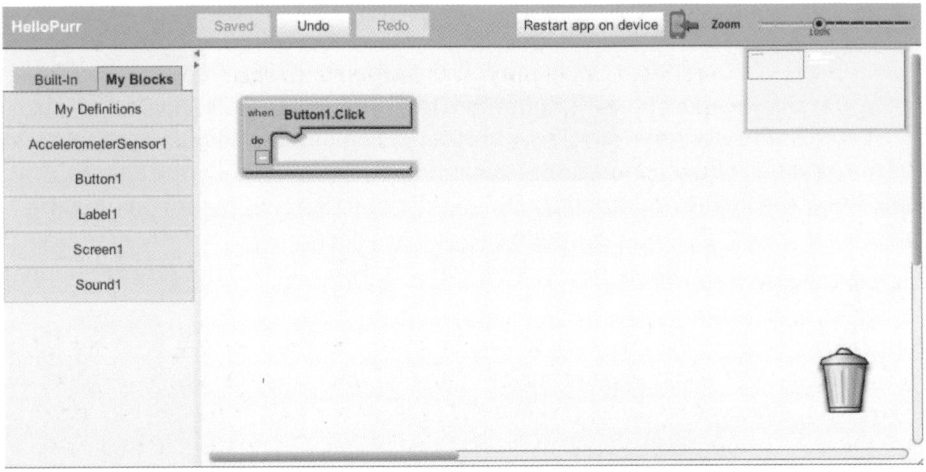

Figure 1-8. You'll specify a response to the user clicking within the Button.Click block

Click Sound1 in My Blocks to open the drawer for the sound component, and drag out the **call Sound1.Play** block. (Remember, earlier we set the property for Sound1 to the meow sound file you downloaded to your computer.) You may notice at this point that the **call Sound1.Play** block is shaped so it can fit into a gap marked "do" in the **Button1.Click** block. App Inventor is set up so that only certain blocks fit together; this way, you always know you're connecting blocks that actually work together. In this case, blocks with the word "call" make components do things. The two blocks should snap together to form a unit, as shown in Figure 1-9, and you'll hear a snapping sound when they connect.

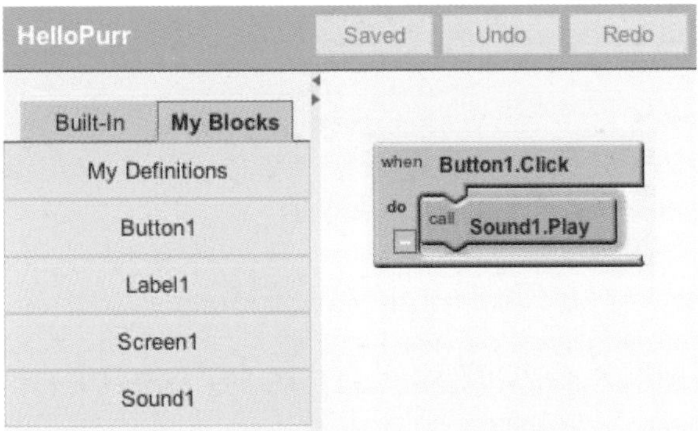

Figure 1-9. Now when someone clicks the button, the meow sound will play

Unlike traditional programming code (which often looks like a jumbled mess of gobbledygook "words"), blocks in App Inventor spell out the behaviors you're trying to create. In this case, we're essentially saying, "Hey, App Inventor, when someone clicks on the kitty button, play the meow sound."

Test your app. *Let's check to make sure everything is working properly—it's important to test your app each time you add something new. Tap the button on the phone (or click it using the emulator). You should hear the kitty meow. Congratulations, your first app is running!*

Adding a Purr

Now we're going to make the kitty purr *and* meow when you tap the button. We'll simulate the purr by making the phone vibrate. That may sound hard, but in fact, it's easy to do because the Sound component we used to play the meow sound can make the phone vibrate as well. App Inventor helps you tap into this kind of core phone functionality without having to deal with *how* the phone actually vibrates. You don't need to do anything different in the Designer; you can just add a second behavior to the button click in the Blocks Editor:

1. Go to the Blocks Editor and click Sound1 in My Blocks to open the drawer.

2. Select **call Sound1.Vibrate** and drag it under the **call Sound1.Play** block in the **Button1.Click** slot. The block should click into place, as shown in Figure 1-10. If it doesn't, try dragging it so that the little dip on the top of **call Sound1.Vibrate** touches the little bump on the bottom of **call Sound1.Play**.

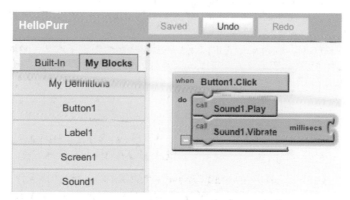

Figure 1-10. Playing the sound and vibrating on the Click event

3. You've likely noticed that the **call Sound1.Vibrate** block includes the text "millisecs" at the top right. An open slot in a block means you can plug something into it to specify more about how the behavior should work. In this case, you must tell the **Vibrate** block how long it should vibrate. You need to input this time in thousandths of a second (milliseconds), which is pretty common for many programming languages. So, to make the phone vibrate for half a second, put in

a value of 500 milliseconds. To put in a value of 500, you need to grab a number block. Click in an empty spot on the Designer screen, and then click the green Math button in the menu that pops up, as shown in Figure 1-11. You should see a drop-down list, with 123 as the first item; 123 indicates a block that represents a number.

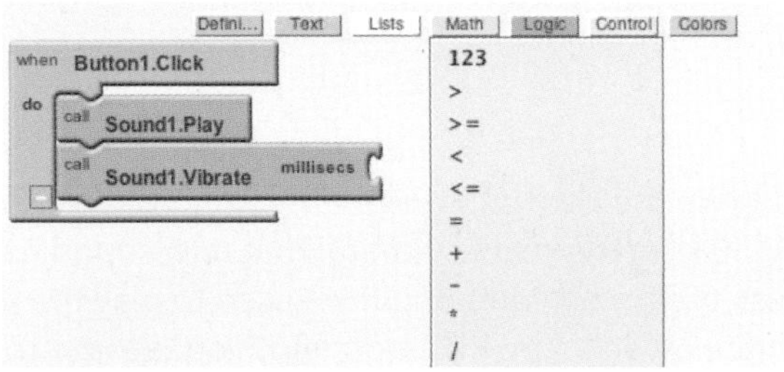

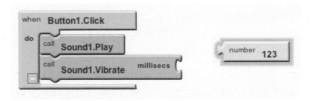

Figure 1-11. Opening the Math drawer

4. Click the 123 at the top of the list and you'll see a green block with the number 123, as shown in Figure 1-12.

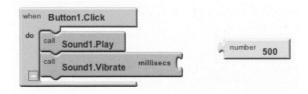

Figure 1-12. Choosing a number block (123 is the default value)

5. Change the 123 to 500 by clicking it and typing a new value, as shown in Figure 1-13.

Figure 1-13. Changing the value to 500

6. Plug the 500 number block into the socket at the right of **call Sound1.Vibrate**, as shown in Figure 1-14.

Figure 1-14. Plugging the 500 into the millisecs slot

Test your app. *Try it! Tap the button on the phone, and you'll feel the purr for half a second.*

Shaking the Phone

Now let's add a final element that taps into another cool feature of Android phones: make the kitty meow when you shake the phone. To do this, you'll use a component called AccelerometerSensor that can sense when you shake or move the phone around.

1. In the Designer, expand the Sensors area in the Palette components list and drag out an AccelerometerSensor. Don't worry about where you drag it—as with any non-visible component, no matter where you place it in the Viewer, it will move to the "Non-visible components" section at the bottom of the Viewer.

2. You'll want to treat someone shaking the phone as a different, separate event from the button click. That means you need a new event handler. Go to the Blocks Editor. There should be a new drawer for AccelerometerSensor1 under My Blocks. Open it and drag out the **AccelerometerSensor1.Shaking** block—it should be the second block in the list.

3. Just as you did with the sound and the button click, drag out a **call Sound1.Play** block and fit it into the gap in **AccelerometerSensor1.Shaking**. Try it out by shaking the phone.

Figure 1-15 shows the blocks for the completed HelloPurr app.

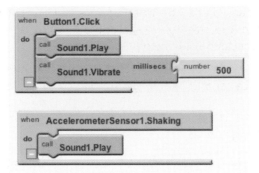

Figure 1-15. The blocks for HelloPurr

Packaging the App for Downloading

App Inventor is a *cloud computing* tool, meaning your app is stored on Google's online servers as you work. So if you close App Inventor, your app will be there when you return; you don't have to save anything on your computer as you would with a Word file or a music track. This also allows you to easily test the app while connected to your phone (what we call *live testing*), without having to download anything to your phone, either. The only problem is that if you disconnect your phone from App Inventor, the app running on the phone will stop, and you won't find an icon for it anywhere because it was never truly installed.

You can package up and install the completed app so that it works on any phone, even when it's not connected to the computer. First, make sure your phone allows apps to be downloaded from places other than the Android Market. Typically, you do this by going to Settings→Applications on your phone and checking the box next to "Unknown sources." Then, go to back into the Designer in App Inventor, click "Package for Phone," and select "Download to Connected Phone." You should see the messages "Saving" and then "Packaging," a process that takes up to a minute. After the "Packaging" message disappears, continue to wait for another 10–15 seconds while the finished app is downloaded to the phone. You'll get a download confirmation when everything is complete.

Once you've downloaded it, look at the apps available on your phone, and you'll now see HelloPurr, the app we just built. You run it just like any other app. (Make sure that you run your new app, not the App Inventor Phone application.) You can now unplug or even reboot the phone and kill all applications, and your new packaged application will still be there.

It's important to understand that this means your packaged app is now separate from the project on App Inventor. You can do more work on the project in App Inventor by connecting the phone with the USB cable as before. But that won't change the packaged app that is now installed on your phone. If you make further changes to your app in App Inventor, you'll want to package the result and download the new version to replace the old one on the phone.

Go ahead and package your HelloPurr app so you have it on your phone. Once you've done this, you can share it with your family and friends, too!

Sharing the App

You can share your app in a couple of ways. To share the executable app, first click "Package for Phone" and choose "Download to this Computer." This will create a file with a *.apk* extension on your computer. You need to upload this file so that it is accessible on the Web. Once the app is on the Web, other people can install it on their phones by opening the phone's browser and downloading it. Just let them know they need to allow "unknown sources" in their phone's Application settings in order to install apps that aren't from the Android Market.

You can also share the *source code* (blocks) of your app with another App Inventor developer. To do this, click My Projects, check the app you want to share (in this case, HelloPurr), and select More Actions→Download Source. The file created on your computer will have a *.zip* extension. You can email this file to someone, and she can open App Inventor, choose More Actions→Upload Source, and select the *.zip* file. This will give the user her own complete copy of your app, which she can then edit and customize without affecting your version.

The process of sharing apps will soon be easier and more fun—work is currently underway on a community sharing site.

Variations

Now that you've built a complete app and had the chance to play with it (and maybe download it to share with other people), you might have noticed a couple of things. Take a look at the following items and consider how you'd address them in your app. As you'll likely soon discover, you'll often build an app, find ways to improve and change it, and then go back into it to program those new ideas. Don't worry, that's a good thing—it means you're on your way to becoming a full-fledged app developer!

- As you shake the phone, the meows will sound strange, as if they are echoing. That's because the accelerometer sensor is triggering the shaking event many times a second, so the meows are overlapping. If you look at the Sound component in the Designer, you'll see a property called Minimum interval. That determines how close together successive sounds can start. It's currently set at a half-second (500 milliseconds), which is less than the duration of a single meow. By playing with the minimum interval, you can change how much the meows overlap.

- If you run the packaged app and walk around with the phone in your pocket, your phone will meow every time you move suddenly—something you might find embarrassing. Android apps are typically designed to keep running even when you're not looking at them; your app continues to communicate with the accelerometer and the meow just keeps going. To really quit the app, bring up HelloPurr and press the phone's menu button. You'll be offered an option to stop the application.

Summary

Here are some of the concepts we've covered in this chapter:

- You build apps by selecting components in the Designer and then telling them what to do and when to do it in the Blocks Editor.

- Some components are visible and some aren't. The visible ones appear in the user interface of the app. The non-visible ones do things like play sounds.

- You define components' behavior by assembling blocks in the Blocks Editor. You first drag out an event handler like **Button1.Click**, and then place command blocks like **Sound.Play** within it. Any blocks within **Button1.Click** will be performed when the user clicks the button.

- Some commands need extra information to make them work. An example is Vibrate, which needs to know how many milliseconds to vibrate. These values are called *arguments*.

- Numbers are represented as number blocks. You can plug these into commands that take numbers as arguments.

- App Inventor has sensor components. The AccelerometerSensor can detect when the phone is moved.

- You can package the apps you build and download them to the phone, where they run independently of App Inventor.

PART I

12 Customizable Apps

This section provides step-by-step instructions for building 12 Android apps. Though the apps are very different in nature, they build upon each other conceptually, the later chapters being the most complex in terms of the programming knowledge required.

At the end of each chapter, there are suggestions for varying and extending the app, the idea being that the best way to learn programming is to switch back and forth between following instructions and exploring on your own. You'll also be pointed to related chapters in the "Inventor's Manual" section of the book that provide in-depth discussion of the concepts learned.

CHAPTER 2

PaintPot

This tutorial introduces the Canvas component for creating simple, two-dimensional (2D) graphics. You'll build PaintPot, an app that lets the user draw on the screen in different colors, and then update it to allow him to take his own picture and draw on that instead. On a historical note, PaintPot was one of the first programs developed to demonstrate the potential of personal computers, as far back as the 1970s. Back then, making something like this simple drawing app was a very complex undertaking, and the results were pretty unpolished. But now with App Inventor, anyone can quickly put together a fairly cool drawing app, which is a great starting point for building 2D games.

Figure 2-1. The PaintPot app

With the PaintPot app shown in Figure 2-1, you can:

- Dip your finger into a virtual paint pot to draw in that color.

- Drag your finger along the screen to draw a line.

- Poke the screen to make dots.

- Use the button at the bottom to wipe the screen clean.

- Change the dot size to large or small with the buttons at the bottom.

- Take a picture with the camera and then draw on that picture.

What You'll Learn

This tutorial introduces the following concepts:

- Using the Canvas component for drawing.

- Handling touch and drag events on the phone's surface.

- Controlling screen layout with arrangement components.

- Using event handlers that take arguments.

- Defining variables to remember things like the dot size the user has chosen for drawing.

Getting Started

Make sure your computer and your phone are set up to use App Inventor, and browse to the App Inventor website at *http://appinventor.googlelabs.com*. Start a new project in the Component Designer window and name it "PaintPot". Open the Blocks Editor, click "Connect to Device," and make sure the phone has started the App Inventor app.

To get started, go to the Properties panel on the right of the Designer and change the screen title to "PaintPot" (no more Screen1 here!). You should see this change on the phone, with the new title displayed in the title bar of your app.

If you're concerned about confusing your project name and the screen name, don't worry! There are three key names in App Inventor:

- The name you choose for your project as you work on it. This will also be the name of the application when you package it for the phone. Note that you can click Save As in the Component Designer to start a new version or rename a project.

- The component name Screen1, which you'll see in the panel that lists the application's components. You can't change this name in the current version of App Inventor.

- The title of the screen, which is what you'll see in the phone's title bar. This starts out being Screen1, which is what you used in HelloPurr. But you can change it, as we just did for PaintPot.

Designing the Components

You'll use these components to make the app:

- Three Button components for selecting red, blue, or green paint, and a HorizontalArrangement component for organizing them.

- One Button component for wiping the drawing clean, and two for changing the size of the dots that are drawn.

- A Canvas component, which is the drawing surface. Canvas has a BackgroundImage property, which we'll set to the *kitty.png* file from the HelloPurr tutorial in Chapter 1. Later in this chapter, you'll modify the app so the background can be set to a picture the user takes.

Creating the Color Buttons

First, create the three color buttons using the following instructions:

1. Drag a Button component onto the viewer and change its Text attribute to "Red" and make its BackgroundColor red.

2. Click Button1 in the components list in the Viewer to highlight it (it might already be highlighted) and click Rename to change its name from Button1 to RedButton. Note that spaces aren't allowed in component names, so it's common to capitalize the first letter of each word in the name.

3. Similarly, make two more buttons for blue and green, named BlueButton and GreenButton, placing them under the red button vertically. Check your work up to this point against Figure 2-2.

Viewer	Components
Screen1 [5:09 PM] Screen1 Red Blue Green	Screen1 RedButton BlueButton GreenButton

Figure 2-2. The Viewer showing the three buttons created

Note that in this project, you're changing the names of the components rather than leaving them as the default names as you did with HelloPurr. Using more meaning-ful names makes your projects more readable, and it will really help when you move to the Blocks Editor and must refer to the components by name. In this book, we'll use the convention of having the component name end with its type (for example, RedButton).

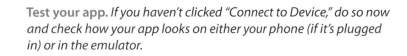

Test your app. *If you haven't clicked "Connect to Device," do so now and check how your app looks on either your phone (if it's plugged in) or in the emulator.*

Using Arrangements for Better Layouts

You should now have three buttons stacked on top of one another. But for this app, you want them all lined up next to one another at the top of the screen, as shown in Figure 2-3. You do this using a HorizontalArrangement component:

1. From the Palette's Screen Arrangement category, drag out a HorizontalArrangement component and place it under the buttons.

2. In the Properties panel, change the Width of the HorizontalArrangement to "Fill parent" so that it fills the entire width of the screen.

3. Move the three buttons one by one into the HorizontalArrangement component. *Hint:* You'll see a blue vertical line that shows where the piece you're dragging will go.

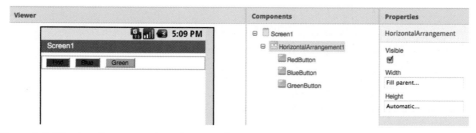

Figure 2-3. The three buttons within a horizontal arrangement

If you look in the list of project components, you'll see the three buttons indented under the HorizontalArrangement component to show that they are now its sub-components. Notice that all the components are indented under Screen1.

Test your app. *You should also see your three buttons lined up in a row on the phone screen, although things might not look exactly as they do on the Designer. For example, the outline around* HorizontalArrangement *appears in the Viewer but not on the phone.*

In general, you use screen arrangements to create simple vertical, horizontal, or tabular layouts. You can also create more complex layouts by inserting (or *nesting*) screen arrangement components within each other.

Adding the Canvas

The canvas is where the user will draw circles and lines. Add it, and add the *kitty.png* file from HelloPurr as the BackgroundImage:

1. From the Palette's Basic category, drag a Canvas component onto the Viewer. Change its name to DrawingCanvas. Set its Width to "Fill parent." Set its Height to 300 pixels.

2. If you've completed the HelloPurr tutorial (Chapter 1), you have already downloaded the *kitty.png* file. If you haven't, you can download it from *http://examples .oreilly.com/0636920016632/*.

3. Set the BackgroundImage of the Canvas to the *kitty.png* file. In the Property editor, the BackgroundImage will be set to None. Click the field and choose Add to upload the *kitty.png* file.

4. Set the PaintColor of the Canvas to red so that when the user starts the app but hasn't clicked on a button yet, his drawings will be red. Check to see that what you've built looks like Figure 2-4.

Figure 2-4. The Canvas component has a BackgroundImage of the kitty picture

Arranging the Bottom Buttons and the Camera Component

1. From the Palette, drag out a second HorizontalArrangement and place it under the canvas. Then drag two more Button components onto the screen and place them in this bottom HorizontalArrangement. Change the name of the first button to TakePictureButton and its Text property to "Take Picture". Change the name of the second button to WipeButton and its Text property to "Wipe".

2. Drag two more Button components from the Palette into the Horizontal Arrangement, placing them next to WipeButton.

3. Name the buttons BigButton and SmallButton, and set their Text to "Big Dots" and "Small Dots", respectively.

4. From the Media Palette, drag a Camera component into the Viewer. It will appear in the non-visible component area.

You've now completed the steps to set the appearance of your app as shown in Figure 2-5.

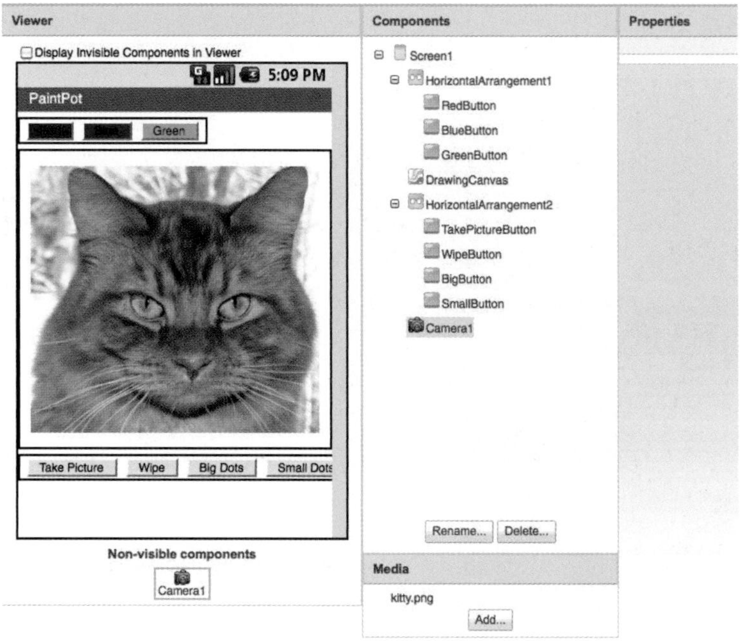

Figure 2-5. The complete user interface for PaintPot

Test your app. *Check the app on the phone. Does the kitty picture now appear under the top row of buttons? Does the bottom row of buttons appear?*

Adding Behaviors to the Components

The next step is to define how the components behave. Creating a painting program might seem overwhelming, but rest assured that App Inventor has done a lot of the heavy lifting for you: there are easy-to-use blocks for handling the user's touches and drags, and for drawing and taking pictures.

In the Designer, you added a Canvas component named DrawingCanvas. Like all canvas components, DrawingCanvas has a Touched event and a Dragged event. You'll program the **DrawingCanvas.Touched** event so that it calls **DrawingCanvas.DrawCircle**. You'll program the **DrawingCanvas.Dragged** event to call **DrawingCanvas.DrawLine**. You'll then program the buttons to set the DrawingCanvas.PaintColor property, clear the DrawingCanvas, and change the BackgroundImage to a picture taken with the camera.

Adding the Touch Event to Draw a Dot

First, you'll arrange things so that when you touch the DrawingCanvas, you draw a dot at the spot you touch:

1. In the Blocks Editor, click My Blocks, select the drawer for the DrawingCanvas, and drag the **DrawingCanvas.Touched** block to the workspace. As soon as you drag the block out, the three plugs on the right automatically fill in with name blocks for x, y, and touchedSprite, as shown in Figure 2-6.

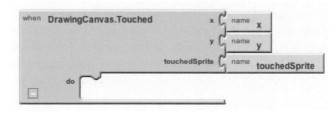

Figure 2-6. The event comes with information about where the screen is touched

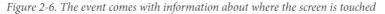

Note. *If you've completed the HelloPurr app in Chapter 1, you're familiar with **Button.Click** events, but not with Canvas events. **Button.Click** events are fairly simple because there's nothing to know about the event other than that it happened. Some event handlers, however, come with information about the event called arguments. The **DrawingCanvas.Touched** event tells you the x and y coordinates of the touch within the canvas. It also tells you if an object within the DrawingCanvas (in App Inventor, this is called a sprite) was touched, but we won't need that until Chapter 3. The x and y coordinates are the arguments we'll use to note where the user touched the screen, so we can then draw the dot at that position.*

2. Drag out a **DrawingCanvas.DrawCircle** command from the DrawingCanvas drawer and place it within the **DrawingCanvas.Touched** event handler, as shown in Figure 2-7.

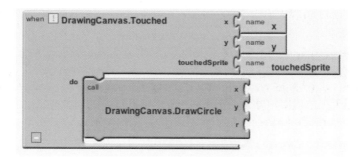

Figure 2-7. When the user touches the canvas, the app draws a circle

On the right side of the **DrawingCanvas.DrawCircle** block, you'll see three slots for the arguments we need to fill in: x, y, and r. The x and y arguments specify the location where the circle should be drawn, and r determines the radius (or size) of the circle. The yellow warning box with the exclamation point at the top of the **DrawingCanvas.Touched** event handler denotes that these slots haven't yet been filled. We'll build the blocks to do that next.

This event handler can be a bit confusing because the **DrawingCanvas .Touched** event also has x and y slots; just keep in mind that the x and y for the **DrawingCanvas.Touched** event tell you where the user touched, while the x and y for the **DrawingCanvas.DrawCircle** event are open slots for you to specify where the circle should be drawn.

Because you want to draw the circle where the user touched, plug in the x and y values from **DrawingCanvas.Touched** as the values of the x and y parameters in **DrawingCanvas.DrawCircle**.

Note. *Do not grab the arguments of the* Touched *event directly, even though this might seem logical! The fact that the arguments can even be grabbed is an unfortunate design aspect of App Inventor. Instead, you want to grab these values from the My Definitions drawer, as shown in Figure 2-8.*

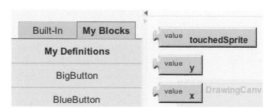

Figure 2-8. The system has added references to the event arguments touchedSprite, y, and x

3. Open the My Definitions drawer within My Blocks and find the blocks for **value x** and **value y**.

   The blocks were automatically created for you by App Inventor when you dragged out the **DrawingCanvas.Touched** event handler block: they are *references* to the x and y arguments (or names) of that event. Drag out the **value x** and **value y** blocks and plug them into the corresponding sockets in the **DrawingCanvas .DrawCircle** block so they resemble what is shown in Figure 2-9.

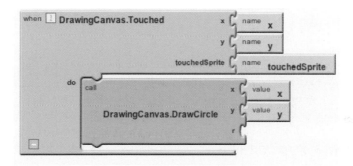

Figure 2-9. The app knows where to draw (x,y), but we still need to specify how big the circle should be

4. You'll also need to specify the radius, r, of the circle to draw. The radius is measured in pixels, which is the tiniest dot that can be drawn on the screen. For now, set it to 5: click in a blank area of the screen to bring up the shortcut menu, and then select the Math folder. Select 123 from the drop-down list to create a number block. Change the 123 to 5 and plug that in for the r slot. When you do, the yellow box in the top-left corner will disappear as all the slots are filled. Figure 2-10 illustrates how the final **DrawingCanvas.Touched** event handler should look.

Note. *Note that you could have created the **number 5** block by simply typing a 5 in the Blocks Editor, followed by Return. This is an example of typeblocking: if you start typing, the Blocks Editor shows a list of blocks whose names match what you are typing; if you type a number, it creates a number block.*

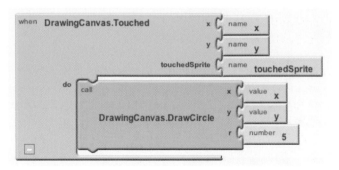

Figure 2-10. When the user touches the canvas, a circle of radius 5 will be drawn at (x,y)

 Test your app. *Try out what you have so far on the phone. Touch the canvas—your finger should leave a dot at each place you touch. The dots will be red if you set the* Canvas.PaintColor *property to red in the Component Designer (otherwise, it's black, as that's the default).*

Adding the Drag Event That Draws a Line

Next, you'll add the drag event handler. Here's the difference between a touch and a drag:

- A *touch* is when you place your finger on the canvas and lift it without moving it.

- A *drag* is when you place your finger on the canvas and move it while keeping it in contact with the screen.

In a paint program, dragging your finger across the screen appears to draw a giant, curved line along your finger's path. What you're actually doing is drawing hundreds of tiny, straight lines; each time you move your finger, even a little bit, you extend the line from your finger's last position to its new position.

1. From the DrawingCanvas drawer, drag the **DrawingCanvas.Dragged** block to the workspace. You should see the event handler as it is shown in Figure 2-11.

   The **DrawingCanvas.Dragged** event comes with seven arguments:

   startx, starty
   : The position of your finger back where the drag started.

   currentx, currenty
   : The current position of your finger.

   prevx, prevy
   : The immediately previous position of your finger.

`draggedSprite`

    The argument that will be true if the user drags directly on an image sprite. We won't use this argument in this tutorial.

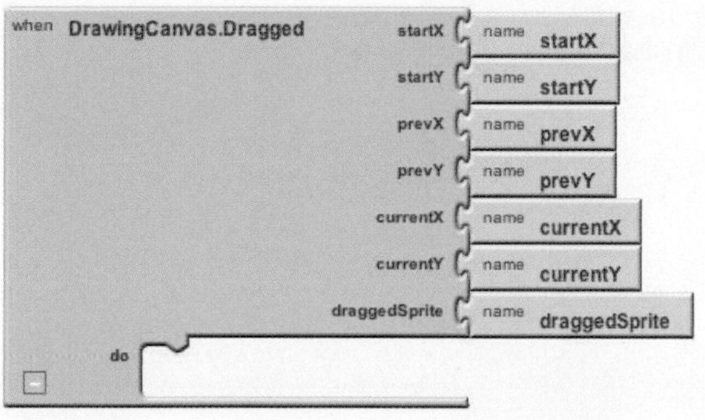

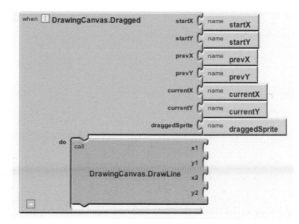

Figure 2-11. A Dragged event has even more arguments than Touched

2. From the DrawingCanvas drawer, drag the **DrawingCanvas.DrawLine** block into the **DrawingCanvas.Dragged** block, as shown in Figure 2-12.

Figure 2-12. Adding the capability to draw lines

The **DrawingCanvas.DrawLine** block has four arguments, two for each point that determines the line: (x1,y1) is one point, while (x2,y2) is the other. Can you figure out what values need to be plugged into each argument? Remember, the **Dragged** event will be called many times as you drag your finger across the canvas: the app draws a tiny line each time your finger moves, from (prevx,prevy) to (currentX,currentY). Let's add those to our **DrawingCanvas.DrawLine** block:

3. Click the My Definitions drawer. You should see the blocks for the arguments you need. Drag the corresponding value blocks to the appropriate slots in DrawingCanvas.Dragged. **value prevX** and **value prevY** should be plugged into the x1 and y1 slots. **value currentX** and **value currentY** should be plugged into the x2 and y2 slots, as shown in Figure 2-13.

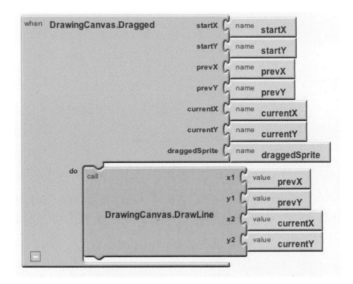

Figure 2-13. As the user drags, the app will draw a line from the previous spot to the current one

Test your app. *Try this behavior on the phone: drag your finger around on the screen to draw lines and curves. Touch the screen to make spots.*

Adding Button Event Handlers

The app you've built lets the user draw, but it always draws in red. Next, add event handlers for the color buttons so users can change the paint color, and another for WipeButton so they can clear the screen and start over.

In the Blocks Editor:

1. Switch to the My Blocks column.

2. Open the drawer for RedButton and drag out the **RedButton.Click** block.

3. Open the DrawingCanvas drawer. Drag out the **set DrawingCanvas.PaintColor to** block (you may have to scroll through the list of blocks in the drawer to find it) and place it in the "do" section of **RedButton.Click**.

4. Switch to the Built-In column. Open the Colors drawer and drag out the block for the color red and plug it into the **set DrawingCanvas.PaintColor to** block.

5. Repeat steps 2–4 for the blue and green buttons.

6. The final button to set up is WipeButton. Switch back to the My Blocks column and drag out a **WipeButton.Click** from the ButtonWipe drawer. From the DrawingCanvas drawer, drag out **DrawingCanvas.Clear** and place it in the **WipeButton.Click** block. Confirm that your blocks show up as they do in Figure 2-14.

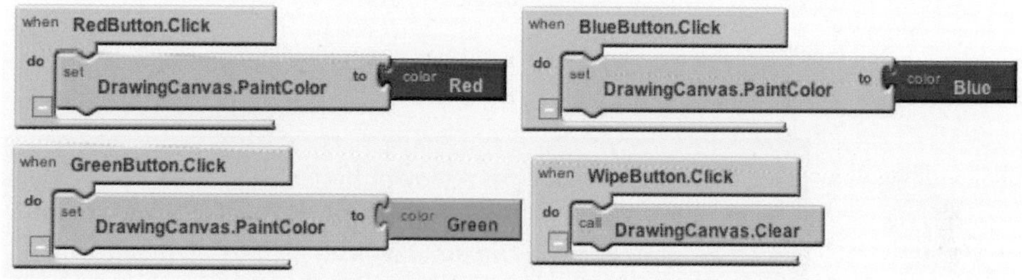

Figure 2-14. Clicking the color buttons changes the canvas's PaintColor; clicking Wipe clears the screen

Letting the User Take a Picture

App Inventor apps can interact with the powerful features of an Android device, including the camera. To spice up the app, we'll let the user set the background of the drawing to a picture she takes with the camera.

1. The Camera component has two key blocks. The **Camera.TakePicture** block launches the camera application on the device. The event **Camera.AfterPicture** is triggered when the user has finished taking the picture. You'll add blocks in the **Camera.AfterPicture** event handler to set the DrawingCanvas.Background Image to the just-taken Switch to the My Blocks column and open the TakePictureButton drawer. Drag the **TakePictureButton.Click** event handler into the workspace.

2. From Camera1, drag out **Camera1.TakePicture** and place it in the **TakePictureButton.click** event handler.

3. From Camera1, drag the **Camera1.AfterPicture** event handler into the workspace.

4. From DrawingCanvas, drag the **set DrawingCanvas.BackgroundImage to** block and place it in the **Camera1.AfterPicture** event handler.

5. **Camera1.AfterPicture** has an argument named image, which is the picture just taken. You can get a reference to it, **value image**, in the My Definitions palette; drag it out and plug it into **DrawingCanvas.BackgroundImage**.

The blocks should look like Figure 2-15.

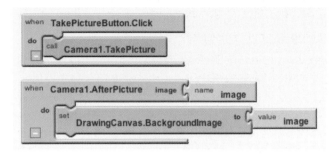

Figure 2-15. When the picture is taken, it's set as the canvas's background image

 Test your app. *Try out this behavior by clicking Take Picture on your phone and taking a picture. The cat should change to the picture you take, and then you can draw on that picture. (Drawing on Professor Wolber is a favorite pastime of his students, as exemplified in Figure 2-16.)*

Changing the Dot Size

The size of the dots drawn on the canvas is determined in the call to **DrawingCanvas.DrawCircle** when the radius argument r is set to 5. To change the thickness, you can put in a different value for r. To test this, try changing the 5 to a 10 and testing it out on the phone to see how it looks.

The catch here is that whatever size you set in the radius argument is the only size the user can use. What if he wants to change the size of the dots? Let's modify the program so that the user, not just the programmer, can change the dot size. We'll change it so that when the user clicks a button labeled "Big Dots," the dot size is 8, and when he clicks a button labeled "Small Dots," it is 2.

To use different values for the radius argument, the app needs to know which one we want to apply. We have to tell it to use a specific value, and it has to store (or remember) that value somehow so it can keep using it. When your app needs to remember

Figure 2-16. The PaintPot app with an "annotated" picture of Professor Wolber

something that's not a property, you can define a *variable*. A variable is a *memory cell*; you can think of it like a bucket in which you can store data that can vary, such as the current dot size (for more information about variables, see Chapter 15).

Let's start by defining a variable dotSize:

1. In the Blocks Editor, open the Definitions drawer in the Built-In column. Drag out a **def variable** block. Change the text "variable" to "dotSize".

2. Notice that the **def dotSize** block has an open slot. This is where you can specify the initial value for the variable, or the value that it defaults to when the app begins. (This is often referred to as "initializing a variable" in programming terms.) For this app, initialize the dotSize to 2 by creating a **number 2** block (by either starting to type the number 2 or dragging a **number 123** block out of the Math drawer) and plugging it into **def dotSize**, as shown in Figure 2-17.

Figure 2-17. Initializing the variable dotSize with a value of 2

Using variables

Next, we want to change the argument of **DrawingCanvas.DrawCircle** in the **DrawingCanvas.Touched** event handler so that it uses the value of **dotSize** rather than always using a fixed number. (It may seem like we've "fixed" dotSize to the value 2 because we initialized it that way, but you'll see in a minute how we can change the value of dotSize and therefore change the size of the dot that gets drawn.)

1. In the Blocks Editor, switch to the My Blocks column and open the My Definitions drawer. You should see two new blocks: (1) a **global dotSize** block that provides the value of the variable, and (2) a **set global dotSize to** block that sets the variable to a new value. These blocks were automatically generated for you when you created the dotSize variable, in the same way that value blocks for the arguments x and y were created when you added the **DrawingCanvas.Touched** event handler earlier.

2. Go to the **DrawingCanvas.Touched** event handler and drag the **number 5** block out of the r slot and place it into the trash. Then replace it with the **global dotSize** block from the My Definitions drawer (see Figure 2-18). When the user touches the canvas, the app will now determine the radius from the variable dotSize.

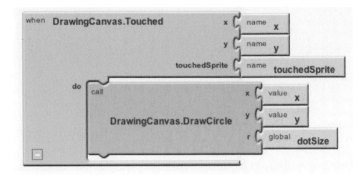

Figure 2-18. Now the size of each circle is dependent on what is stored in the variable dotSize

Changing the values of variables

Here's where the magic of variables really comes into play—the variable `dotSize` allows the user to choose the size of the circle, and your event handler will draw the circle accordingly. We'll implement this behavior by programming the **SmallButton .Click** and **BigButton.Click** event handlers:

1. Drag out a **SmallButton.Click** event handler from the SmallButton drawer of My Blocks. Then drag out a **set global dotSize to** block from My Definitions and plug it into **SmallButton.Click**. Finally, create a **number 2** block and plug it into the **set global dotSize to** block.

2. Make a similar event handler for **BigButton.Click**, but set `dotSize` to 8. Both event handlers should now show up in the Blocks Editor, as shown in Figure 2-19.

 Note. *The "global" in the **set global dotSize to** refers to the fact that the variable can be used in all the event handlers of the program (globally). Some programming languages allow you to define variables that are "local" to a particular part of the program; App Inventor currently does not.*

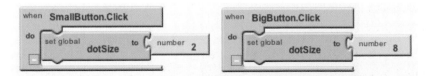

Figure 2-19. Clicking the buttons changes the dotSize; successive touches will draw at that size

Test your app. *Try clicking the size buttons and then touching the canvas. Are the circles drawn with different sizes? Are the lines? The line size shouldn't change because you programmed* dotSize *to only be used in the **DrawingCanvas.DrawCircle** block. Based on that, can you think of how you'd change your blocks so users could change the line size as well? (Note that Canvas has a property named LineWidth.)*

The Complete App: PaintPot

Figure 2-20 illustrates our completed PaintPot app.

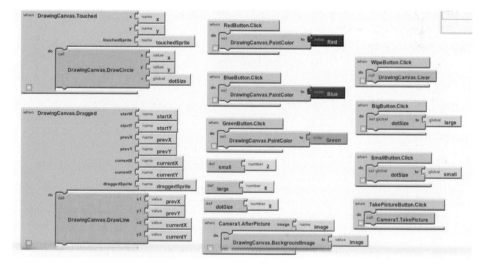

Figure 2-20. The final set of blocks for PaintPot

Variations

Here are some variations you can explore:

- The app's user interface doesn't provide much information about the current settings (for example, the only way to know the current dot size or color is to draw something). Modify the app so that these settings are displayed to the user.

- Let the user enter the dot size within a TextBox component. This way, she can change it to other values besides 2 and 8. For more information on input forms and the TextBox component, see Chapter 4.

Summary

Here are some of the ideas we've covered in this chapter:

- The Canvas component lets you draw on it. It can also sense touches and drags, and you can map these events to drawing functions.

- You can use screen arrangement components to organize the layout of components instead of just placing them one under the other.

- Some event handlers come with information about the event, such as the coordinates of where the screen was touched. This information is represented by arguments. When you drag out an event handler that has arguments, App Inventor creates value blocks for them and places them in the My Definitions drawer.

- You create variables by using **def variable** blocks from the Definitions drawer. Variables let the app remember information, like dot size, that isn't stored in a component property.

- For each variable you define, App Inventor automatically supplies a **global value** block that gives the value of the variable, and a **set global variable to** block for changing the value of the variable. These blocks can be found in the My Definitions drawer. To learn more about variables, see Chapter 16.

This chapter showed how the Canvas component can be used for a painting program. You can also use it to program animations such as those you'd find in 2D games. To learn more, check out the Ladybug Chase game in Chapter 5 and the discussion of animation in Chapter 17.

CHAPTER 3

MoleMash

This chapter shows you how to create MoleMash, a game inspired by the arcade classic Whac-A-Mole, in which mechanical critters pop briefly out of holes, and players score points by whacking them with a mallet. MoleMash was created by a member of the App Inventor team, nominally to test the sprite functionality (which she implemented), but really because she is a fan of the game.

When Ellen Spertus joined the App Inventor team at Google, she was eager to add support for creating games, so she volunteered to implement *sprites*. The term, originally reserved for mythological creatures such as fairies and pixies, emerged in the computing community in the 1970s, where it referred to images capable of movement on a computer screen (for video games). Ellen first worked with sprites when she attended a computer camp in the early 1980s and programmed a TI 99/4. Her work on sprites and MoleMash was motivated by double nostalgia—for both the computers and games of her childhood.

What You'll Build

For the MoleMash app shown in Figure 3-1, you'll implement the following functionality:

- A mole pops up at random locations on the screen, moving once every second.

- Touching the mole causes the phone to vibrate, the display of hits to be incremented (increased by one), and the mole to move immediately to a new location.

- Touching the screen but missing the mole causes the display of misses to be incremented.

- Pressing the Reset button resets the counts of hits and misses.

Figure 3-1. The MoleMash user interface

What You'll Learn

The tutorial covers the following components and concepts:

- The ImageSprite component for touch-sensitive movable images.
- The Canvas component, which acts as a surface on which to place the ImageSprite.
- The Clock component to move the sprite around.
- The Sound component to produce a vibration when the mole is touched.
- The Button component to start a new game.
- Procedures to implement repeated behavior, such as moving the mole.
- Generating random numbers.
- Using the addition (+) and subtraction (-) blocks.

Getting Started

Connect to the App Inventor website and start a new project. Name it "MoleMash" and also set the screen's title to "MoleMash". Open the Blocks Editor and connect to the phone.

Download this picture of a mole from this book's site (*http://examples.oreilly .com/0636920016632/*), naming it *mole.png* and noting where you save it on your computer. In the Media section of the Component Designer, click Add, browse to where the file is located on your computer, and upload it to App Inventor.

Designing the Components

You'll use these components to make MoleMash:

- A Canvas that serves as a playing field.
- An ImageSprite that displays a picture of a mole and can move around and sense when the mole is touched.
- A Sound that vibrates when the mole is touched.
- Labels that display "Hits: ", "Misses: ", and the actual numbers of hits and misses.
- HorizontalArrangements to correctly position the Labels.
- A Button to reset the numbers of hits and misses to 0.
- A Clock to make the mole move once per second.

Table 3-1 shows the complete list of components.

Table 3-1. The complete list of components for MoleMash

Component type	Palette group	What you'll name it	Purpose
Canvas	Basic	Canvas1	The container for ImageSprite.
ImageSprite	Animation	Mole	The user will try to touch this.
Button	Basic	ResetButton	The user will press this to reset the score.
Clock	Basic	Clock1	Control the mole's movement.
Sound	Media	Sound1	Vibrate when the mole is touched.
Label	Basic	HitsLabel	Display "Hits: ".
Label	Basic	HitsCountLabel	Display the number of hits.
Horizontal-Arrangement	Screen Arrangement	HorizontalArrangement1	Position HitsLabel next to HitsCountLabel.
Label	Basic	MissesLabel	Display "Misses: ".
Label	Basic	MissesCountLabel	Display the number of misses.
Horizontal-Arrangement	Screen Arrangement	HorizontalArrangement2	Position MissesLabel next to MissesCountLabel.

Placing the Action components

In this section, we will place the components necessary for the game's action. In the next section, we will place the components for displaying the score.

1. Drag in a Canvas component, leaving it with the default name Canvas1. Set its Width property to "Fill parent" so it is as wide as the screen, and set its Height to 300 pixels.

2. Drag in an ImageSprite component from the Animation group on the Palette. Place it anywhere on Canvas1. Click Rename at the bottom of the Components list and change its name to "Mole". Set its Picture property to *mole.png*, which you uploaded earlier.

3. Drag in a Button component from the Basic group on the Palette, placing it beneath Canvas1. Rename it to "ResetButton" and set its Text property to "Reset".

4. Drag in a Clock component. It will appear at the bottom of the Viewer in the "Non-visible components" section.

5. Drag in a Sound component from the Media group on the Palette. It, too, will appear in the "Non-visible components" section.

Your screen should now look something like Figure 3-2 (although your mole may be in a different position).

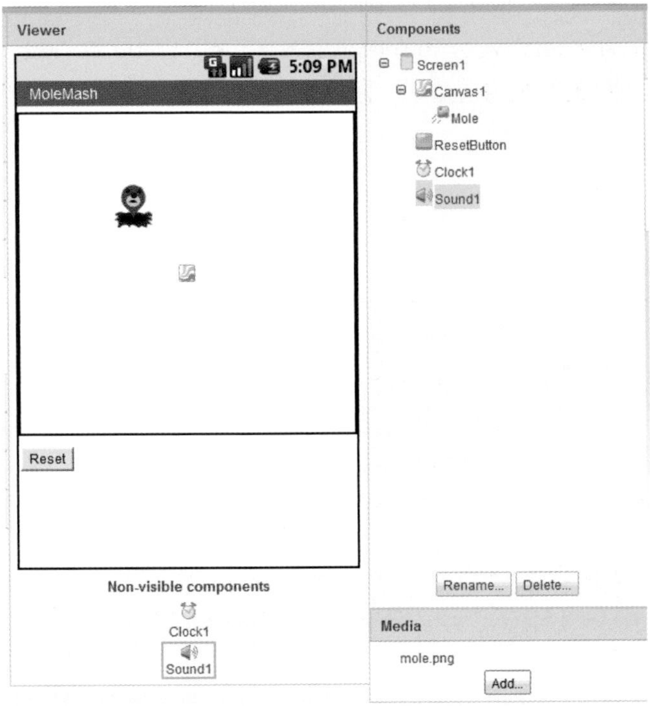

Figure 3-2. The Component Designer view of the "action" components

Placing the Label components

We will now place components for displaying the user's score—specifically, the number of hits and misses.

1. Drag in a HorizontalArrangement from the Screen Arrangement group, placing it beneath the Button and keeping the default name of HorizontalArrangement1.

2. Drag two Labels from the Basic group into HorizontalArrangement1.

   a. Rename the left Label to "HitsLabel" and set its Text property to "Hits: " (making sure to include a space after the colon).

   b. Rename the right Label to "HitsCountLabel" and set its Text property to "0".

3. Drag in a second HorizontalArrangement, placing it beneath Horizontal Arrangement1.

4. Drag two Labels into HorizontalArrangement2.

    a. Rename the left Label to "MissesLabel" and set its Text property to "Misses: " (making sure to include a space after the colon).

    b. Rename the right Label to "MissesCountLabel" and set its Text property to "0".

Your screen should now look like something like Figure 3-3.

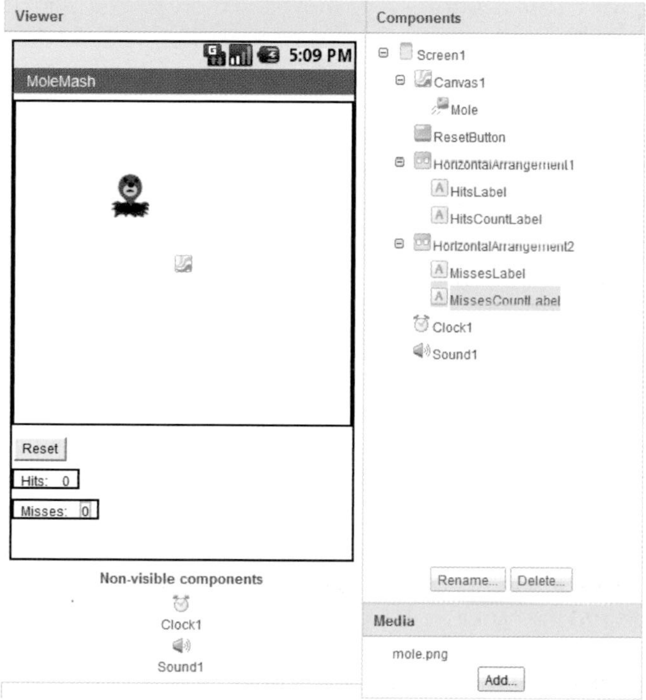

Figure 3-3. The Component Designer view of all the MoleMash components

Adding Behaviors to the Components

After creating the preceding components, we can move to the Blocks Editor to implement the program's behavior. Specifically, we want the mole to move to a random location on the canvas every second. The user's goal is to tap on the mole wherever it appears, and the app will display the number of times the user hits or misses the mole. (*Note*: We recommend using your finger, not a mallet!) Pressing the Reset button resets the number of hits and misses to 0.

Moving the Mole

In the programs you've written thus far, you've called built-in procedures, such as Vibrate in HelloPurr. Wouldn't it be nice if App Inventor had a procedure that moved an ImageSprite to a random location on the screen? The bad news: it doesn't. The good news: you can create your own procedures! Just like the built-in procedures, your procedure will show up in a drawer and can be used anywhere in the app.

Specifically, we will create a procedure to move the mole to a random location on the screen, which we will name MoveMole. We want to call MoveMole at the start of the game, when the user successfully touches the mole, and once per second.

Creating MoveMole

To understand how to move the mole, we need to look at how Android graphics work. The canvas (and the screen) can be thought of as a grid with x (horizontal) and y (vertical) coordinates, where the (x, y) coordinates of the upper-left corner are (0, 0). The x coordinate increases as you move to the right, and the y coordinate increases as you move down, as shown in Figure 3-4. The X and Y properties of an ImageSprite indicate where its upper-left corner should be, so the top-left mole has X and Y values of 0.

To determine the maximum available X and Y values so that Mole fits on the screen, we need to make use of the Width and Height properties of Mole and Canvas1. (The mole's Width and Height properties are the same as the size of the image you uploaded. When you created Canvas1, you set its Height to 300 pixels and its Width to "Fill parent," which copies the width of its "parent" element, the screen.) If the mole is 36 pixels wide and the canvas is 200 pixels wide, the x coordinate of the left side of the mole can be as low as 0 (all the way to the left) or as high as 164 (200 – 36, or Canvas1.Width – Mole.Width) without the mole extending off the right edge of the screen. Similarly, the y coordinate of the top of the mole can range from 0 to Canvas1.Height – Mole.Height.

Figure 3-5 shows the procedure you will create, annotated with descriptive comments (which you can optionally add to your procedure).

To randomly place the mole, we will want to select an x coordinate in the range from 0 to Canvas1.Width – Mole.Width. Similarly, we will want the y coordinate to be in the range from 0 to Canvas1.Height – Mole.Height. We can generate a random number through the built-in procedure random integer, found in the Math drawer. You will need to change the default "from" parameter from 1 to 0 and replace the "to" parameters, as shown in Figure 3-5.

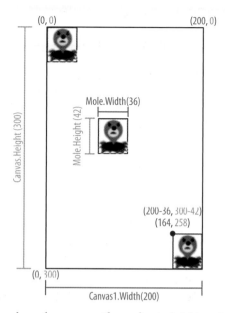

Figure 3-4. Positions of the mole on the screen, with coordinate, height, and width information; x coordinates and widths are shown in blue, while y coordinates and heights are shown in orange

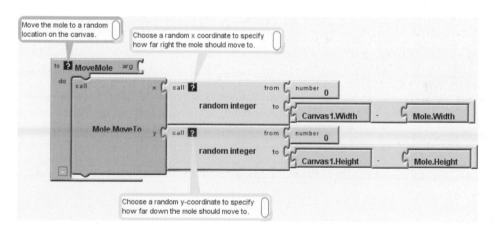

Figure 3-5. The MoveMole procedure, which places the mole in a random location

To create the procedure:

1. Click the Definition drawer under the Built-In tab in the Blocks Editor.

2. Drag out the **to procedure** block (not **to procedureWithResult**).

3. Click the text "procedure" on the new block and enter "MoveMole" to set the name of the procedure.

4. Since we want to move the mole, click the My Blocks tab, click the Mole drawer, and drag **Mole.MoveTo** into the procedure, to the right of "do." Note that we need to provide *x* and *y* coordinates.

5. To specify that the new *x* coordinate for the mole should be between 0 and Canvas1.Width – Mole.Width, as discussed earlier:

   a. Click the Built-In tab to get to the built-in procedures.

   b. Click the Math drawer.

   c. Drag out the **random integer** block, putting the plug (protrusion) on its left side into the "x" socket on **Mole.MoveTo**.

   d. Change the **number 1** on the "from" socket by clicking it and then entering 0.

   e. Discard the **number 100** by clicking it and pressing your keyboard's Del or Delete button, or by dragging it to the trash can.

   f. Click the Math drawer and drag a subtraction (-) block into the "to" socket.

   g. Click My Blocks to get to your components.

   h. Click the Canvas1 drawer and scroll down until you see **Canvas1.Width**, which you should drag to the left side of the subtraction operation.

   i. Similarly, click the Mole drawer and drag **Mole.Width** into the right side of the subtraction block.

6. Follow a similar procedure to specify that the *y* coordinate should be a random integer in the range from 0 to Canvas1.Height – Mole.Height.

7. Check your results against Figure 3-5.

To try out your **Mole.MoveTo** call, right-click the block and choose Do It. (You may need to restart the app by clicking "Connect to Device" first.) You should see the mole move on your phone screen, going to a different location each time (except in the extremely unlikely case that the random-number generator chooses the same place twice in a row).

Calling MoveMole when the app starts

Now that you've written the MoveMole procedure, let's make use of it. Because it's so common for programmers to want something to happen when an app starts, there's a block for that very purpose: **Screen1.Initialize**.

1. Click My Blocks, click the Screen1 drawer, and drag out **Screen1.Initialize**.

2. Click the My Definitions drawer, where you'll see a **call MoveMole** block. (It's pretty cool that you've created a new block, isn't it?!) Drag it out, putting it in **Screen1.Initialize**, as shown in Figure 3-6.

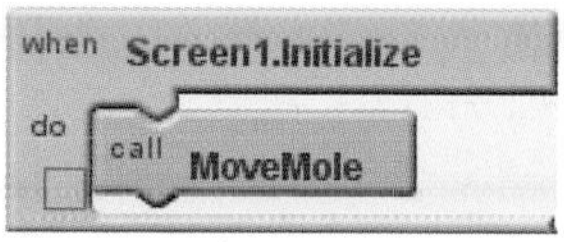

Figure 3-6. Calling the MoveMole procedure when the application starts

Calling MoveMole every second

Making the mole move every second will require the Clock component. We left Clock1's TimerInterval property at its default value of 1,000 (milliseconds), or 1 second. That means that every second, whatever is specified in a **Clock1.Timer** block will take place. Here's how to set that up:

1. Click My Blocks, click the Clock1 drawer, and drag out **Clock1.Timer**.

2. Click the My Definitions drawer and drag a **call MoveMole** block into the **Clock1 .Timer** block, as shown in Figure 3-7.

Figure 3-7. Calling the MoveMole procedure when the timer goes off (every second)

If that's too fast or slow for you, you can change Clock1's TimerInterval property in the Component Designer to make it move more or less frequently.

Keeping Score

As you may recall, you created two labels, HitsCountsLabel and MissesCountsLabel, which had initial values of 0. We'd like to increment the numbers in these labels whenever the user successfully touches the mole (a hit) or taps the screen without touching the mole (a miss). To do so, we will use the **Canvas1.Touched** block, which indicates that the canvas was touched, the *x* and *y* coordinates of where it was touched (which we don't need to know), and whether a sprite was touched (which we do need to know). Figure 3-8 shows the code you will create.

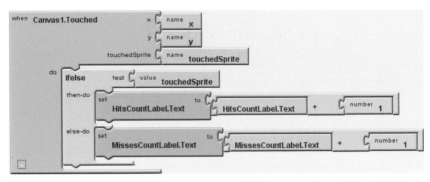

Figure 3-8. Incrementing the number of hits (HitsCountLabel) or misses (MissesCountLabel) when Canvas1 is touched

Figure 3-8's translation is whenever the canvas is touched, check whether a sprite was touched. Since there's only one sprite in our program, it has to be Mole1. If Mole1 is touched, add one to the number in HitsCountLabel.Text; otherwise, add one to MissesCountLabel.Text. (The value of touchedSprite is false if no sprite was touched.)

Here's how to create the blocks:

1. Click My Blocks, click the Canvas1 drawer, and drag out **Canvas1.Touched**.

2. Click Built-In, click the Control drawer, and drag out **ifelse**, placing it within **Canvas1.Touched**.

3. Click My Blocks, click the My Definitions drawer, and drag out **touchedSprite** and place it in **ifelse**'s test socket.

4. Since we want HitsCountLabel.Text to be incremented if the test succeeded (if the mole was touched):

    a. From the HitsCountLabel drawer, drag out the **set HitsCountLabel.Text to** block, putting it to the right of "then-do."

    b. Click Built-In, click the Math drawer, and drag out a plus sign (+), placing it in the "to" socket.

    c. Click My Blocks, click the HitsCountLabel drawer, and drag the **HitsCountLabel.Text** block to the left of the plus sign.

    d. Click Built-In, click the Math drawer, and drag a **number 123** block to the right of the plus sign. Click 123 and change it to 1.

5. Repeat step 4 for MissesCountLabel in the "else-do" section of the **ifelse**.

Test your app. *You can test this new code on your phone by touching the canvas, on and off the mole, and watching the score change.*

Procedural Abstraction

The ability to name and later call a set of instructions like MoveMole is one of the key tools in computer science and is referred to as *procedural abstraction*. It is called "abstraction" because the caller of the procedure (who, in real-world projects, is likely to be different from the author of the procedure) only needs to know what the procedure does (moves the mole), not how it does it (by making two calls to the random-number generator). Without procedural abstraction, big computer programs would not be possible, because they contain too much code for one person to hold in his head at a time. This is analogous to the division of labor in the real world, where, for example, different engineers design different parts of a car, none of them understanding all of the details, and the driver only has to understand the interface (e.g., pressing the brake pedal to stop the car), not the implementation.

Some advantages of procedural abstraction over copying and pasting code are:

- It is easier to test code if it is neatly segregated from the rest of the program.

- If there's a mistake in the code, it only needs to be fixed in one place.

- To change the implementation, such as making sure that the mole doesn't move somewhere that it appeared recently, you only have to modify the code in one place.

- Procedures can be collected into a library and used in different programs. (Unfortunately, this functionality is not currently supported in App Inventor.)

- Breaking code into pieces helps you think about and implement the application ("divide and conquer").

- Choosing good names for procedures helps document the code, making it easier for someone else (or you, a month later) to read.

In later chapters, you will learn ways of making procedures even more powerful: adding arguments, providing return values, and having procedures call themselves. For an overview, see Chapter 21.

Resetting the Score

A friend who sees you playing MoleMash will probably want to give it a try too, so it's good to have a way to reset the number of hits and misses to 0. Depending on which tutorials you've already worked through, you may be able to figure out how to do this without reading the following instructions. Consider giving it a try before reading ahead.

What we need is a **ResetButton.Click** block that sets the values of HitsCountLabel.Text and MissesCountLabel.Text to 0. Create the blocks shown in Figure 3-9.

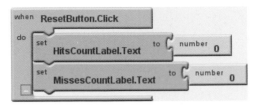

Figure 3-9. Resetting the number of hits (HitsCountLabel) and Misses (MissesCountLabel) when the Reset button is pressed

At this point, you probably don't need step-by-step instructions for creating a button click event handler with text labels, but here's a tip to help speed up the process: instead of getting your number from the Math drawer, just type 0, and the block should be created for you. (These kinds of keyboard shortcuts exist for other blocks, too.)

 Test your app. *Try hitting and missing the mole and then pressing the Reset button.*

Adding Behavior When the Mole Is Touched

We said earlier that we want the phone to vibrate when the mole is touched, which we can do with the **Sound1.Vibrate** block, as shown in Figure 3-10. Note that the parameter names x1 and y1 are used in **Mole.Touched** because x and y have already been used in **Canvas1.Touched**.

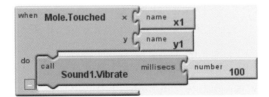

Figure 3-10. Making the phone vibrate briefly (for 100 milliseconds) when the mole is touched

 Test your app. *See how the vibration works when you actually touch the mole. If the vibration is too long or too short for your taste, change the number of milliseconds in **Sound1.Vibrate**.*

The Complete App: MoleMash

Figure 3-11 illustrates the blocks for the complete MoleMash app.

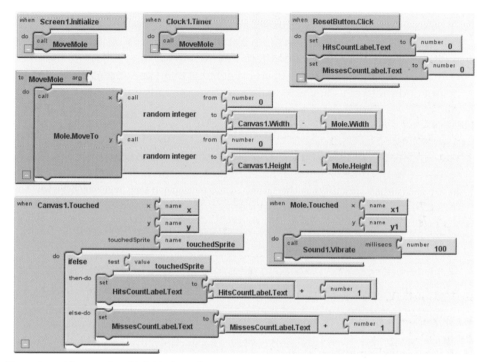

Figure 3-11. The complete MoleMash application

Variations

Here are some ideas for additions to MoleMash:

- Add buttons to let the user make the mole move faster or slower.

- Add a label to keep track of and display the number of times the mole has appeared (moved).

- Add a second ImageSprite with a picture of something that the user should *not* hit, such as a flower. If the user touches it, penalize him by reducing his score or ending the game.

- Instead of using a picture of a mole, let the user select a picture with the ContactPicker component.

Summary

In this chapter, we've covered a number of techniques useful for apps in general and games in particular:

- The Canvas component makes use of an x-y coordinate system, where x represents the horizontal direction (from 0 at the left to Canvas.Width-1 at the right) and y the vertical direction (from 0 at the top to Canvas.Height-1 at the bottom). The height and width of an ImageSprite can be subtracted from the height and width of a Canvas to make sure the sprite fits entirely on the Canvas.

- You can take advantage of the phone's touchscreen through the Canvas and ImageSprite components' Touched methods.

- You can create real-time applications that react not just to user input but also in response to the phone's internal timer. Specifically, the **Clock.Timer** block runs at the frequency specified in the Clock.Interval property and can be used to move ImageSprite (or other) components.

- Labels can be used to display scores, which go up (or down) in response to the player's actions.

- Tactile feedback can be provided to users through the Sound.Vibrate method, which makes the phone vibrate for the specified number of milliseconds.

- Instead of just using the built-in methods, you can create procedures to name a set of blocks (**MoveMole**) that can be called just like the built-in ones. This is called procedural abstraction and is a key idea in computer science, enabling code reuse and making complex applications possible.

- You can generate unpredictable behavior with the **random integer** block in the Math drawer, making a game different every time it is played.

You'll learn more techniques for games, including detecting collisions between moving ImageSprite components, in Chapter 5 (Ladybug Chase).

CHAPTER 4

No Texting While Driving

This chapter walks you through the development of No Texting While Driving, an app that autoresponds to text messages you receive while you're driving. The app, first created with App Inventor by a beginning computer science student, is similar to a now-mass-produced app developed by State Farm Insurance. It is a prime example of how App Inventor provides access to some of the great features of the Android phone, including SMS text processing, database management, text-to-speech, and the location sensor.

In January 2010, the National Safety Council (NSC) announced the results of a study that found that at least 28 percent of all traffic accidents—close to 1.6 million crashes every year—are caused by drivers using cell phones, and at least 200,000 of those accidents occurred while drivers were texting.[1] As a result, many states have banned drivers from using cell phones altogether.

Daniel Finnegan, a student in the Fall 2010 session of the University of San Francisco App Inventor programming class, came up with a great app idea to help with the driving and texting epidemic. The app he created, which is shown in Figure 4-1, responds automatically (and hands-free) to any text with a message such as "I'm driving right now, I'll contact you shortly."

Figure 4-1. The No Texting While Driving app

---

1 *http://www.nsc.org/pages/nscestimates16millioncrashescausedbydriversusingcellphonesandtexting.aspx*

Some in-class brainstorming led to a few additional features that were developed for a tutorial posted on the App Inventor site:

The user can change the response for different situations
For example, if you're going into a meeting or a movie instead of driving, the response can be modified accordingly.

The app speaks the text aloud
Even if you know the app will autorespond, the jingle of incoming texts can kill you with curiosity.

The response message can contain your current location
If your partner is at home making dinner, he or she would probably like to know how much longer your commute will last, without endangering you by having you answer the text.

Some weeks after the app was posted on the App Inventor site, State Farm Insurance created an Android app called "On the Move," which has similar functionality to No Texting While Driving.[2] The service is free to anyone, as part of State Farm's updated Pocket Agent→ for Android™ application, which the company announced in a YouTube video that can be found here: *http://www.youtube.com/watch?v=3xtjzO0-Hfw*.

We don't know if Daniel's app or the tutorial on the App Inventor site influenced "On the Move," but it's interesting to consider the possibility that an app created in a beginning programming course (by a creative writing student, no less!) might have inspired this mass-produced piece of software, or at least contributed to the ecosystem that brought it about. It certainly demonstrates how App Inventor has lowered the barrier of entry so that anyone with a good idea can quickly and inexpensively turn his idea into a tangible, interactive app.

What You'll Learn

This is a more complex app than those in the previous chapters, so you'll build it one piece of functionality at a time, starting with the autoresponse message. You'll learn about:

- The Texting component for sending texts and processing received texts.
- An input form for submitting the custom response message.
- The TinyDB database component for saving the customized message even after the app is closed.

---

2 *http://www.statefarm.com/aboutus/newsroom/20100819.asp*

- The **Screen.Initialize** event for loading the custom response when the app launches.
- The Text-to-Speech component for speaking the texts aloud.
- The LocationSensor component for reporting the driver's current location.

Getting Started

For this app to work, you need a text-to-speech module, *Text-To-Speech Extended*, on your phone. This module is included in Android version 2 or higher, but if you are running an Android 1.*x* operating system, you'll need to download it from the Android Market. On your phone:

1. Open the Market app.
2. Search for TTS.
3. Select the app *Text-To-Speech Extended* to install.

Once the Text-To-Speech module is installed, open it to test its features. When it opens, set the default language as desired. Then select "Listen to Preview." If you don't hear anything, make sure the volume on your phone is turned up. You can also change the way the voice sounds by changing the setting for the TTS Default Engine property.

After you've set up the Text-To-Speech module to your liking, connect to the App Inventor website and start a new project. Name it "NoTextingWhileDriving" (project names can't have spaces) and set the screen's title to "No Texting While Driving". Open the Blocks Editor and connect to the phone.

Designing the Components

The user interface for the app is relatively simple: it has a label that displays the automated response, along with a text box and a button for submitting a change. You'll also need to drag in a Texting component, a TinyDB component, a TextToSpeech component, and a LocationSensor component, all of which will appear in the "Non-visible components" area. You can see how this should look in the snapshot of the Component Designer shown in Figure 4-2.

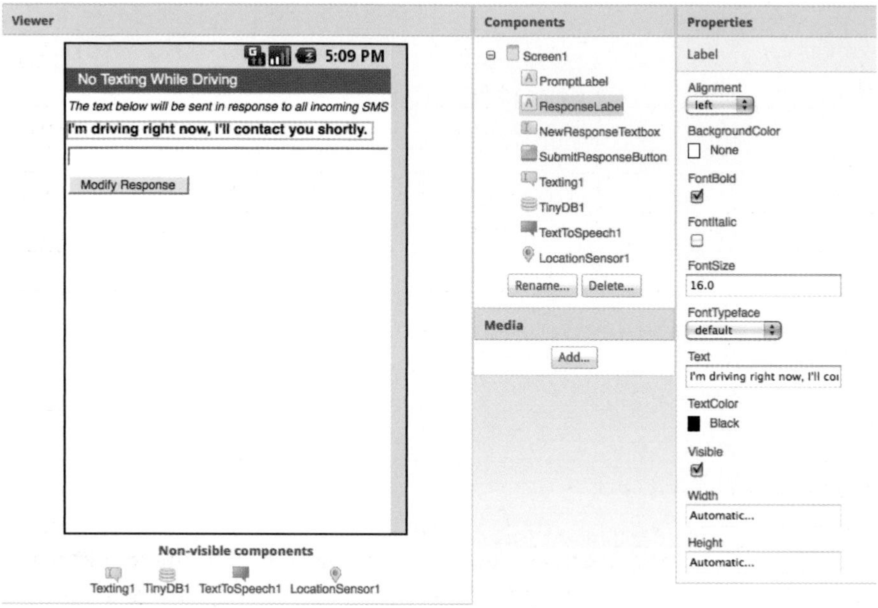

Figure 4-2. The No Texting While Driving app in the Component Designer

You can build the user interface shown in Figure 4-2 by dragging out the components listed in Table 4-1.

Set the properties of the components in the following way:

- Set the `Text` of `PromptLabel` to "The text below will be sent in response to all SMS texts received while this app is running."

- Set the `Text` of `ResponseLabel` to "I'm driving right now, I'll contact you shortly." Check its `boldness` property.

- Set the `Text` of `NewResponseTextbox` to "". (This leaves the text box blank for the user's input.)

- Set the `Hint` of `NewResponseTextbox` to "Enter new response text."

- Set the `Text` of `SubmitResponseButton` to "Modify Response."

Adding Behaviors to the Components

You'll start by programming the basic text autoresponse behavior, and then successively add more functionality.

Table 4-1. All the components for the No Texting While Driving app

Component type	Palette group	What you'll name it	Purpose
Label	Basic	PromptLabel	Let the user know how the app works.
Label	Basic	ResponseLabel	The response that will be sent back to the sender of original text.
TextBox	Basic	NewResponseTextbox	The user will enter the custom response here.
Button	Basic	SubmitResponseButton	The user clicks this to submit response.
Texting	Social	Texting1	Process the texts.
TinyDB	Basic	TinyDB1	Store the response in the database.
TextToSpeech	Other stuff	TextToSpeech1	Speak the texts aloud.
LocationSensor	Sensors	LocationSensor1	Sense where the phone is.

Programming an autoresponse

For the autoresponse behavior, you'll use App Inventor's Texting component. You can think of this component as a little person inside your phone that knows how to read and write texts. For reading texts, the component provides a **Texting .MessageReceived** event block. You can drag this block out and place blocks inside it to show what should happen when a text is received. In the case of this app, we want to automatically send back a prewritten response text.

To program the response text, you'll place a **Texting1.SendMessage** block within the **Texting1.MessageReceived** block. **Texting1.SendMessage** actually sends the text—so you'll first need to tell the component what message to send, and who to send it to, before calling **Texting1.SendMessage**. Table 4-2 lists all the blocks you'll need for this autoresponse behavior, and Figure 4-3 shows how they should look in the Blocks Editor.

Table 4-2. The blocks for sending an autoresponse

Block type	Drawer	Purpose
Texting1.MessageReceived	Texting	The event handler that is triggered when the phone receives a text.
set Texting1.PhoneNumber to	Texting	Set the PhoneNumber property before sending.
value number	My Definitions	The phone number of the person who sent the text.
set Texting1.Message to	Texting	Set the Message property before sending.
ResponseLabel.Text	ResponseLabel	The message the user has entered.
Texting1.SendMessage	Texting	Send the message.

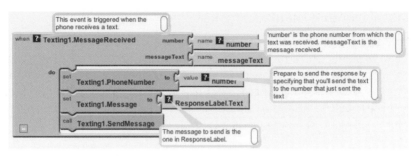

Figure 4-3. Responding to an incoming text

How the blocks work

When the phone receives a text message, the **Texting1.MessageReceived** event is triggered. As shown in Figure 4-3, the phone number of the sender is in the argument number, and the message received is in the argument messageText. For the autoresponse, the app needs to send a text message to the sender. To send the text, you first need to set the two key properties of the Texting component: PhoneNumber and Message.Texting.PhoneNumber is set to the number of the sender, and Texting.Message is set to the text you typed into ResponseLabel: "I'm driving right now, I'll contact you shortly." Once these are set, the app calls **Texting.SendMessage** to actually send the response.

You may be wondering about the yellow boxes that we have in the Blocks Editor. Those are *comments*, and you can add them by right-clicking a block and selecting Add Comment. Once you add a comment, you can show or hide it by clicking the black question mark that appears. You don't have to add comments in your app— we've simply included them here to help describe each block and what it does.

Most people use comments to document how they are building their app; comments explain how the program works, but they won't make the app behave differently. Comments are important, both for you as you build the app and modify it later, and for other people who might customize it. The one thing everyone agrees on about software is that it changes and transforms often. For this reason, commenting code is very important in software engineering, and especially so with open source software like App Inventor.

Test your app. *You'll need a second phone to test this behavior. If you don't have one, you can register with Google Voice or a similar service and send texts from that service to your phone.*

From the second phone, send a text to the phone running the app. Does the second phone receive the response text?

Entering a Custom Response

Next, let's add blocks so the user can enter her own custom response. In the Component Designer, you added a TextBox component named NewResponseTextbox; this is where the user will enter the custom response. When the user clicks on the SubmitResponseButton, you need to copy her entry (NewResponseTextbox) into the ResponseLabel, which is used to respond to texts. Table 4-3 lists the blocks you'll need for transferring a newly entered response into the ResponseLabel.

Table 4-3. Blocks for displaying the custom response

Block type	Drawer	Purpose
SubmitResponseButton .Click	SubmitResponseButton	The user clicks this button to submit a new response message.
set ResponseLabel.Text to	ResponseLabel	Move (set) the newly input value to this label.
NewResponseTextbox.Text	NewResponseTextbox	The user has entered the new response here.

How the blocks work

Think of how a typical input form works: you first enter something in a text box, and then click a submit button to tell the system to process it. The input form for this app is no different. Figure 4-4 shows how the blocks are programmed so that when the user clicks the SubmitResponseButton, the **SubmitResponseButton.Click** event is triggered.

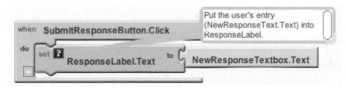

Figure 4-4. Setting the response to the user's entry

The event handler in this case copies (or *sets*, in programming terms) what the user has entered in NewResponseTextbox into the ResponseLabel. Recall that ResponseLabel holds the message that will be sent out in the autoresponse, so you want to be sure to place the newly entered custom message there.

 Test your app. *Enter a custom response and submit it, and then use the second phone to send another text to the phone running the app. Was the custom response sent?*

Storing the Custom Response in a Database

You've built a great app already, with one catch: if the user enters a custom response, and then closes the app and relaunches it, the custom response will not appear (instead, the default one will). This behavior is not what your users will expect; they'll want to see the custom response when they restart the app. To make this happen, you need to store that custom response *persistently*.

You might think that placing data in the `ResponseLabel.Text` property is technically "storing" it, but the issue is that data stored in component properties is *transient* data. Transient data is like your short-term memory; the phone "forgets" it as soon as an app closes. If you want your app to remember something *persistently*, you have to transfer it from short-term memory (a component property or variable) to long-term memory (a database).

To store data persistently, you'll use the `TinyDB` component, which stores data in a database that's already on the Android device. `TinyDB` provides two functions: `StoreValue` and `GetValue`. The former allows the app to store information in the device's database, while the latter lets the app retrieve information that has already been stored.

For many apps, you'll use the following scheme:

1. Store data to the database each time the user submits a new value.

2. When the app launches, load the data from the database into a variable or property.

You'll start by modifying the **SubmitResponseButton.Click** event handler so that it stores the data persistently, using the blocks listed in Table 4-4.

Table 4-4. Blocks for storing the custom response with TinyDB

Block type	Drawer	Purpose
TinyDB1.StoreValue	TinyDB1	Store the custom message in the phone's database.
text ("responseMessage")	Text	Use this as the tag for the data.
ResponseLabel.Text	ResponseLabel	The response message is now here.

How the blocks work

This app uses **TinyDB** to take the text it just put in `ResponseLabel` and store it in the database. As shown in Figure 4-5, when you store something in the database, you provide a tag with it; in this case, the tag is "responseMessage." Think of the tag as the name for the data's spot in the database; it uniquely identifies the data you are storing. As you'll see in the next section, you'll use the same tag ("responseMessage") when you load the data back in from the database.

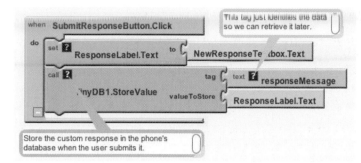

Figure 4-5. Storing the custom response persistently

Retrieving the Custom Response When the App Opens

The reason for storing the custom response in the database is so it can be loaded back into the app the next time the user opens it. App Inventor provides a special event block that is triggered when the app opens: **Screen1.Initialize** (if you completed MoleMash in Chapter 3, you've seen this before). If you drag this event block out and place blocks in it, those blocks will be executed right when the app launches.

For this app, your **Screen1.Initialize** event handler should check to see if a custom response has been put in the database. If so, the custom response should be loaded in using the **TinyDB.GetValue** function. The blocks you'll need for this are shown in Table 4-5.

Table 4-5. Blocks for loading the data back in when the app is opened

Block type	Drawer	Purpose
def variable ("response")	Definition (don't forget: this is different than the My Definitions drawer)	A temporary variable to hold the retrieved data.
text ("")	Text	The initial value for the variable can be anything.
Screen1.Initialize	Screen1	This is triggered when the app begins.
set global response to	My Definitions	Set this variable to the value retrieved from the database.
TinyDB1.GetValue	TinyDB1	Get the stored response text from the database.
text ("responseMessage")	Text	Plug this into the tag slot of **TinyDB .GetValue**, making sure the text is the same as that used in **TinyDB.Store Value** earlier.
if	Control	Ask if the retrieved value has some text.
>	Math	Check if the length of the retrieved value is greater than (>) 0.

Table 4-5. Blocks for loading the data back in when the app is opened (continued)

Block type	Drawer	Purpose
length text	Text	Check if the length of the retrieved value is greater than 0.
global response	My Definitions	This variable holds the value retrieved from **TinyDB1.GetValue**.
number (0)	Math	Compare this with the length of the response.
set ResponseLabel.Text to	ResponseLabel	If we retrieved something, place it in `ResponseLabel`.
global response	My Definitions	This variable holds the value retrieved from **TinyDB1.GetValue**.

How the blocks work

The blocks are shown in Figure 4-6. To understand them, you must envision a user opening the app for the first time, entering a custom response, and opening the app subsequent times. The first time the user opens the app, there won't be any custom response in the database to load, so you want to leave the default response in the `ResponseLabel`. On successive launches, you want to load the previously stored custom response from the database and place it in the `ResponseLabel`.

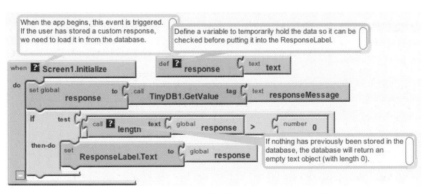

Figure 4-6. Loading the custom response from the database upon app initialization

When the app begins, the **Screen1.Initialize** event is triggered. The app calls the **TinyDB1.GetValue** with a tag of "responseMessage," the same tag you used when you stored the user's custom response entry earlier. The retrieved value is placed in the variable `response` so that it can be checked before we place it as the `ResponseLabel`. Can you think of why you'd want to check what you get back from the database before displaying it as the custom message to the user?

TinyDB returns empty text if there is no data for a particular tag in the database. There won't be data the first time the app is launched; this will be the case until the user enters a custom response. Because the variable response now holds the returned value, we can use the **if** block to check if the length of what was returned by the database is greater than 0. If the length of the value contained in response is greater than 0, the app knows that TinyDB did return something, and the retrieved value can be placed into the ResponseLabel. If the length isn't greater than 0, the app knows there is no previously stored response, so it doesn't modify the ResponseLabel (leaving the default response in it).

Test your app. *You cannot test this behavior through live testing, as the database gets emptied each time you "Connect to Device" to restart the app.*

Instead, select "Package for Phone"→Show Barcode, and then download the app to your phone by scanning the barcode. Once the app is installed, enter a new response message in the NewResponseTextbox *and click the* SubmitResponseButton. *Then close the app and restart it. Does your custom message appear?*

Speaking the Incoming Texts Aloud

In this section, you'll modify the app so that when you receive a text, the sender's phone number, along with the message, is spoken aloud. The idea here is that when you're driving and hear a text come in, you might be tempted to check the text even if you know the app is sending an autoresponse. With text-to-speech, you can hear the incoming texts and keep your hands on the wheel.

Android devices provide text-to-speech capabilities and App Inventor provides a component, TextToSpeech, that will speak any text you give it. (Note that here "text" is meant in the general sense of the word—a sequence of letters, digits, and punctuation—not an SMS text.)

In the "Getting Started" section of this app, we asked you to download a text-to-speech module from the Android Market. If you didn't do so then, you'll need to now. Once that module is installed and configured as desired, you can use the TextToSpeech component within App Inventor.

The TextToSpeech component is very simple to use—you just call its Speak function and plug in the text you want spoken into its *message* slot. For instance, the function shown in Figure 4-7 would say, "Hello World."

Figure 4-7. Blocks for speaking "Hello World" aloud

For the No Texting While Driving app, you'll need to provide a more complicated message to be spoken, one that includes both the text received and the phone number of the person who sent it. Instead of plugging in a static text object like the "Hello World" text block, you'll plug in a **make text** block. An incredibly useful function, **make text** allows you to combine separate pieces of text (or numbers and other characters) into a single text object.

You'll need to make the call to **TextToSpeech.Speak** within the **Texting.Message Received** event handler you programmed earlier. The blocks you programmed previously handle this event by setting the PhoneNumber and Message properties of the Texting component appropriately and then sending the response text. You'll extend that event handler by adding the blocks listed in Table 4-6.

Table 4-6. Blocks for speaking the incoming text aloud

Block type	Drawer	Purpose
TextToSpeech1.Speak	TextToSpeech1	Speak the message received out loud.
make text	Text	Build the words that will be spoken.
text ("SMS text received from")	Text	The first words spoken.
value number	My Definitions	The number from which the original text was received.
text (".The message is")	Text	Put a period in after the phone number and then say, "The message is."
value messageText	My Definitions	The original message received.

How the blocks work

After the response is sent, the **TextToSpeech1.Speak** function is called, as shown at the bottom of Figure 4-8. You can plug any text object into the message slot of the **TextToSpeech1.Speak** function. In this case, **make text** is used to build the words to be spoken—it *concatenates* (or adds) together the text "SMS text received from" and the phone number from which the message was received (**value number**), plus the text ".The message is," and finally the message received (**value messageText**). So, if the text "hello" was sent from the number "111–2222," the phone would say, "SMS text received from 111–2222. The message is hello."

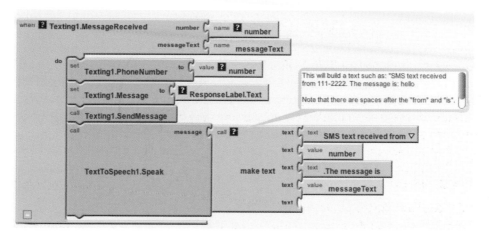

Figure 4-8. Speaking the incoming text aloud

 Test your app. *You'll need a second phone to test your app. From the second phone, send a text to the phone running the app. Does the phone running the app speak the text aloud? Does it still send an automated response?*

Adding Location Information to the Response

Apps like Facebook's Place and Google's Latitude use GPS information to help people track one another's location. There are major privacy concerns with such apps, one reason being that location tracking kindles people's fear of a "Big Brother" apparatus that a totalitarian government might set up to track its citizens' whereabouts. But apps that use location information can be quite useful—think of a lost child, or hikers who've gotten off the trail in the woods.

In the No Texting While Driving app, location tracking can be used to convey a bit more information in response to incoming texts. Instead of just "I'm driving," the response message can be something like "I'm driving and I'm at 3413 Cherry Avenue." For someone awaiting the arrival of a friend or family member, this extra information can be helpful.

App Inventor provides the LocationSensor component for interfacing with the phone's GPS (or *geographical positioning system*). Besides latitude and longitude information, the LocationSensor can also tap into Google Maps to provide the driver's current street address.

It's important to note that LocationSensor doesn't always have a reading. For this reason, you need to take care to use the component properly. Specifically, your app should respond to the **LocationSensor.LocationChanged** event handler. A **LocationChanged** event occurs when the phone's location sensor first gets a reading, and when the phone is moved to generate a new reading. Using the blocks listed in Table 4-7, our scheme will respond to the **LocationChanged** event by placing the current address in a variable we'll name **lastKnownLocation**. Later, we'll change the response message to incorporate the address we get from this variable.

Table 4-7. Blocks to set up the location sensor

Block type	Drawer	Purpose
def variable ("lastKnownLocation")	Definitions	Create a variable to hold the last read address.
text ("unknown")	Text	Set the default value in case the phone's sensor is not working.
LocationSensor1.LocationChanged	LocationSensor1	This is triggered on the first location reading and every location change.
set global lastKnownLocation to	My Definitions	Set this variable to be used later.
LocationSensor1.CurrentAddress	LocationSensor1	This is a street address such as "2222 Willard Street, Atlanta, Georgia."

How the blocks work

The **LocationSensor1.LocationChanged** event is triggered the first time the sensor gets a location reading and when the device is moved so that a new reading is generated. Since you eventually want to send a street address as part of the response message, Figure 4-9 shows how the **LocationSensor1.CurrentAddress** function is called to get that information and store it in the lastKnownLocation variable. Behind the scenes, this function makes a call to Google Maps (via an *API*, something you'll learn about in Chapter 24) to determine the closest street address for the latitude and longitude that the sensor reads.

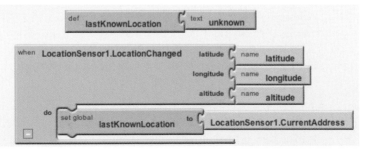

Figure 4-9. Recording the phone's location in a variable each time the GPS location is sensed

Note that with these blocks, you've finished only half of the job. The app still needs to incorporate the location information into the autoresponse text that will be sent back to the sender. Let's do that next.

Sending the Location As Part of the Response

Using the variable lastKnownLocation, you can modify the **Texting1.Message Received** event handler to add location information to the response. Table 4-8 lists the blocks you'll need for this.

Table 4-8. Blocks to display location information in the autoresponse

Block type	Drawer	Purpose
make text	Text	If there is a location reading, build a compound text object.
ResponseLabel.Text	MessageTextBox	This is the (custom) message in the text box.
text ("My last known location is:")	Text	This will be spoken after the custom message (note the leading space).
global lastKnownLocation	LocationSensor	This is an address such as "2222 Willard Street, Atlanta, Georgia."

How the blocks work

This behavior works in concert with the **LocationSensor1.LocationChanged** event and the variable lastKnownLocation. As you can see in Figure 4-10, instead of directly sending a message containing the text in ResponseLabel.Text, the app first builds a message using **make text**. It combines the response text in ResponseLabel.Text with the text "My last known location is:" followed by the variable lastKnownLocation.

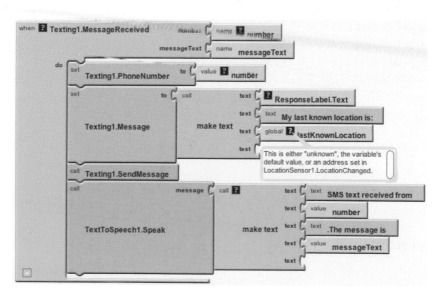

Figure 4-10. Including location information in the response text

The default value of **lastKnownLocation** is "unknown," so if the location sensor hasn't yet generated a reading, the second part of the response message will contain the text "My last known location is: unknown." If there has been a reading, the second part of the response will be something like "My last known location is: 876 Willard Street, San Francisco, CA 95422."

 Test your app. *From the second phone, send a text to the phone running the app. Does the second phone receive the response text with the location information? If it doesn't, make sure you've turned GPS on in the first phone's Location settings.*

The Complete App: No Texting While Driving

Figure 4-11 shows the final block configuration for No Texting While Driving.

Variations

Once you get the app working, you might want to explore some variations. For example:

- Write a version that lets the user define custom responses for particular incoming phone numbers. You'll need to add conditional (if) blocks that check for those numbers. For more information on conditional blocks, see Chapter 18.

- Write a version that sends custom responses based on whether the user is within certain latitude/longitude boundaries. So, if the app determines that you're in room 222, it will send back "Bob is in room 222 and can't text right now." For more information on the LocationSensor and determining boundaries, see Chapter 23.

- Write a version that sounds an alarm when a text is received from a number in a "notify" list. For help working with lists, see Chapter 19.

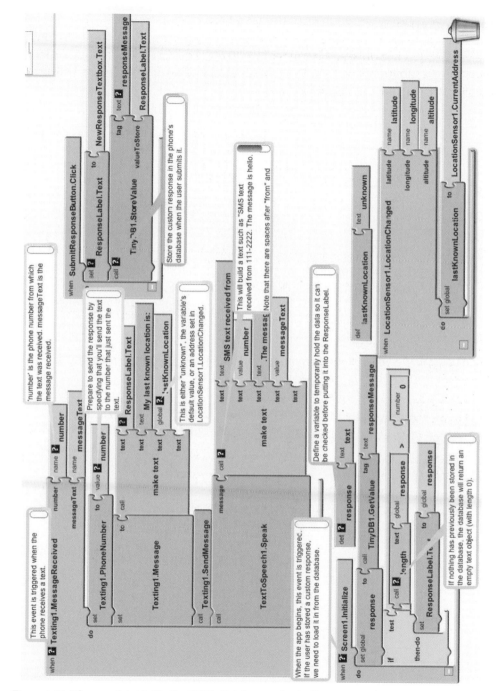

Figure 4-11. The complete No Texting While Driving app (with all comments showing)

Summary

Here are some of the concepts we've covered in this tutorial:

- The Texting component can be used to both send text messages and process the ones that are received. Before calling **Texting.SendMessage**, you should set the PhoneNumber and Message properties of the Texting component. To respond to an incoming text, program the **Texting.MessageReceived** handler.

- The TinyDB component is used to store information persistently—in the phone's database—so that the data can be reloaded each time the app is opened. For more information on TinyDB, see Chapter 22.

- The TextToSpeech component takes any text object and speaks it aloud.

- **make text** is used to piece together (or concatenate) separate text items into a single text object.

- The LocationSensor component can report the phone's latitude, longitude, and current street address. To ensure that it has a reading, you should access its data within the **LocationSensor.LocationChanged** event handler, which is triggered the first time a reading is made and upon every change thereafter. For more information on the LocationSensor, see Chapter 23.

If you're interested in exploring SMS-processing apps further, check out the Broadcast Hub app in Chapter 11.

CHAPTER 5

Ladybug Chase

Games are among the most exciting mobile phone apps, both to play and to create. The recent smash hit Angry Birds was downloaded 50 million times in its first year and is played more than a million hours every day, according to Rovio, its developer. (There is even talk of making it into a feature film!) While we can't guarantee that kind of success, we can help you create your own games with App Inventor, including this one involving a ladybug eating aphids while avoiding a frog.

What You'll Build

With the Ladybug Chase app shown in Figure 5-1, the user can:

- Control a ladybug by tilting the phone.

- View an energy-level bar on the screen, which decreases over time, leading to the ladybug's starvation.

- Make the ladybug chase and eat aphids to gain energy and prevent starvation.

- Help the ladybug avoid a frog that wants to eat it.

Figure 5-1. The Ladybug Chase game in the Designer

What You'll Learn

You should work through the MoleMash app in Chapter 3 before delving into this chapter, as it assumes you know about procedure creation, random-number generation, the **ifelse** block, and the ImageSprite, Canvas, Sound, and Clock components.

In addition to reviewing material from MoleMash and other previous chapters, this chapter introduces:

- Using multiple ImageSprite components and detecting collisions between them.

- Detecting phone tilts with an OrientationSensor component and using it to control an ImageSprite.

- Changing the picture displayed for an ImageSprite.

- Drawing lines on a Canvas component.

- Controlling multiple events with a Clock component.

- Using variables to keep track of numbers (the ladybug's energy level).

- Creating and using procedures with parameters.

- Using the **and** block.

Designing the Components

This application will have a Canvas that provides a playing field for three ImageSprite components: one for the ladybug, one for the aphid, and one for the frog, which will also require a Sound component for its "ribbit." The OrientationSensor will be used to measure the phone's tilt to move the ladybug, and a Clock will be used to change the aphid's direction. There will be a second Canvas that displays the ladybug's energy level. A Reset button will restart the game if the ladybug starves or is eaten. Table 5-1 provides a complete list of the components in this app.

Table 5-1. All of the components for the Ladybug Chase game

Component type	Palette group	What you'll name it	Purpose
Canvas	Basic	FieldCanvas	Playing field.
ImageSprite	Animation	Ladybug	User-controlled player.
OrientationSensor	Sensors	OrientationSensor1	Detect the phone's tilt to control the ladybug.
Clock	Basic	Clock1	Determines when to change the Image Sprites' headings
ImageSprite	Animation	Aphid	The ladybug's prey.
ImageSprite	Animation	Frog	The ladybug's predator.
Canvas	Basic	EnergyCanvas	Display the ladybug's energy level.
Button	Basic	RestartButton	Restart the game.
Sound	Media	Sound1	"Ribbit" when the frog eats the ladybug.

Getting Started

Download the images of the ladybug, aphid, and frog from the book's website (*http://examples.oreilly.com/0636920016632/*). You'll also need to download the sound file for the frog's ribbit.

Connect to the App Inventor website and start a new project. Name it "LadybugChase" and also set the screen's title to "Ladybug Chase". Open the Blocks Editor and connect to the phone. Add the images you found or created, as well as the sound file, to the Media panel.

If you will be using a phone, you'll need to disable autorotation of the screen, which changes the display direction when you turn the phone. On most phones, you do this by going to the home screen, pressing the menu button, selecting Settings, selecting Display, and unchecking the box labeled "Auto-rotate screen."

Animating the Ladybug

In this "first-person chewer" game, the user will be represented by a ladybug, whose movement will be controlled by the phone's tilt. This brings the user into the game in a different way from MoleMash, in which the user was outside the phone, reaching in.

Adding the Components

While previous chapters have had you create all the components at once, that's not how developers typically work. Instead, it's more common to create one part of a program at a time, test it, and then move on to the next part of the program. In this section, we will create the ladybug and control its movement.

- Create a Canvas in the Component Designer, name it FieldCanvas, and set its Width to "Fill parent" and its Height to 300 pixels.

- Place an ImageSprite on the Canvas, renaming it Ladybug and setting its Picture property to the (live) ladybug image. Don't worry about the values of the X and Y properties, as those will depend on where on the canvas you placed the ImageSprite.

As you may have noticed, ImageSprites also have Interval, Heading, and Speed properties, which we will use in this program:

- The Interval property, which you can set to 10 (milliseconds) for this game, specifies how often the ImageSprite should move itself (as opposed to being moved by the MoveTo procedure, which you used for MoleMash).

- The Heading property indicates the direction in which the ImageSprite should move, in degrees. For example, 0 means due right, 90 means straight up, 180 means due left, and so on. Leave the Heading as-is right now; we will change it in the Blocks Editor.

- The Speed property specifies how many pixels the ImageSprite should move whenever its Interval (10 milliseconds) passes. We will also set the Speed property in the Blocks Editor.

For more details on image sprites, see Chapter 17.

The ladybug's movement will be controlled by an OrientationSensor, which detects how the phone is tilted. We want use the Clock component to check the phone's orientation every 10 milliseconds (100 times per second) and change the ladybug's Heading (direction) accordingly. We will set this up in the Blocks Editor as follows:

1. Add an OrientationSensor, which will appear in the "Non-visible components" section.

2. Add a Clock, which will also appear in the "Non-visible components" section, and set its TimerInterval to 10 milliseconds. Check what you've added against Figure 5-2.

Adding the Behavior

Moving to the Blocks Editor, create the procedure UpdateLadybug and a **Clock1 .Timer** block, as shown in Figure 5-3. Try typing the names of some of the blocks (such as "Clock1.Timer") instead of dragging them out of the drawers. (Note that the operation applied to the number 100 is multiplication, indicated by an asterisk, which may be hard to see in the figure.) You do not need to create the yellow comment callouts, although you can by right-clicking a block and selecting Add Comment.

The UpdateLadybug procedure makes use of two of the OrientationSensor's most useful properties:

- Angle, which indicates the direction in which the phone is tilted (in degrees).

- Magnitude, which indicates the amount of tilt, ranging from 0 (no tilt) to 1 (maximum tilt).

Multiplying the Magnitude by 100 tells the ladybug that it should move between 0 and 100 pixels in the specified Heading (direction) whenever its TimerInterval, which you previously set to 10 milliseconds in the Component Designer, passes.

Although you can try this out on the connected phone, the ladybug's movement might be both slower and jerkier than if you package and download the app to the phone. If, after doing that, you find the ladybug's movement too sluggish, increase the speed multiplier. If the ladybug seems too jerky, decrease it.

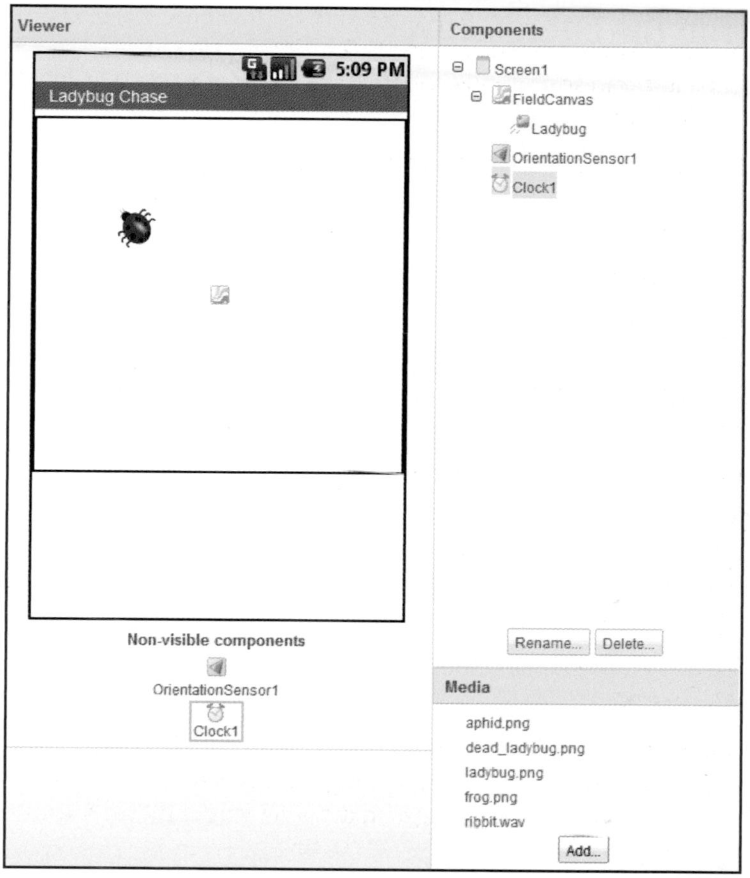

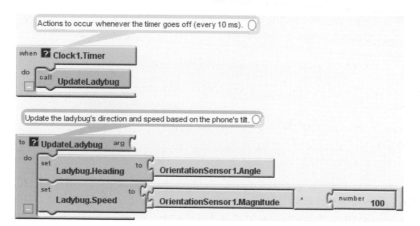

Figure 5-2. *Setting up the user interface in the Component Designer for animating the ladybug*

Figure 5-3. *Changing the ladybug's heading and speed every 10 milliseconds*

Displaying the Energy Level

We will display the ladybug's energy level with a red bar in a second canvas. The line will be 1 pixel high, and its width will be the same number of pixels as the ladybug's energy, which ranges from 200 (well fed) to 0 (dead).

Adding a Component

In the Designer, create a new Canvas, placing it beneath FieldCanvas and naming it EnergyCanvas. Set its Width property to "Fill parent" and its Height to 1 pixel.

Creating a Variable: Energy

In the Blocks Editor, you will need to create a variable energy with an initial value of 200 to keep track of the ladybug's energy level. (As you may recall, we first used a variable, dotSize, in Chapter 2's PaintPot app.) Here's how to do it:

1. In the Blocks Editor, in the Built-In column, open the Definitions drawer. Drag out a **def variable** block. Change the text "variable" to "energy".

2. If there is a block in the socket on the right side of **def energy**, delete it by selecting it and either pressing the Delete key or dragging it to the trash can.

3. Create a **number 200** block (by either starting to type the number 200 or dragging a **number** block out of the Math drawer) and plug it into **def energy**, as shown in Figure 5-4.

Figure 5-4. Initializing the variable energy to 200

Figure 5-5 shows how creating the variable also added blocks to the My Definitions drawer to set or get the value of **energy**.

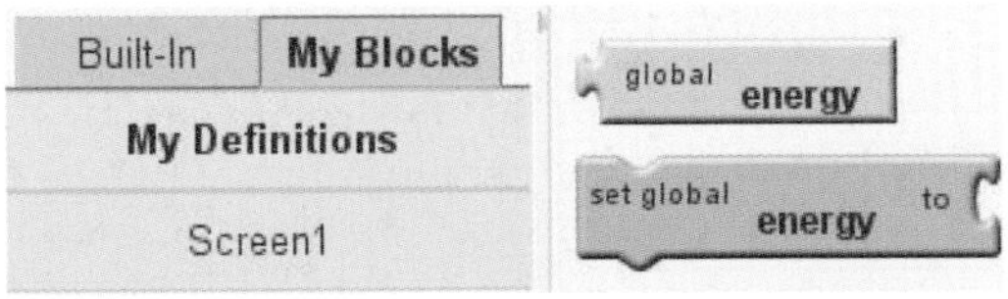

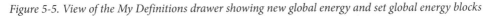

Figure 5-5. View of the My Definitions drawer showing new global energy and set global energy blocks

Drawing the Energy Bar

We want to communicate the energy level with a red bar whose length in pixels is the energy value. To do so, we could create two similar sets of blocks as follows:

1. Draw a red line from (0, 0) to (energy, 0) in FieldCanvas to show the current energy level.

2. Draw a white line from (0, 0) to (EnergyCanvas.Width, 0) in FieldCanvas to erase the current energy level before drawing the new level.

However, a better alternative is to create a procedure that can draw a line of any length and of any color in FieldCanvas. To do this, we must specify two arguments, length and color, when our procedure is called, just as we needed to specify parameter values in MoleMash when we called the built-in random integer procedure. Here are the steps for creating a DrawEnergyLine procedure, which is shown in Figure 5-6.

1. Go to the Definition drawer and drag out a **to procedure** block.

2. Click its name (probably "procedure1") and change it to "DrawEnergyLine".

3. Go back to the Definition drawer and drag out a **name** block, snapping it into the *arg* (short for *argument*) socket. Click its name and change it to "color".

4. Repeat step 3 to add a second argument and name it "length".

5. Fill in the rest of the procedure as shown in Figure 5-6. You can find the new **color** and **length** blocks in the My Definitions drawer.

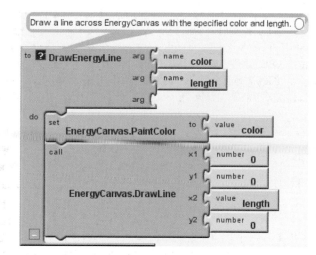

Figure 5-6. Defining the procedure DrawEnergyLine

Now that you're getting the hang of creating your own procedures, let's also write a DisplayEnergyLevel procedure that calls DrawEnergyLine twice, once to erase the old line (by drawing a white line all the way across the canvas) and once to display the new line, as shown in Figure 5-7.

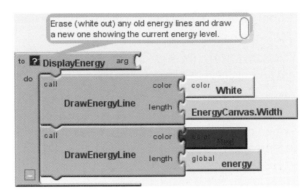

Figure 5-7. Defining the procedure DisplayEnergyLevel

The DisplayEnergyLevel procedure consists of four lines that do the following:

1. Set the paint color to white.

2. Draw a line all the way across EnergyCanvas (which is only 1 pixel high).

3. Set the paint color to red.

4. Draw a line whose length in pixels is the same as the energy value.

Note. *The process of replacing common code with calls to a new procedure is called refactoring, a set of powerful techniques for making programs more maintainable and reliable. In this case, if we ever wanted to change the height or location of the energy line, we would just have to make a single change to* DrawEnergyLine, *rather than making changes to every call to it. For more information on procedures, see Chapter 21.*

Starvation

Unlike the apps in previous chapters, this game has a way to end: it's over if the ladybug fails to eat enough aphids or is eaten by the frog. In either of these cases, we want the ladybug to stop moving (which we can do by setting Ladybug.Enabled to false) and for the picture to change from a live ladybug to a dead one (which we can do by changing Ladybug.Picture to the name of the appropriate uploaded image). Create the GameOver procedure as shown in Figure 5-8.

```
to GameOver    arg
do    set                              to
         Ladybug.Enabled                    false
      set                              to    text
         Ladybug.Picture                        dead_ladybug.png
```

Figure 5-8. Defining the procedure GameOver

Next, add the code outlined in red in Figure 5-9 to UpdateLadybug (which, as you may recall, is called by Clock.Timer every 10 milliseconds) to:

- Decrement its energy level.

- Display the new level.

- End the game if energy is 0.

 Test your app. *You should be able to test this code on your phone and verify that the energy level decreases over time, eventually causing the ladybug's demise. If you want to restart the application, press the "Connect to Device…" button in the Blocks Editor.*

```
Decrement and display the ladybug's energy level, ending
the game if it reaches zero.  Otherwise, update the
ladybug's direction and speed based on the phone's tilt.

to ? UpdateLadybug    arg
do    set global            to    global
         energy                       energy    -    number  1

      call  DisplayEnergy

      if    test    global
                       energy    =    number  0
      then-do  call  GameOver

      set                  to
         Ladybug.Heading       OrientationSensor1.Angle
      set                  to
         Ladybug.Speed         OrientationSensor1.Magnitude  *  number  100▽
```

Figure 5-9. Second version of the procedure UpdateLadybug

Adding an Aphid

The next step is to add an aphid. Specifically, an aphid should flit around FieldCanvas. If the ladybug runs into the aphid (thereby "eating" it), the ladybug's energy level should increase and the aphid should disappear, to be replaced by another one a little later. (From the user's point of view, it will be a different aphid, but it will really be the same ImageSprite component.)

Adding an ImageSprite

The first step to add an aphid is to go back to the Designer and create another ImageSprite, being sure not to place it on top of the ladybug. It should be renamed Aphid and its properties set as follows:

1. Set its Picture property to the aphid image file you uploaded.

2. Set its Interval property to 10, so, like the ladybug, it moves every 10 milliseconds.

3. Set its Speed to 2, so it doesn't move too fast for the ladybug to catch it.

Don't worry about its X and Y properties (as long as it's not on top of the ladybug) or its Heading property, which will be set in the Blocks Editor.

Controlling the Aphid

By experimenting, we found it worked best for the aphid to change directions approximately once every 50 milliseconds (5 "ticks" of Clock1). One approach to enabling this behavior would be to create a second clock with a TimerInterval of 50 milliseconds. However, we'd like you to try a different technique so you can learn about the **random fraction** block, which returns a random number greater than or equal to 0 and less than 1 each time it is called. Create the UpdateAphid procedure shown in Figure 5-10 and add a call to it in **Clock1.Timer**.

How the blocks work

Whenever the timer goes off (100 times per second), both **UpdateLadybug** (like before) and **UpdateAphid** are called. The first thing that happens in **UpdateAphid** is that a random fraction between 0 and 1 is generated—for example, 0.15. If this number is less than 0.20 (which will happen 20% of the time), the aphid will change its direction to a random number of degrees between 0 and 360. If the number is *not* less than 0.20 (which will be the case the remaining 80% of the time), the aphid will stay the course.

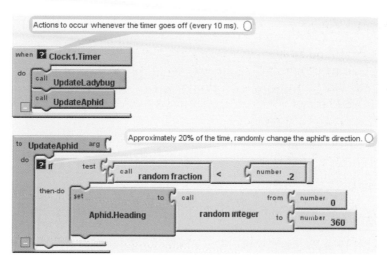

Figure 5-10. Adding the procedure UpdateAphid

Having the Ladybug Eat the Aphid

The next step is having the ladybug "eat" the aphid when they collide. Fortunately, App Inventor provides blocks for detecting collisions between ImageSprite components, which raises the question: what should happen when the ladybug and the aphid collide? You might want to stop and think about this before reading on.

To handle what happens when the ladybug and aphid collide, let's create a procedure, EatAphid, that does the following:

- Increases the energy level by 50 to simulate eating the tasty treat.
- Causes the aphid to disappear (by setting its Visible property to false).
- Causes the aphid to stop moving (by setting its Enabled property to false).
- Causes the aphid to move to a random location on the screen. (This follows the same pattern as the code to move the mole in MoleMash).

Check that your blocks match Figure 5-11. If you had other ideas of what should happen, such as sound effects, you can add those too.

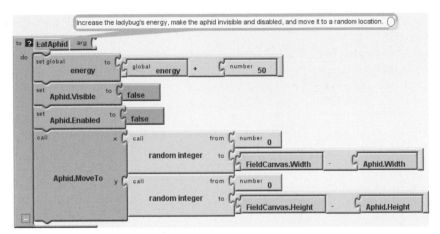

Figure 5-11. Adding the procedure EatAphid

How the blocks work

Whenever **EatAphid** is called, it adds 50 to the variable energy, staving off starvation for the ladybug. Next, the aphid's Visible and Enabled properties are set to false so it seems to disappear and stops moving. Finally, random *x* and *y* coordinates are generated for a call to **Aphid.MoveTo** so that, when the aphid reappears, it's in a new location (otherwise, it will be eaten as soon as it reemerges).

Detecting a Ladybug–Aphid Collision

Figure 5-12 shows the code to detect collisions between the ladybug and the aphid. Note that when you add a condition to the "and" block, a new test socket appears.

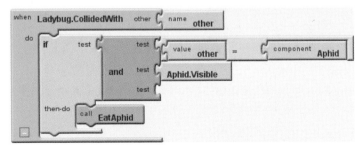

Figure 5-12. Detecting and acting on collisions between the ladybug and aphid

How the blocks work

When the ladybug collides with another ImageSprite, **Ladybug.CollidedWith** gets called, with the parameter "other" bound to whatever the ladybug collided with. Right now, the only thing it can collide with is the aphid, but we'll be adding a frog later. We'll use *defensive programming* and explicitly check that the collision was with the aphid before calling **EatAphid**. There's also a check to confirm that the aphid is visible. Otherwise, after an aphid is eaten but before it reappears, it could collide with the ladybug again. Without the check, the invisible aphid would be eaten again, causing another jump in energy without the user understanding why.

 Note. *Defensive programming is the practice of writing code in such a way that it is still likely to work even if the program gets modified. In Figure 5-12, the test* **other = Aphid** *is not strictly necessary because the only thing the ladybug can currently collide with is the aphid, but having the check will prevent our program from malfunctioning if we add another* ImageSprite *and forget to change* **Ladybug.CollidedWith***. Programmers generally spend more time fixing bugs than writing new code, so it is well worth taking a little time to write code in a way that prevents bugs.*

The Return of the Aphid

To make the aphid eventually reappear, you should modify UpdateAphid as shown in Figure 5-13 so it changes the aphid's direction only if it is visible. (Changing it if it's invisible is a waste of time.) If the aphid is not visible (as in, it has been eaten recently), there is a 1 in 20 (5%) chance that it will be reenabled—in other words, made eligible to be eaten again.

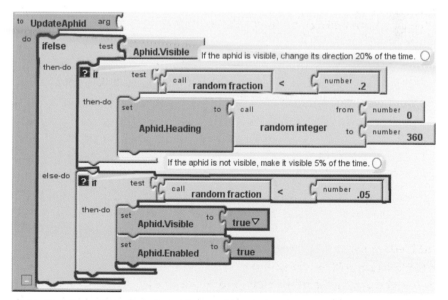

Figure 5-13. Modifying UpdateAphid to make invisible aphids come back to life

How the blocks work

UpdateAphid is getting pretty complex, so let's carefully step through its behavior:

- If the aphid is visible (which will be the case unless it was just eaten), UpdateAphid behaves as we first wrote it. Specifically, there is a 20% chance of its changing direction.

- If the aphid is not visible (was recently eaten), then the "else-do" part of the **ifelse** block will run. A random number is then generated. If it is less than .05 (which it will be 5% of the time), the aphid becomes visible again and is enabled, making it eligible to be eaten again.

Because UpdateAphid is called by Clock1.Timer, which occurs every 10 milliseconds, and there is a 1 in 20 (5%) chance of the aphid becoming visible again, the aphid will take on average 200 milliseconds (1/5 of a second) to reappear.

Adding a Restart Button

As you may have noticed from testing the app with your new aphid-eating functionality, the game really needs a Restart button. (This is another reason why it's helpful to design and build your app in small chunks and then test it—you often discover things that you may have overlooked, and it's easier to add them as you progress than to go back in and change them once the app is "complete.") In the Component Designer, add a Button component underneath EnergyCanvas, rename it "RestartButton", and set its Text property to "Restart".

In the Blocks Editor, create the code shown in Figure 5-14 to do the following when the RestartButton is clicked:

1. Set the energy level back to 200.

2. Reenable the aphid and make it visible.

3. Reenable the ladybug and change its picture back to the live ladybug (unless you want zombie ladybugs!).

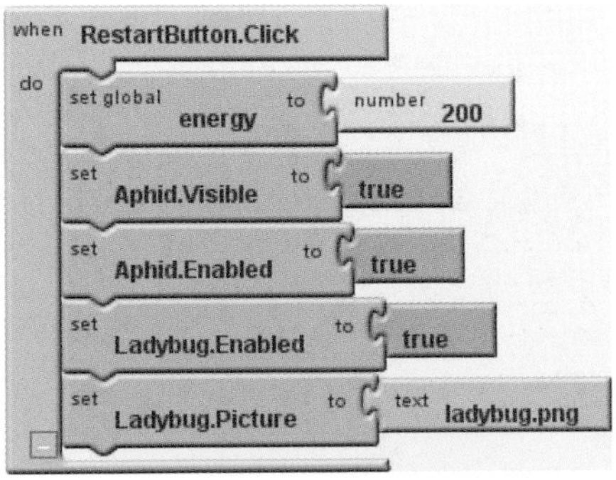

Figure 5-14. Restarting the game when RestartButton is pressed

Adding the Frog

Right now, keeping the ladybug alive isn't too hard. We need a predator. Specifically, we'll add a frog that moves directly toward the ladybug. If they collide, the ladybug gets eaten, and the game ends.

Having the Frog Chase the Ladybug

The first step to having the frog chase the ladybug is returning to the Component Designer and adding a third ImageSprite—Frog—to FieldCanvas. Set its Picture property to the appropriate picture, its Interval to 10, and its Speed to 1, since it should be slower-moving than the other creatures.

Figure 5-15 shows UpdateFrog, a new procedure you should create and call from Clock1.Timer.

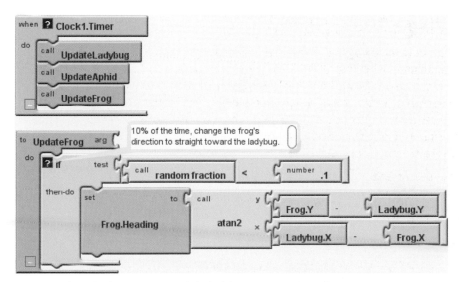

Figure 5-15. Making the frog move toward the ladybug

How the blocks work

By now, you should be familiar with the use of the **random fraction** block to make an event occur with a certain probability. In this case, there is a 10% chance that the frog's direction will be changed to head straight toward the ladybug. This requires trigonometry, but don't panic—you don't have to figure it out yourself! App Inventor handles a ton of math functions for you, even stuff like trig. In this case, you want to use the **atan2** (arctangent) block, which returns the angle corresponding to a given set of *x* and *y* values.

(For those of you familiar with trigonometry, the reason the y argument to **atan2** has the opposite sign of what you'd expect—the opposite order of arguments to subtract—is that the y coordinate increases in the downward direction on an Android Canvas, the opposite of what would occur in a standard x–y coordinate system.)

Having the Frog Eat the Ladybug

We now need to modify the collision code so that if the ladybug collides with the frog, the energy level and bar goes to 0 and the game ends, as shown in Figure 5-16.

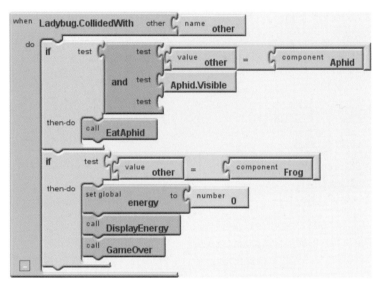

Figure 5-16. Making the frog eat the ladybug

How the blocks work

In addition to the first **if**, which checks if the ladybug collided with the aphid, there is now a second **if**, which checks if the ladybug has collided with the frog. If the ladybug and the frog collide, three things happen:

1. The variable energy goes down to 0, since the ladybug has lost its life force.

2. **DisplayEnergy** is called, to erase the previous energy line (and draw the new—empty—one).

3. The procedure we wrote earlier, **GameOver**, is called to stop the ladybug from moving and changes its picture to that of a dead ladybug.

The Return of the Ladybug

RestartButton.Click already has code to replace the picture of the dead ladybug with the one of the live ladybug. Now you need to add code to move the live lady-bug to a random location. (Think about what would happen if you didn't move the ladybug at the beginning of a new game. Where would it be in relation to the frog?) Figure 5-17 shows the blocks to move the ladybug when the game restarts.

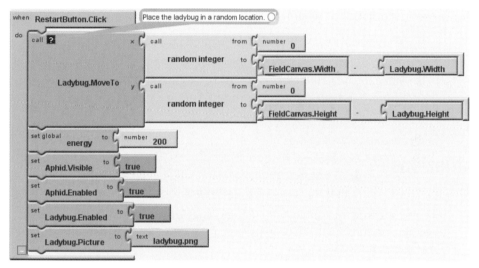

Figure 5-17. The final version of RestartButton.Click

How the blocks work

The only difference between this version of **RestartButton.Click** and the previ-ous version is the **Ladybug.MoveTo** block and its arguments. The built-in function **random integer** is called twice, once to generate a legal *x* coordinate and once to generate a legal *y* coordinate. While there is nothing to prevent the ladybug from being placed on top of the aphid or the frog, the odds are against it.

 Test your app. *Restart the game and make sure the ladybug shows up in a new random location.*

Adding Sound Effects

When you tested the game, you may have noticed there isn't very good feedback when an animal gets eaten. To add sound effects and tactile feedback, do the following:

1. In the Component Designer, add a Sound component. Set its Source to the sound file you uploaded.

2. Go to the Blocks Editor, where you will:

    a. Make the phone vibrate when an aphid is eaten by adding a **Sound1 .Vibrate** block with an argument of 100 (milliseconds) in **EatAphid**.

    b. Make the frog ribbit when it eats the ladybug by adding a call to **Sound1.Play** in **Ladybug.CollidedWith** just before the call to **GameOver**.

Variations

Here are some ideas of how to improve or customize this game:

- Currently, the frog and aphid keep moving after the game has ended. Prevent this by setting their Enabled properties to false in **GameOver** and back to true in **RestartButton.Click**.

- Display a score indicating how long the ladybug has remained alive. You can do this by creating a label that you increment in **Clock1.Timer**.

- Make the energy bar more visible by increasing the Height of EnergyCanvas to 2 and drawing two lines, one above the other, in DrawEnergyLine. (This is another benefit of having a procedure rather than duplicated code to erase and redraw the energy line: you just need to make a change in one place to change the size—or color, or location—of the line.)

- Add ambiance with a background image and more sound effects, such as nature sounds or a warning when the ladybug's energy level gets low.

- Have the game get harder over time, such as by increasing the frog's Speed property or decreasing its Interval property.

- Technically, the ladybug should disappear when it is eaten by the frog. Change the game so that the ladybug becomes invisible if eaten by the frog but not if it starves to death.

- Replace the ladybug, aphid, and frog pictures with ones more to your taste, such as a hobbit, orc, and evil wizard or a rebel starfighter, energy pod, and Imperial starfighter.

Summary

With two games now under your belt (if you completed the MoleMash tutorial), you now know how to create your own games, which is the goal of many new programmers or wannabes! Specifically, you learned:

- You can have multiple ImageSprite components (the ladybug, the aphid, and the frog) and can detect collisions between them.

- The tilt of the phone can be detected by the OrientationSensor, and the value can be used to control the movement of a sprite (or anything else you can imagine).

- A single Clock component can control multiple events that occur at the same frequency (changes in the ladybug's and frog's directions), or at different frequencies, by using the **random fraction** block. For example, if you want an event to occur approximately one-fourth (25 percent) of the time, put it in the body of an **if** block that is only executed when the result of **random fraction** is less than .25.

- You can have multiple Canvas components in a single app, which we did to have both a playing field and to display a variable graphically (instead of through a Label).

- User-defined procedures can be defined with parameters (such as "color" and "length" in DrawEnergyLine) that control the behavior, greatly expanding the power of procedural abstraction.

Another component useful for games is Ball, which only differs from ImageSprite in having the appearance of a filled circle rather than an arbitrary image.

CHAPTER 6

Paris Map Tour

In this chapter, you'll build an app that lets you create your own custom guide for a dream trip to Paris. And since a few of your friends can't join you, we'll create a companion app that lets them take a virtual tour of Paris as well. Creating a fully functioning map app might seem really complicated, but App Inventor lets you use the ActivityStarter *component to launch Google Maps for each virtual location. First, you'll build an app that launches maps for the Eiffel Tower, the Louvre, and Notre Dame Cathedral with a single click. Then you'll modify the app to create a virtual tour of satellite maps that are also available from Google Maps.*

What You'll Learn

This chapter introduces the following App Inventor components and concepts:

- The Activity Starter component for launching other Android apps from your app. You'll use this component here to launch Google Maps with various parameters.

- The ListPicker component for allowing the user to choose from a list of locations.

Designing the Components

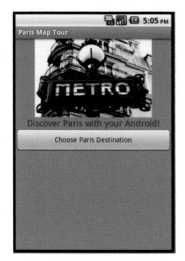

Create a new project in App Inventor and call it "ParisMapTour". The user interface for the app has an Image component with a picture of Paris, a Label component with some text, a ListPicker component that comes with an associated button, and an ActivityStarter (non-visible) component. You can design the components using the snapshot in Figure 6-1.

The components listed in Table 6-1 were used to create this Designer window. Drag each component from the Palette into the Viewer and name it as specified.

Figure 6-1. TheParis Map Tour app running in the emulator

Table 6-1. Components for the Paris Map Tour

Component type	Palette group	What you'll name it	Purpose
Image	Basic	Image1	Show a static image of a Paris map on screen.
Label	Basic	Label1	Display the text "Discover Paris with your Android!"
ListPicker	Basic	ListPicker1	Display the list of destination choices.
ActivityStarter	Other stuff	ActivityStarter1	Launch the Maps app when a destination is chosen.

Setting the Properties of ActivityStarter

ActivityStarter is a component that lets you launch any Android app—a browser, Google Maps, or even another one of your own apps. When a user launches another app from your app, he can click the back button to return to your app. You'll build ParisMapTour so that the Maps application is launched to show particular maps based on the user's choice. The user can then hit the back button to return to your app and choose a different destination.

ActivityStarter is a relatively low-level component in that you'll need to set some properties with information familiar to a Java Android SDK programmer, but foreign to the other 99.999% of the world. For this app, enter the properties as specified in Table 6-2, and *be careful*—even the upper-/lowercase letters are important.

Table 6-2. ActivityStarter properties for launching Google Maps

Property	Value
Action	android.intent.action.VIEW
ActivityClass	com.google.android.maps.MapsActivity
ActivityPackage	com.google.android.apps.maps

In the Blocks Editor, you'll set one more property, DataUri, which lets you launch a specific map in Google Maps. This property must be set in the Blocks Editor instead of the Component Designer because it needs to be dynamic; it will change based on whether the user chooses to visit the Eiffel Tower, the Louvre, or the Notre Dame Cathedral.

We'll get to the Blocks Editor in just a moment, but there are a couple more details to take care of before you can move on to programming the behavior for your components:

1. Download the file *metro.jpg* from the book site (*http://examples.oreilly.com/ 0636920016632/*) onto your computer, and then choose Add in the Media section to load it into your project. You'll then need to set it as the Picture property of Image1.

2. The ListPicker component comes with a button; when the user clicks it, the choices are listed. Set the text of that button by changing the Text property of ListPicker1 to "Choose Paris Destination".

Adding Behaviors to the Components

In the Blocks Editor, you'll need to define a list of destinations, and two behaviors:

- When the app begins, the app loads the destinations into the ListPicker component so the user can choose one.

- When the user chooses a destination from the ListPicker, the Maps application is launched and shows a map of that destination. In this first version of the app, you'll just open Maps and tell it to run a search for the chosen destination.

Creating a List of Destinations

Open the Blocks Editor and create a variable with the list of Paris destinations using the blocks listed in Table 6-3.

Table 6-3. Blocks for creating a destinations variable

Block type	Drawer	Purpose
def variable ("Destina-tions")	Definitions	Create a list of the destinations.
make a list	Lists	Add the items to the list.
text ("Tour Eiffel")	Text	The first destination.
text ("Musée du Louvre")	Text	The second destination.
text ("Cathédrale Notre Dame")	Text	The third destination.

The destinations variable will call the make a list function, into which you can plug the text values for the three destinations in your tour, as shown in Figure 6-2.

Figure 6-2. Creating a list is easy in App Inventor

Letting the User Choose a Destination

The purpose of the ListPicker component is to display a list of items for the user to choose from. You preload the choices into the ListPicker by setting the property Elements to a list. For this app, you want to set the ListPicker's Elements property to the destinations list you just created. Because you want to display the list when the app launches, you'll define this behavior in the **Screen1.Initialize** event. You'll need the blocks listed in Table 6-4.

Table 6-4. Blocks for launching the ListPicker when the app starts

Block type	Drawer	Purpose
Screen1.Initialize	Screen1	This event is triggered when the app starts.
set ListPicker1 .Elements to	ListPicker1	Set this property to the list you want to appear.
global destinations	My Definitions	The list of destinations.

How the blocks work

Screen1.Initialize is triggered when the app begins. As shown in Figure 6-3, the event handler sets the Elements property of ListPicker so that the three destinations will appear.

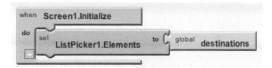

Figure 6-3. Put anything you want to happen when the app starts in a Screen1.Initialize event handler

> **Test your app.** *First, you'll need to restart the app by clicking "Connect to Device. . ." in the Blocks Editor. Then, on the phone, click the button labeled "Choose Paris Destination." The list picker should appear with the three items.*

Opening Maps with a Search

Next, you'll program the app so that when the user chooses one of the destinations, the ActivityStarter launches Google Maps and searches for the selected location.

When the user chooses an item from the ListPicker component, the **ListPicker .AfterPicking** event is triggered. In the event handler for AfterPicking, you need to set the DataUri of the ActivityStarter component so it knows which map to open, and then you need to launch Google Maps using **ActivityStarter.StartActivity**. The blocks for this functionality are listed in Table 6-5.

Table 6-5. Blocks to launch Google Maps with the Activity Starter

Block type	Drawer	Purpose
ListPicker1.After Picking	ListPicker1	This event is triggered when the user chooses from ListPicker.
set ActivityStarter1 .DataUri to	ActivityStarter1	The DataUri tells Maps which map to open on launch.
make text	Text	Build the DataUri from two pieces of text.
text ("geo:0,0?q=")	Text	The first part of the DataUri expected by Maps.
ListPicker1.Selection	ListPicker1	The item the user chose.
ActivityStarter1 .StartActivity	ActivityStarter1	Launch Maps.

How the blocks work

When the user chooses from the ListPicker, the chosen item is stored in **ListPicker .Selection** and the AfterPicking event is triggered. As shown in Figure 6-4, the DataUri property is set to a text object that combines "http://maps.google.com/?q=" with the chosen item. So, if the user chose the first item, "Tour Eiffel," the DataUri would be set to "http://maps.google.com/?q=Tour Eiffel."

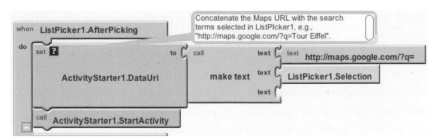

Figure 6-4. *Setting the DataURI to launch the selected map*

Since you already set the other properties of the ActivityStarter so that it knows to open Maps, the **ActivityStarter1.StartActivity** block launches the Maps app and invokes the search proscribed by the DataUri.

Test your app. *Restart the app and click the "Choose Paris Destination" button again. When you choose one of the destinations, does a map of that destination appear? Google Maps should also provide a back button to return you to your app to choose again—does that work? (You may have to click the back button a couple of times.)*

Setting Up a Virtual Tour

Now let's spice up the app and have it open some great zoomed-in and street views of the Paris monuments so your friends at home can follow along while you're away. To do this, you'll first explore Google Maps to obtain the URLs of some specific maps. You'll still use the same Parisian landmarks for the destinations, but when the user chooses one, you'll use the *index* (the position in the list) of her choice to select and open a specific zoomed-in or street-view map.

Before going on, you may want to save your project (using Save As) so you have a copy of the simple map tour you've created so far. That way, if you do anything that causes issues in your app, you can always go back to this working version and try again.

Finding the DataUri for Specific Maps

The first step is to open Google Maps on your computer to find the specific maps you want to launch for each destination:

1. On your computer, browse to *http://maps.google.com*.

2. Search for a landmark (e.g., the Eiffel Tower).

3. Zoom in to the level you desire.

4. Choose the type of view you want (e.g., Address, Satellite, or Street View).

5. Click the Link button near the top right of the Maps window and copy the URL for the map. You'll use this URL (or parts of it) to launch the map from your app.

Using this scheme, Table 6-6 shows the URLs you'll use.

Table 6-6. Virtual tour URLs for Google Maps

Landmark	Maps URL
Tour Eiffel	http://maps.google.com/maps?f=q&source=s_q&hl=en&geocode=&q=eiffel+tower&sll=37.0625,-95.677068&sspn=48.909425,72.333984&ie=UTF8&hq=Tour+Eiffel&hnear=Tour+Eiffel,+Quai+Branly,+75007+Paris,+Ile-de-France,+France&ll=48.857942,2.294748&spn=0.001249,0.002207&t=h&z=19
Musée du Louvre	http://maps.google.com/maps?f=q&source=s_q&hl=en&q=louvre&sll=48.86096,2.335421&sspn=0.002499,0.004415&ie=UTF8&t=h&split=1&filter=0&rq=1&ev=zi&radius=0.12&hq=louvre&hnear=&ll=48.86096,2.335421&spn=0.002499,0.004415&z=18
Cathédrale Notre Dame (Street View)	http://maps.google.com/maps?f=q&source=s_q&hl=en&q=french+landmarks&sll=48.853252,2.349111&sspn=0.002411,0.004415&ie=UTF8&t=h&radius=0.12&split=1&filter=0&rq=1&ev=zi&hq=french+landmarks&hnear=&ll=48.853252,2.349111&spn=0,0.004415&z=18&layer=c&cbll=48.853046,2.348861&panoid=74fLTqeYdgkPYj6KKLlqgQ&cbp=12,63.75,,0,-35.58

To view any of these maps, paste the URLs from Table 6-6 into a browser. The first two are zoomed-in satellite views, while the third is a street view.

You can use these URLs directly to launch the maps you want, or you can define cleaner URLs using the Google Maps protocols outlined at *http://mapki.com*. For example, you can show the Eiffel Tower map using only the GPS coordinates found in the long URL in Table 6-6 and the Maps geo: protocol:

```
geo:48.857942,2.294748?t=h&z=19
```

Using such a DataUri, you'll get essentially the same map as the map based on the full URL from which the GPS coordinates were extracted. The t=h specifies that Maps should show a hybrid map with both satellite and address views, and the z=19 specifies the zoom level. If you're interested in the details of setting parameters for various types of maps, check out the documentation at *http://mapki.com*.

To get comfortable using both types of URLs, we'll use the geo: format for the first two DataUri settings in our list, and the full URL for the third.

Defining the dataURIs List

You'll need a list named dataURIs, containing one DataURI for each map you want to show. Create this list as shown in Figure 6-5 so that the items correspond to the items in the destinations list (i.e., the first dataURI should correspond to the first destination, the Eiffel Tower).

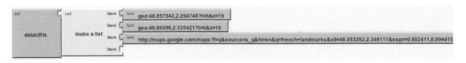

Figure 6-5. The list of maps for your virtual tour

The first two items shown are DataURIs for the Eiffel Tower and the Louvre. They both use the geo: protocol. The third DataURI is not shown completely because the block is too long for this page; you should copy this URL from the entry for "Notre Dame, Street View" in Table 6-6 and place it in a **text** block.

Modifying the ListPicker.AfterPicking Behavior

In the first version of this app, the **ListPicker.AfterPicking** behavior set the DataUri to the *concatenation* (or combination) of "http://maps.google.com/?q=" and the destination the user chose from the list (e.g., Tour Eiffel). In this second version, the AfterPicking behavior must be more sophisticated, because the user is choosing from one list (destinations), but the DataUri must be selected from another list (dataURIs). Specifically, when the user chooses an item from the ListPicker, you need to know the *index* of his choice so you can use it to select the correct DataUri from the dataURIs list. We'll explain more about what an index is in a moment, but it helps to set up the blocks first to better illustrate the concept. There are quite a few blocks required for this functionality, all of which are listed in Table 6-7.

Table 6-7. Blocks for choosing a list item based on the user's selection

Block type	Drawer	Purpose
def variable ("index")	Definitions	This variable will hold the index of the user's choice.
number (1)	Math	Initialize the index variable to 1.
ListPicker1 .AfterPicking	ListPicker1	This event is triggered when the user chooses an item.
set global index to	My Definitions	Set this variable to the position of the selected item.
position in list	Lists	Get the position (index) of a selected item.
ListPicker1 .Selection	ListPicker1	The selected item—for example, "Tour Eiffel." Plug this into the "thing" slot of **position in list**.
global destinations	My Definitions	Plug this into the "list" slot of **position in list**.
set ActivityStarter .DataUri	ActivityStarter	Set this before starting the activity to open the map.
select list item	Lists	Select an item from the **dataURIs** list.
global DataURIs	My Definitions	The list of DataURIs.

Table 6-7. Blocks for choosing a list item based on the user's selection (continued)

Block type	Drawer	Purpose
global index	My Definitions	Hold the position of the chosen item.
ActivityStarter .StartActivity	ActivityStarter	Launch the Maps app.

How the blocks work

When the user chooses an item from the ListPicker, the AfterPicking event is triggered, as shown in Figure 6-6. The chosen item—e.g., "Tour Eiffel"—is in **ListPicker.Selection**. The event handler uses this to find the position of the selected item, or the *index* value, in the destinations list. The index corresponds to the position of the chosen destination in the list. So if "Tour Eiffel" is chosen, the index will be 1; if "Musée du Louvre" is chosen, it will be 2; and if "Cathédrale Notre Dame de Paris" is chosen, the index will be 3.

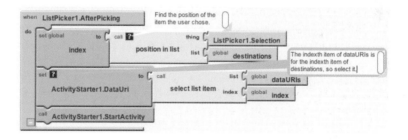

Figure 6-6. Choosing a list item based on the user's selection

The index can then be used to select an item from another list—in this case, data URIs—and to set that entry as the ActivityStarter's DataUri. Once this is set, the map can be launched with **ActivityStarter.StartActivity**.

Test your app. *On the phone, click the button labeled "Choose Paris Destination." The list should appear with the three items. Choose one of the items and see which map appears.*

Variations

Here are some suggested variations to try:

- Create a virtual tour of some other exotic destination, or of your workplace or school.

- Create a customizable Virtual Tour app that lets a user create a guide for a location of her choice by entering the name of each destination along with the URL of a corresponding map. You'll need to store the data in a TinyWebDB database and create a Virtual Tour app that works with the entered data. For an example of how to create a TinyWebDB database, see the MakeQuiz/TakeQuiz app in Chapter 10.

Summary

Here are some of the ideas we've covered in this chapter:

- List variables can be used to hold data like map destinations and URLs.

- The ListPicker component lets the user choose from a list of items. The ListPicker's Elements property holds the list, the Selection property holds the selected item, and the AfterPicking event is triggered when the user chooses an item from the list.

- The ActivityStarter component allows your app to launch other apps. This chapter demonstrated its use with the Maps application, but you can launch a browser or any other Android app as well, even another one you created yourself. See *http://appinventor.googlelabs.com/learn/reference/other/activitystarter.html* for more information.

- You can launch a particular map in Google Maps by setting the DataUri property. You can find URIs by configuring a particular map in the browser and then choosing the Link button to find the URI. You can either place such a URI directly into the DataUri of your ActivityStarter, or build your own URI using the protocols defined at *http://mapki.com*.

- You can identify the *index* of a list item using the **position in list** block. With ListPicker, you can use list position to find the index of the item the user chooses. This is important when, as in this chapter, you need the index to choose an item from a second, related list. For more information on List variables and the ListPicker component, see Chapter 19.

CHAPTER 7

Android, Where's My Car?

You parked as close to the stadium as you possibly could, but when the concert ends, you don't have a clue where your car is. Your friends are equally clueless. Fortunately, you haven't lost your Android phone, which never forgets anything, and you remember you have the hot new app, "Android, Where's My Car?" With this app, you click a button when you park your car, and the Android uses its location sensor to record the car's GPS coordinates and address. Later, when you reopen the app, it gives you directions from where you currently are to the remembered location—problem solved!

What You'll Learn

This app covers the following concepts:

- Determining the location of the Android device using the LocationSensor component.

- Recording data in a database directly on the device using TinyDB.

- Using the ActivityStarter component to open Google Maps from your app and show directions from one location to another.

Getting Started

Connect to the App Inventor website and start a new project. Name it "AndroidWhere" (project names can't have spaces) and also set the screen's title to "Android, Where's My Car?" Open the Blocks Editor and connect to the phone.

Designing the Components

The user interface for "Android, Where's My Car?" consists of labels to show your current and remembered locations, and buttons to record a location and show directions to it. You'll need some labels that just show static text; for example, GPSLabel will provide the text "GPS:" that appears in the user interface. Other labels, such as CurrentLatLabel, will display data from the location sensor. For these labels, you'll provide a default value, (0,0), which will change as the GPS acquires location information.

You'll also need three non-visible components: a LocationSensor for obtaining the current location, a TinyDB for storing locations persistently, and an ActivityStarter for launching Google Maps to get directions between the current and stored locations.

You can build the components from the snapshot of the Component Designer in Figure 7-1.

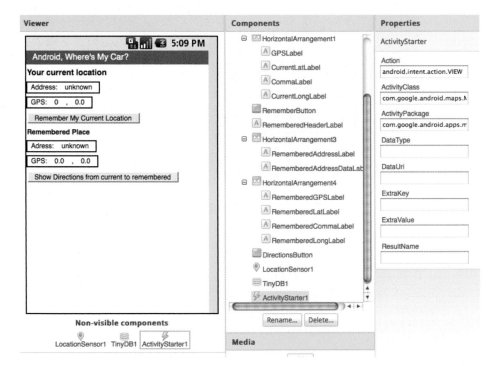

Figure 7-1. The "Android, Where's My Car?" app in the Component Designer

You can build the user interface shown in Figure 7-1 by dragging out the components in Table 7-1.

Table 7-1. All of the components for the app

Component type	Palette group	What you'll name it	Purpose
Label	Basic	CurrentHeaderLabel	Display the header "Your current location".
HorizontalArrangement	Screen Arrangement	HorizontalArrangement1	Arrange the address info.
Label	Basic	CurrentAddressLabel	Display the text "Address:".
Label	Basic	CurrentAddressDataLabel	Display dynamic data: the current address.
HorizontalArrangement	Screen Arrangement	HorizontalArrangement2	Arrange the GPS info.
Label	Basic	GPSLabel	Display the text "GPS:".
Label	Basic	CurrentLatLabel	Display dynamic data: the current latitude.
Label	Basic	CommaLabel	Display ",".
Label	Basic	CurrentLongLabel	Display dynamic data: the current longitude.
Button	Basic	RememberButton	Click to record the current location.
Label	Basic	HorizontalArrangement2	Arrange remembered address info.
Label	Basic	RememberedAddressLabel	Display the text "Remembered Place".
Label	Basic	RememberedAddressData Label	Display dynamic data: the remembered address.
Label	Basic	RememberedGPSLabel	Display the text "GPS".
Label	Basic	RememberedLatLabel	Display dynamic data: the remembered latitude.
Label	Basic	Comma2Label	Display ",".
Label	Basic	RememberedLongLabel	Display dynamic data: the remembered longitude.
Button	Basic	DirectionsButton	Click to show the map.
LocationSensor	Sensors	LocationSensor1	Sense GPS info.
TinyDB	Basic	TinyDB1	Store the remembered location persistently.
ActivityStarter	Other stuff	ActivityStarter1	Launch Maps.

Set the properties of the components in the following way:

- Set the Text property for the labels with fixed text as specified in Table 7-1.

- Set the Text property of the labels for dynamic GPS data to "0.0".

- Set the Text property of the labels for dynamic addresses to "unknown".

- Uncheck the Enabled property of the RememberButton and DirectionsButton.

- Set the ActivityStarter properties so that ActivityStarter.StartActivity will open Google Maps. (The ActivityStarter's properties are only partially visible in the user interface shown in Figure 7-1.) Table 7-2 describes how they should be specified; you can leave blank any properties not listed in the table.

Table 7-2. ActivityStarter properties for launching Google Maps

Property	Value
Action	android.intent.action.VIEW
ActivityClass	com.google.android.maps.MapsActivity
ActivityPackage	com.google.android.apps.maps

Note. *The* ActivityStarter *component lets your app open any Android app installed on the device. The properties indicated in Table 7-2 can be used verbatim to open Maps; to open other apps, see the App Inventor documentation at http://appinventor.google labs.com/learn/reference/other/activitystarter.html.*

Adding Behaviors to the Components

You'll need the following behaviors for this app:

- When the LocationSensor gets a reading, place the current location data into the appropriate labels of the user interface. This will let the user know the sensor has read a location and is ready to remember it.

- When the user clicks the RememberButton, copy the current location data into the labels for the remembered location. You'll also need to store the remembered location data so it will be there if the user closes and relaunches the app.

- When the user clicks the DirectionsButton, launch Google Maps so it shows directions to the remembered location.

- When the app is relaunched, load the remembered location from the database into the app.

Displaying the Current Location

The **LocationSensor.LocationChanged** event occurs not just when the device's location changes, but also when the sensor first gets a reading. Sometimes that first reading will take a few seconds, and sometimes you won't get a reading at all if the sight lines to GPS satellites are blocked (and depending on the device settings). For more information about GPS and LocationSensor, see Chapter 23.

When you do get a location reading, the app should place the data into the appropriate labels. Table 7-3 lists all the blocks you'll need to do this.

Table 7-3. Blocks for getting a location reading and displaying it in the app's UI

Block type	Drawer	Purpose
LocationSensor1.Location Changed	LocationSensor	This is the event handler that is triggered when the phone receives a new GPS reading.
set CurrentAddressData Label.Text to	CurrentAddressDataLabel	Place the new data into the label for the current address.
LocationSensor1.Current Address	LocationSensor	This property gives you a street address.
set CurrentLatLabel.Text to	CurrentLatLabel	Place the latitude into the appropriate label.
value latitude	My Definitions	Plug into **set CurrentLatLabel.Text to**.
set CurrentLongLabel .Text to	CurrentLongLabel	Place the longitude into the appropriate label.
value longitude	My Definitions	Plug into **set CurrentLongLabel.Text to**.
set RememberButton .Enabled to	RememberButton	Remember the reading for current location.
true	Logic	Plug into **set RememberButton.Enabled to**.

How the blocks work

As you can see in Figure 7-2, latitude and longitude are arguments of the **LocationChanged** event, so you grab references to those in the My Definitions drawer. CurrentAddress is not an argument, but rather a property of the LocationSensor, so you grab it from LocationSensor's drawer. The LocationSensor does some additional work for you by calling Google Maps to get a street address corresponding to the GPS location.

This event handler also enables the RememberButton. We initialized it as disabled (unchecked) in the Component Designer because there is nothing for the user to remember until the sensor gets a reading, so now we'll program that behavior.

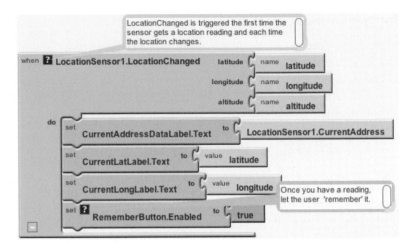

Figure 7-2. Using the LocationSensor to read the current location

 Test your app. *Live testing—testing your app on a phone connected to your computer—doesn't work for location-sensing apps. You need to package and download the app to your phone by selecting "Package for Phone"→"Download to Connected Phone" in the Component Designer. Some GPS data should appear and the* RememberButton *should be enabled.*

If you don't get a reading, check your Android settings for Location & Security and try going outside. For more information, see Chapter 23.

Recording the Current Location

When the user clicks the RememberButton, the most current location data should be placed into the labels for displaying the remembered data. Table 7-4 shows you which blocks you'll need for this functionality.

Table 7-4. Blocks for recording and displaying the current location

Block type	Drawer	Purpose
RememberButton.Click	RememberButton	Triggered when the user clicks "Remember."
set RememberedAddress DataLabel.Text to	RememberedAddressDataLabel	Place the sensor's address data into the label for the remembered address.
LocationSensor1.Current Address	LocationSensor	This property gives you a street address.
set RememberedLatLabel .Text to	RememberedLatLabel	Place the latitude sensed into the "remembered" label.

Table 7-4. Blocks for recording and displaying the current location (continued)

Block type	Drawer	Purpose
LocationSensor.Latitude	LocationSensor	Plug into **set RememberedLat Label.Text to**.
set RememberedLongLabel .Text to	RememberedLongLabel	Place the longitude sensed into the "remembered" label.
LocationSensor.Longitude	My Definitions	Plug into **set RememberedLong Label.Text to**.
set DirectionsButton.Enabled to	DirectionsButton	Map the remembered place.
true	Logic	Plug into **set DirectionsButton .Enabled to**.

How the blocks work

When the user clicks the RememberButton, the location sensor's current readings are put into the "remembered" labels, as shown in Figure 7-3.

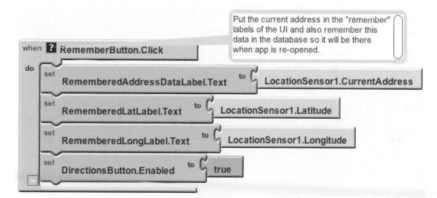

Figure 7-3. Placing the current location information in the "remembered" labels

You'll notice also that the DirectionsButton is enabled. This could get tricky, because if the user clicks the DirectionsButton immediately, the remembered location will be the same as the current location, so the map that appears won't provide much in terms of directions. But that's not something anyone is likely to do; after the user moves (e.g., walks to the concert), the current location and remembered location will diverge.

> **Test your app.** *Download the new version of the app to your phone and test again. When you click the* RememberButton, *is the data from the current settings copied into the remembered settings?*

Displaying Directions to the Remembered Location

When the user clicks the `DirectionsButton`, you want the app to open Google Maps with the directions from the user's current location to the remembered location (in this case, where the car is parked).

The `ActivityStarter` component can open any Android app, including Google Maps. You have to set some configuration data to use it, but to open something like a browser or map, the data you need to specify is fairly straightforward.

To open a map, the key property to configure is the `ActivityStarter.DataUri` property. You can set the property to any URL that you might enter directly in a browser. If you want to explore this, open *http://maps.google.com* in your browser and ask for directions between, say, San Francisco and Oakland. When they appear, click the Link button at the top right of the map and check the URL that appears. This is the kind of URL you need to build in your app.

The difference for your app is that the directions map you'll create will be from one specific set of GPS coordinates to another (not city to city). The URL must be in the following form:

```
http://maps.google.com/maps?saddr=37.82557,-122.47898&daddr=37.81079,-122.47710
```

Type that URL into a browser—can you tell which famous landmark it directs you across?

For this app, you need to build the URL and set its source address (`saddr`) and destination address (`daddr`) parameters dynamically. You've put text together before in earlier chapters using **make text**; we'll do that here as well, plugging in the GPS data for the remembered and current locations. You'll put the URL you build in as the `ActivityStarter.DataUri` property, and then call **ActivityStarter.StartActivity**. Table 7-5 lists all the blocks you'll need for this.

How the blocks work

When the user clicks the `DirectionsButton`, the event handler builds a URL for a map and calls `ActivityStarter` to launch the Maps application and load the map, as shown in Figure 7-4. **make text** is used to build the URL to send to the Maps application.

The resulting URL consists of the Maps domain (*http://maps.google.com/maps*) along with two URL parameters, `saddr` and `daddr`, which specify the source and destination locations for the directions. For this app, the `saddr` is set to the latitude and longitude of the current location, and the `daddr` is set to the latitude and longitude of the location stored for the car.

Table 7-5. Blocks for recording and displaying the current location

Block type	Drawer	Purpose
DirectionsButton.Click	DirectionsButton	Triggered when the user clicks "Directions."
set ActivityStarter.Data Uri to	ActivityStarter	Set the URL for the map you want to bring up.
make text	Text	Build a URL from multiple parts.
text ("http://maps.google.com/ maps?saddr=")	Text	The fixed part of the URL, the source address.
CurrentLatLabel.Text	CurrentLatLabel	The current latitude.
text (",")	Text	Put a comma between the latitude and longitude values.
CurrentLongLabel.Text	CurrentLongLabel	The current longitude.
text ("&daddr=")	Text	The second parameter of the URL, the destination address.
RememberedLatLabel .Text	RememberedLatLabel	The remembered latitude.
text (",")	Text	Put a comma between the values for latitude and longitude.
RememberedLongLabel .Text	RememberedLongLabel	The remembered longitude.
ActivityStarter.Start Activity	ActivityStarter	Open Maps.

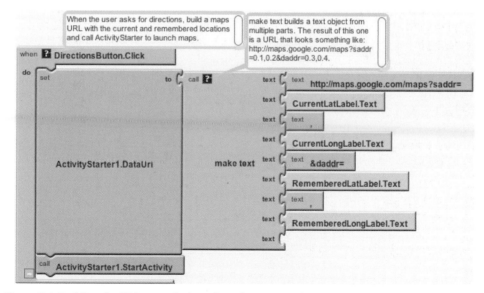

Figure 7-4. Building the URL to use for launching the Maps application

Test your app. *Download the new version of the app to your phone and test again. When a reading comes in, click the* RememberButton *and then take a walk. When you click the* DirectionsButton, *does the map show you how to retrace your steps? After looking at the map, click the back button a few times. Do you get back to your app?*

Storing the Remembered Location Persistently

So now you've got a fully functioning app that remembers a start location and draws a map back to that location from wherever the user is. But if the user "remembers" a location and then closes the app, the remembered data will not be available when he reopens it. Really, you want the user to be able to record the location of his car, close the app and go to some event, and then relaunch the app to get directions to the recorded location.

If you're already thinking back to the No Texting While Driving app (Chapter 4), you're on the right track here—we need to store the data *persistently* in a database using TinyDB. You'll use a scheme similar to the one we used in that app:

1. When the user clicks the RememberButton, store the location data to the database.

2. When the app launches, load the location data from the database into a variable or property.

You'll start by modifying the **RememberButton.Click** event handler so that it stores the remembered data. To store the latitude, longitude, and address, you'll need three calls to **TinyDB.StoreValue.** Table 7-6 lists the additional blocks you'll need.

Table 7-6. Blocks for recording and displaying the current location

Block type	Drawer	Purpose
TinyDB1.StoreValue (3)	TinyDB	Store the data in the device database.
text ("address")	Text	Plug this into the "tag" slot of **TinyDB1.StoreValue.**
LocationSensor.Current Address	LocationSensor	The address to store persistently; plug this into the "value" slot of **TinyDB1.StoreValue.**
text ("lat")	Text	Plug this into the "tag" slot of the second **TinyDB1 .StoreValue.**
LocationSensor.Current Latitude	LocationSensor	The latitude to store persistently; plug this into the "value" slot of the second **TinyDB1.StoreValue.**
text ("long")	Text	Plug this into the "tag" slot of the third **TinyDB1. StoreValue.**
LocationSensor.Current Longitude	LocationSensor	The longitude to store persistently; plug this into the "value" slot of the third **TinyDB1.StoreValue.**

How the blocks work

As shown in Figure 7-5, **TinyDB1.StoreValue** copies the location data from the
LocationSensor properties into the database. As you may recall from No Texting
While Driving, the StoreValue function has two arguments, the tag and the value.
The *tag* identifies which data you want to store, and the *value* is the actual data you
want saved—in this case, the LocationSensor data.

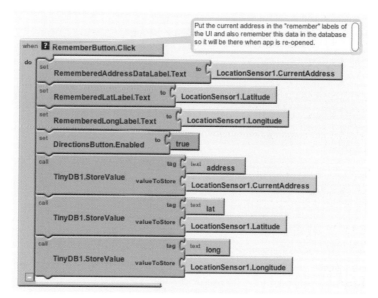

Figure 7-5. Storing the remembered location data in a database

Retrieving the Remembered Location When the App Launches

You store data in a database so you can recall it later. In this app, if a user stores a
location and then closes the app, you want to recall that information from the database and show it to her when she relaunches the app.

As discussed in previous chapters, the **Screen.Initialize** event is triggered when
your app launches. Retrieving data from a database is a very common thing to do on
startup, and it's exactly what we want to do for this app.

You'll use the **TinyDB.GetValue** function to retrieve the stored GPS data. Because
you need to retrieve the stored address, latitude, and longitude, you'll need three
calls to GetValue. As with No Texting While Driving, you'll need to check if there is
indeed data there (if it's the first time your app is being launched, **TinyDB.GetValue**
will return an empty text).

As a challenge, see if you can create these blocks and then compare your creation to
the blocks shown in Figure 7-6.

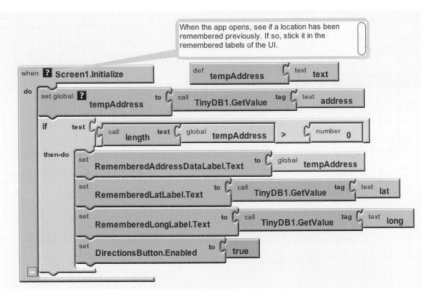

Figure 7-6. Adding the remembered location to a database so it's available when the app is closed and reopened

How the blocks work

To understand these blocks, you can envision a user opening the app the first time, and opening it later after previously recording location data. The first time the user opens the app, there won't be any location data in the database to load, so you don't want to set the "remembered" labels or enable the DirectionsButton. On successive launches, if there is data stored, you do want to load the previously stored location data from the database.

The blocks first call the **TinyDB1.GetValue** with a tag of "address," which is one of the tags used when you stored the location data earlier. The retrieved value is placed in the variable tempAddress, where it is checked to see whether it's empty or contains data.

The **if** block is necessary because TinyDB returns an empty text if there is no data for a particular tag; there isn't any data the first time the app is launched and there won't be until the user clicks the RememberButton. Since the variable tempAddress now holds the returned value, the blocks check to see if the length of tempAddress is greater than 0. If the length is greater than 0, the app knows that TinyDB did return something, and the retrieved value is placed into RememberedAddressDataLabel. The app also knows that if an address has been stored, it has a latitude and longitude. Thus, those values are also retrieved using **TinyDB.GetValue**. Finally, if data has indeed been retrieved, the DirectionsButton is enabled.

Test your app. *Download the new version of the app to your phone and test again. Click the* RememberButton *and make sure the readings are recorded. Then close the app and reopen it. Does the remembered data appear?*

The Complete App: Android, Where's My Car?

Figure 7-7 shows the final blocks for the complete "Android, Where's My Car?" app.

Variations

Here are some variations you can experiment with:

- Create "Android, Where Is Everyone?", an app that lets a group of people track one another's whereabouts. Whether you're hiking or at the park, this app could help save time and possibly even lives. The data for this app is shared, so you'll need to use a web database and the TinyWebDB component instead of TinyDB. See Chapter 22 for more information.

- Create a Breadcrumb app that tracks your whereabouts by recording each location change in a list. You should only record a new breadcrumb if the location has changed by a certain amount, or a certain amount of time has elapsed, because even slight movement can generate a new location reading. You'll need to store the recorded locations in a list—see Chapter 19 for help.

Summary

Here are some of the ideas we've covered in this tutorial:

- The LocationSensor component can report the user's latitude, longitude, and current street address. Its LocationChanged event is triggered when the sensor gets its first reading and when the reading changes (the device has moved). For more information on the LocationSensor, see Chapter 23.

- The ActivityStarter component can launch any app, including Google Maps. For Maps, you set the DataUri property to the URL of the map you want to display. If you want to show directions between GPS coordinates, the URL will be in the following format, but you'd replace the sample data shown here with actual GPS coordinates:

      http://maps.google.com/maps/?saddr=0.1,0.1&daddr=0.2,0.2

- **make text** is used to piece together (concatenate) separate text items into a single text object. It allows you to concatenate dynamic data with static text. With the Maps URL, the GPS coordinates are the dynamic data.

- TinyDB allows you to store data persistently in the phone's database. Whereas the data in a variable or property is lost when an app closes, data stored in the database can be loaded each time the app is opened. For more information on TinyDB and databases, see Chapter 22.

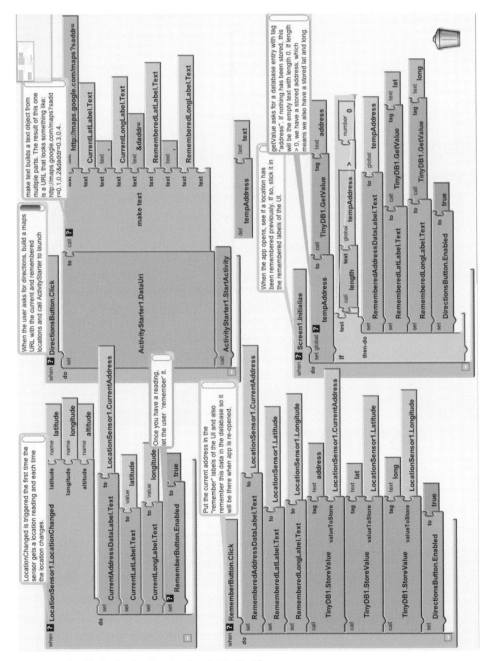

Figure 7-7. The blocks for "Android, Where's My Car?"

CHAPTER 8

Presidents Quiz

The Presidents Quiz is a trivia game about former leaders of the United States. Though this quiz is about presidents, you can use it as a template to build quizzes on any topic.

In the previous chapters, you've been introduced to some fundamental programming concepts. Now you're ready for something more challenging. You'll find that this chapter requires a conceptual leap in terms of programming skills and abstract thinking. In particular, you'll use two list variables to store the data—in this case, the quiz questions and answers—and you'll use an index variable to track where the user is in the quiz. When you finish, you'll be armed with the knowledge to create quiz apps and many other apps that require list processing.

This chapter assumes you're familiar with the basics of App Inventor: using the Component Designer to build the user interface, and using the Blocks Editor to specify event handlers and program the component behavior. If you are not familiar with these fundamentals, be sure to review the previous chapters before continuing.

You'll design the quiz so that the user proceeds from question to question by clicking a Next button and receives feedback on whether each answer he inputs is correct or incorrect.

What You'll Learn

This app, shown in Figure 8-1, covers:

- Defining list variables for storing the questions and answers in lists.

- Sequencing through a list using an index; each time the user clicks Next, you'll display the next question.

- Using conditional (`if`) behaviors: performing certain operations only under specific conditions. You'll use an **if** block to handle the app's behavior when the user
reaches the end of the quiz.

- Switching an image to show a different picture for each quiz question.

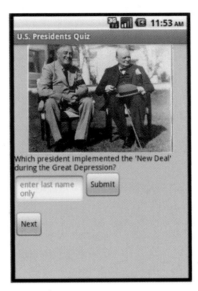

Figure 8-1. The Presidents Quiz running in the emulator

Getting Started

Connect to the App Inventor website and start a new project. Name it "PresidentsQuiz"
and set the screen's title to "Presidents Quiz". Open the Blocks Editor and connect
to the phone. Also download the pictures for the quiz from the book's site (*http://
examples.oreilly.com/0636920016632/*) onto your computer: *roosChurch.gif*, *nixon.gif*,
carterChina.gif, and *atomic.gif*. You'll load these images into your project in the next
section.

Designing the Components

The Presidents Quiz app has a simple interface for displaying the question and allowing the user to answer. You can build the components from the snapshot of the
Component Designer shown in Figure 8-2.

Figure 8-2. The Presidents Quiz in the Designer

To create this interface, first load the images you downloaded into the project. Click Add in the Media area and select one of the downloaded files (e.g., *roosChurch.gif*). Do the same for the other three images. Then add the components listed in Table 8-1.

Table 8-1. Components for the Presidents Quiz app

Component type	Palette group	What you'll name it	Purpose
Image	Basic	Image1	The picture displayed with the question.
Label	Basic	QuestionLabel	Display the current question.
Horizontal Arrangement	Screen Arrangement	Horizontal Arrangement1	Organize the AnswerPrompt and Text.
TextBox	Basic	AnswerText	The user will enter his answer here.
Button	Basic	AnswerButton	The user clicks this to submit an answer.
Label	Basic	RightWrongLabel	Display "correct!" or "incorrect!"
Button	Basic	NextButton	The user clicks this to proceed to the next question.

Set the properties of the components as follows:

1. Set Image1.Picture to the image file *roosChurch.gif*, the first picture that should appear. Set its Width to "Fill parent" and its Height to 200.

2. Set QuestionLabel.Text to "Question…" (you'll input the first question in the Blocks Editor).

3. Set AnswerText.Hint to "Enter an answer". Set its Text property to blank. Move it into HorizontalArrangement1.

4. Change `AnswerButton.Text` to "Submit" and move it into `Horizontal Arrangement1`.

5. Change `NextButton.Text` to "Next".

6. Change `RightWrongLabel.Text` to blank.

Adding Behaviors to the Components

You'll need to program the following behaviors:

- When the app starts, the first question appears, including its corresponding image.

- When the user clicks the `NextButton`, the second question appears. When he clicks it again, the third question appears, and so on.

- When the user reaches the last question and clicks the `NextButton`, the first question should appear again.

- When the user answers a question, the app will report whether it is correct or not.

To start, you'll define two list variables based on the items listed in Table 8-2: `QuestionList` to hold the list of questions, and `AnswerList` to hold the list of corresponding answers. Figure 8-3 shows the two lists you'll create in the Blocks Editor.

Table 8-2. Variables for holding question and answer lists

Block type	Drawer	Purpose
def variable ("QuestionList")	Definitions	Store the list of questions (rename it `QuestionList`).
def variable ("AnswerList")	Definitions	Store the list of answers (rename it `AnswerList`).
make a list	Lists	Insert the items of the `QuestionList`.
text (three of them)	Text	The questions.
make a list	Lists	Insert the items of the `AnswerList`.
text (three of them)	Text	The answers.

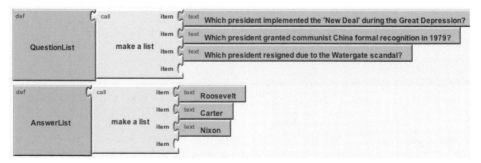

Figure 8-3. The lists for the quiz

Defining the Index Variable

The app needs to keep track of the current question as the user clicks the NextButton to proceed through the quiz. You'll define a variable named currentQuestionIndex for this, and the variable will serve as the index into both the QuestionList and AnswerList. Table 8-3 lists the blocks you'll need to do this, and Figure 8-4 shows what that variable will look like.

Table 8-3. Creating the index

Block type	Drawer	Purpose
def variable ("currentQuestionIndex")	Definitions	Hold the index (position) of the current question/answer.
number (1)	Math	Set the initial value of currentQuestionIndex to 1 (the first question).

Figure 8-4. Initiating the index blocks with a value of 1

Displaying the First Question

Now that you've defined the variables you need, you can specify the app's interactive behavior. As with any app, it's important to work incrementally and define one behavior at a time. To start, let's think only about the questions—specifically, displaying the first question in the list when the app launches. We'll come back and deal with the images a bit later.

You want your code blocks to work regardless of the specific questions that are in the list. That way, if you decide to change the questions or create a new quiz by copying and modifying this app, you'll only need to change the actual questions in the list definitions, and you won't need to change any event handlers.

So, for this first behavior, you don't want to refer directly to the first question, "Which president implemented the 'New Deal' during the Great Depression?" Instead, you want to refer, abstractly, to the first *slot* in the QuestionList (regardless of the specific question there). That way, the blocks will still work even if you modify the question in that first slot.

You select particular items in a list with the **select list item** block. The block asks you to specify the list and an index (a position in the list). If a list has three items, you can enter 1, 2, or 3 as the index.

For this first behavior, when the app launches, you want to select the first item in QuestionList and place it in the QuestionLabel. As you'll recall from the "Android, Where's My Car?" app in Chapter 7, if you want something to happen when your app launches, you program that behavior in the **Screen1.Initialize** event handler using the blocks listed in Table 8-4.

Table 8-4. Blocks to load the initial question when the app starts

Block type	Drawer	Purpose
Screen1.Initialize	Screen1	Event handler triggered when the app begins.
set QuestionLabel .Text to	QuestionLabel	Put the first question in `QuestionLabel`.
select list item	Lists	Select the first question from `QuestionList`.
Global QuestionList	My Definitions	The list to select questions from.
number (1)	Math	Select the first question by using an index of 1.

How the blocks work

The **Screen1.Initialize** event is triggered when the app begins. As shown in Figure 8-5, the first item of the variable `QuestionList` is selected and placed into `QuestionLabel.Text`. So, when the app begins, the user will see the first question.

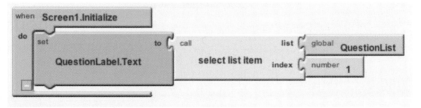

Figure 8-5. Selecting the first question

Test your app. *Plug in your phone to the computer or click "New emulator" to open an Android emulator, and then click "Connect to Device." When your app loads, do you see the first item of* `QuestionList`, *"Which president implemented the 'New Deal' during the Great Depression?"*

Iterating Through the Questions

Now program the behavior of the `NextButton`. You've already defined the `current QuestionIndex` to remember which question the user is on. When the user clicks the `NextButton`, the app needs to *increment* (add one to) the `currentQuestionIndex` (i.e., change it from 1 to 2 or from 2 to 3, and so on). You'll then use the resulting value of `currentQuestionIndex` to select the new question to display.

As a challenge, see if you can build these blocks on your own. When you're finished, compare your results against Figure 8-6.

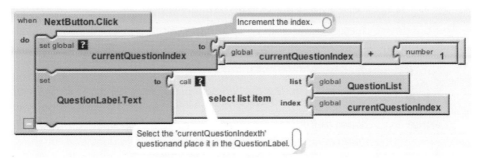

Figure 8-6. Moving to the next question

How the blocks work

The first row of blocks increments the variable currentQuestionIndex. If current QuestionIndex has a 1 in it, it is changed to 2. If it has a 2, it is changed to 3, and so on. Once the currentQuestionIndex variable has been changed, the app uses it to select the new question to display.

When the user clicks NextButton for the first time, the increment blocks will change currentQuestionIndex from 1 to 2, so the app will select the second item from QuestionList, "Which president granted communist China formal recognition in 1979?" The second time NextButton is clicked, currentQuestionIndex will be set from 2 to 3, and the app will select the third question in the list, "Which president resigned due to the Watergate scandal?"

Note. *Take a minute to compare the blocks of **NextButton.Click** to those in the **Screen.Initialize** event handler. In the **Screen.Initialize** blocks, the app used **select list item** with a concrete number (1) to select the list item. In these blocks, you're selecting the list item using a variable as the index. The app doesn't choose the first item in the list, or the second or third; it chooses the* currentQuestion Index*th item, and thus a different item will be selected each time the* NextButton *is clicked. This is a very common use for an index— incrementing its value to find and display items in a list.*

The problem with the app is that it simply increments to the next question each time without any concern for the end of the quiz. When currentQuestionIndex is already 3 and the user clicks the NextButton, the app changes currentQuestionIndex from 3 to 4. It then calls **select list item** to get the currentQuestionIndex*th* item—in this case, the fourth item. Since there are only three items in the variable `QuestionList`, the Android device doesn't know what to do and forces the app to quit. So how can we let the app know that it has reached the end of the quiz?

 Test your app. *Test the behavior of the* `NextButton` *to see if the app is working correctly. Click the* `NextButton` *on the phone. Does the phone display the second question, "Which president granted communist China formal recognition in 1979?" It should, and the third question should appear when you click the* `NextButton` *again. But if you click again, you should see an error: "Attempting to get item 4 of a list of length 3." The app has a bug! Do you know what the problem is? Try figuring it out before moving on.*

The app needs to ask a question when the `NextButton` is clicked, and execute different blocks depending on the answer. Since you know your app contains three questions, one way to ask the question would be, "Is the variable `currentQuestionIndex` greater than 3?" If the answer is yes, you should set `currentQuestionIndex` back to 1 so the user is taken back to the first question. The blocks you'll need for this are listed in Table 8-5.

Table 8-5. Blocks for checking the index value for the end of the list

Block type	Drawer	Purpose
if	Control	Figure out if the user is on the last question.
=	Math	Test if `currentQuestionIndex` is 3.
global currentQuestion Index	My Definitions	Put this into the left side of =.
number 3	Math	Put this into the right side of = since 3 is the number of items in the list.
set global current QuestionIndex to	My Definitions	Set to 1 to revert to the first question.
number 1	Math	Set the index to 1.

Test your app. *Because variables like* currentQuestionIndex *aren't visible when you run an app, they are often the source of bugs in a program. Fortunately, App Inventor provides a way to "watch" variables during testing. Specifically, you can right-click a **def variable** block and select Watch, and a little box will appear, showing the value of the variable. In this case, right-click the **def current QuestionIndex** definition to watch it. Then click on the "Connect to Device..." button in the Blocks Editor to restart the app. The **def current QuestionIndex** block will appear with a watch box displaying the initial value of* currentQuestionIndex *(1), as shown in Figure 8-8.*

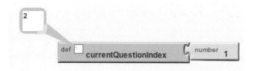

Figure 8 8. Watching a variable while testing your app

Now pick up the phone and click the NextButton. *The second question, "Which president granted communist China formal recognition in 1979?" should appear in the* QuestionLabel *on the phone, as before. On the App Inventor screen, a 2 should appear in the* current QuestionIndex *watch box, as shown in Figure 8-9.*

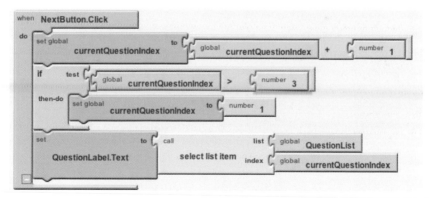

Figure 8-9. Confirming that the index is incrementing

When you click again, the third question should appear on the phone and a 3 should appear in the watch box. Now for the behavior you're really testing: if you click again, you should see 1 in currentQuestionIndex, *and the first question ("Which president implemented the 'New Deal' during the Great Depression?") should appear on the phone.*

When the user clicks the NextButton, the app increments the index as it did before. But then, as shown in Figure 8-7, it checks to see if currentQuestionIndex is larger than 3, the number of questions. If it is larger than 3, currentQuestionIndex is set back to 1, and the first question is displayed. If it is 3 or less, the blocks within the **if** block are not performed, and the current question is displayed as usual.

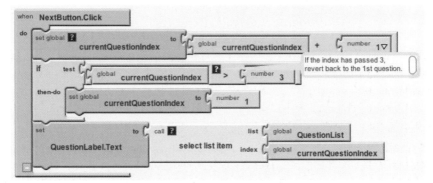

Figure 8-7. Checking if the last (third) question has been reached

Making the Quiz Easy to Modify

If your blocks for the NextButton work, pat yourself on the back—you are on your way to becoming a programmer! But what if you added a new question (and answer) to the quiz? Would your blocks still work?

To explore this, first add a fourth question to QuestionList and a fourth answer into AnswerList, as shown in Figure 8-10.

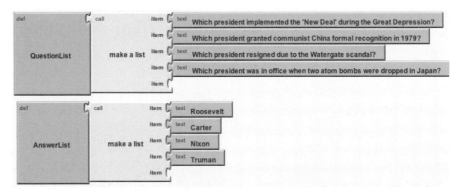

Figure 8-10. Adding an item to both lists

Test your app. *Click the* NextButton *several times. You'll notice that the fourth question never appears, no matter how many times you click Next.*

Do you know what the problem is? Before reading on, see if you can fix the blocks so the fourth question appears.

The problem is that the test to determine whether the user is on the last question is too specific; it asks if the currentQuestionIndex variable is 3. You could just change the number 3 to a 4, and the app would work correctly again. The problem with that solution, however, is that each time you modify the questions and answers, you also have to remember to make this change. Such dependencies in a computer program often lead to bugs, especially as an app grows in complexity.

A much better strategy is to design the blocks so that they will work no matter how many questions there are. Such generality makes it easier if you, as a programmer, want to customize your quiz for some other topic. It is also essential if the list you are working with changes dynamically—for example, think of a quiz app that allows the user to add new questions (you'll build this in Chapter 10).

For a program to be more general, it can't refer to concrete numbers like 3, as that only works for quizzes of three questions. So, instead of asking if the value of currentQuestionIndex is larger than the specific number 3, ask if it is as large as the *number of items* in QuestionList. If the app asks this more general question, it will work even when you add to or remove items from the QuestionList. So modify the **NextButton.Click** event handler to replace the previous test that referred directly to 3. You'll need the blocks listed in Table 8-6.

Table 8-6. Blocks to check the length of the list

Block type	Drawer	Purpose
length of list	Lists	Ask how many items are in QuestionList.
global Question List	My Definitions	Put this into the "list" slot of **length of list**.

How the Blocks Work

The **if** test now compares the currentQuestionIndex to the length of the QuestionList, as shown in Figure 8-11. So, if currentQuestionIndex is 5, and the length of the QuestionList is 4, then the currentQuestionIndex will be set back to 1. Note that, because the blocks no longer refer to 3 or any specific number, the behavior will work no matter how many items are in the list.

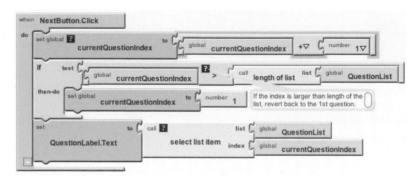

Figure 8-11. Checking for the end of the list in a generic way

 Test your app. *When you click the* NextButton, *does the app now cycle through the four questions, moving to the first one after the fourth?*

Switching the Image for Each Question

Now that you've programmed all the behaviors for moving through the questions (and you've made your code smarter and more flexible by making it more *abstract*), let's get the images working properly, too. Right now, the app shows the same image no matter what question is being asked. You can change this so an image pertaining to each question appears when the user clicks the NextButton. Earlier, you added four pictures as media for the project. Now, you'll create a third list, PictureList, with the image filenames as its items. You'll also modify the **NextButton.Click** event handler to switch the picture each time, just as you switch the question text each time. (If you're already thinking about using the currentQuestionIndex here, you're on the right track!)

First, create a PictureList and initialize it with the names of the image files. Be sure that the names are exactly the same as the filenames you loaded into the Media section of the project. Figure 8-12 shows how the blocks for the PictureList should look.

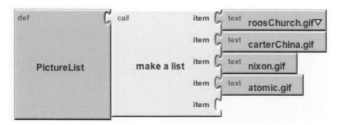

Figure 8-12. The PictureList with image filenames as items

Next, modify the **NextButton.Click** event handler so that it changes the picture that appears depending on the question index. The **Image.Picture** property is used to change the picture displayed. To modify **NextButton.Click**, you'll need the blocks listed in Table 8-7.

Table 8-7. Blocks to add the image that accompanies the question

Block type	Drawer	Purpose
set Image1.Picture to	Image1	Set this to change the picture.
select list item	Lists	Select the picture corresponding to the current question.
global PictureList	My Definitions	Select a filename from this list.
global current QuestionIndex	My Definitions	Select the currentQuestionIndex*th* item.

How the Blocks Work

The currentQuestionIndex serves as the index for both the QuestionList and the PictureList. As long as you've set up your lists properly such that the first question corresponds to the first picture, the second to the second, and so on, the single index can serve both lists, as shown in Figure 8-13. For instance, the first picture, *roosChurch .gif*, is a picture of President Franklin Delano Roosevelt (sitting with British Prime Minister Winston Churchill), and "Roosevelt" is the answer to the first question.

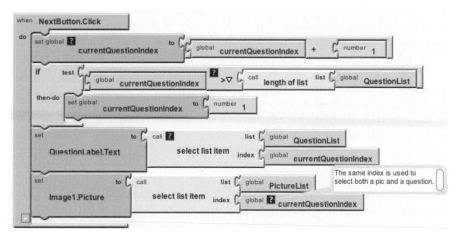

Figure 8-13. Selecting the currentQuestionIndexth picture each time

Test your app. *Click next a few times. Now does a different image appear each time you click the* NextButton?

Checking the User's Answers

Thus far, we've created an app that simply cycles through questions and answers (paired with an image of the answer). It's a great example of apps that use lists, but to be a true quiz app, it needs to give users feedback on whether they're right or wrong. So now let's add blocks that report whether the user has answered a question correctly or not. Our interface is set up so the user enters her answer in AnswerText and then clicks the AnswerButton. The app must compare the user's entry with the answer to the current question, using an **ifelse** block to check. The RightWrongLabel should then be modified to report whether or not the answer is correct. There are quite a few blocks needed to program this behavior, all of which are listed in Table 8-8.

Table 8-8. Blocks for indicating whether an answer is correct or not

Block type	Drawer	Purpose
AnswerButton.Click	AnswerButton	Triggered when the user clicks the AnswerButton.
ifelse	Control	If the answer is correct, do one thing; otherwise, do another.
=	Math	Ask if the answer is correct.
AnswerText.Text	AnswerText	Contains the user's answer.
select list item	Lists	Select the current answer from AnswerList.
global AnswerList	My Definitions	The list to select from.
global currentQuestion Index	My Definitions	The question (and answer) number the user is on.
set RightWrongLabel .Text to	RightWrongLabel	Report the answer here.
text ("correct!")	Text	Display this if the answer is right.
set RightWrongLabel .Text to	RightWrongLabel	Report the answer here.
text ("incorrect!")	Text	Display this if the answer is wrong.

How the Blocks Work

As shown in Figure 8-14, the **ifelse** test asks whether the answer the user entered (**AnswerText.Text**) is equal to the currentQuestionIndexth item in the AnswerList. If currentQuestionIndex is 1, the app will compare the user's answer with the first item in AnswerList, "Roosevelt." If currentQuestionIndex is 2, the app will compare the user's answer with the second answer in the list, "Carter," and so on. If the test result is positive, the "then-do" blocks are executed and the RightWrongLabel is set to "correct!" If the test is false, the "else-do" blocks are executed and the RightWrongLabel is set to "incorrect!"

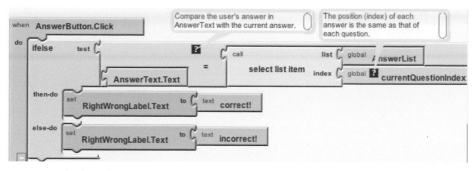

Figure 8-14. Checking the answer

 Test your app. *Try answering one of the questions. It should report whether or not you answered the question exactly as specified in the* AnswerList. *Test with both a correct and incorrect answer. You'll likely notice that for an answer to be marked as correct, it has to be an exact match (meaning case-specific and including any punctuation or spaces) to what you entered in the* AnswerList. *Be sure to also test that things work on successive questions.*

The app should work, but you might notice that when you click the NextButton, the "correct!" or "incorrect!" text and the previous answer are still there, as shown in Figure 8-15, even though you're looking at the next question. It's fairly innocuous, but your app users will definitely notice such user interface issues.

To blank out the RightWrongLabel and the AnswerText, you'll put the blocks listed in Table 8-9 within the **NextButton.Click** event handler.

Figure 8-15. The first answer and "correct!" still appear when user moves to the next question.

Table 8-9. Blocks to clear the RightWrongLabel

Block type	Drawer	Purpose
set RightWrongLabel.Text to	RightWrongLabel	This is the label to blank out.
text ("")	Text	When the user clicks NextButton, erase the previous answer's feedback.
set AnswerText.Text to	AnswerText	The user's answer from the previous question.
text ("")	Text	When the user clicks the NextButton, erase the previous answer.

How the Blocks Work

As shown in Figure 8-16, when the user clicks the NextButton, he is moving on to the next question, so the top two rows of the event handler blank out the RightWrongLabel and the AnswerText.

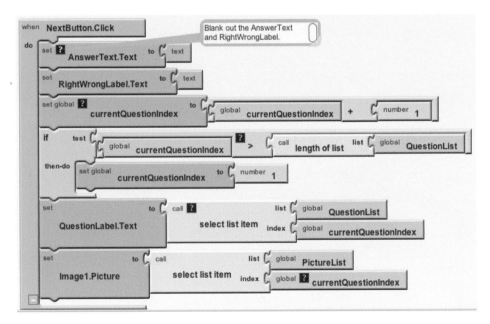

Figure 8-16. Blanking out the answer and correct/incorrect label for the next question

Test your app. *Answer a question and click "Submit", then click the* NextButton. *Did your previous answer and its feedback disappear?*

The Complete App: The Presidents Quiz

Figure 8-17 shows the final block configuration for the Presidents Quiz.

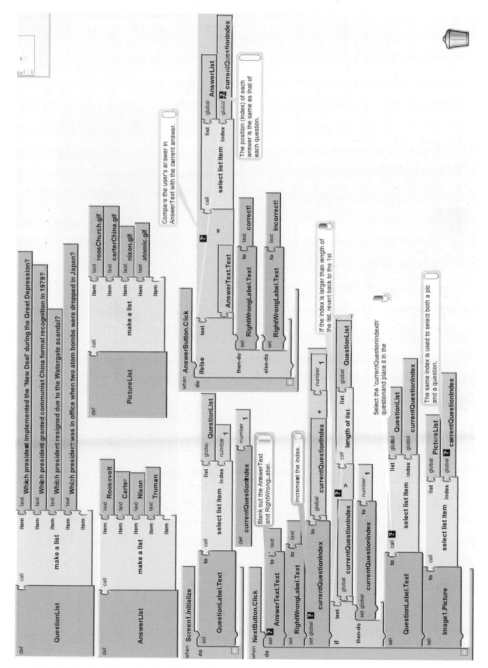

Figure 8-17. The blocks for the Presidents Quiz

Variations

Once you get this quiz working, you might want to explore some variations. For example:

- Instead of just showing images for each question, try playing a sound clip or a short video. With sound, you can turn your quiz into a Name That Tune app.

- The quiz is very rigid in terms of what it accepts as a valid answer. There are a number of ways to modify this. One is to use the **text.contains** block to see if the user's answer is contained in the actual answer. Another option is to provide multiple answers for each question, and check by iterating (**foreach**) through them to see if any match. You could also figure out how to deal with any extra spaces your user entered in the answer or allow upper- or lowercase characters (i.e., make the answers case-insensitive).

- Transform the quiz so that it is multiple choice. You'll need an additional list to hold the answer choices for each question. The possible answers will be a list of lists, with each sublist holding the answer choices for a particular question. Use the ListPicker component to allow the user to choose an answer. You can read more about lists in Chapter 19.

Summary

Here are some of the ideas we've covered in this tutorial:

- Separate an app into its data (often stored in a list) and its event handlers. Use an **ifelse** block to check conditions. For more information on conditionals, see Chapter 18.

- The blocks in event handlers should refer only *abstractly* to list items and list size so that the app will work even if the data in the list is changed.

- Index variables track the current position of an item within a list. When you increment them, be careful about using an **if** block to handle the app's behavior when the user reaches the end of the list.

CHAPTER 9

Xylophone

It's hard to believe that using technology to record and play back music only dates back to 1878, when Edison patented the phonograph. We've come so far since then—with music synthesizers, CDs, sampling and remixing, phones that play music, and even long-distance jamming over the Internet. In this chapter, you'll take part in this tradition by building a Xylophone app that records and plays music.

What You'll Build

With the app shown in Figure 9-1 (originally created by Liz Looney of the App Inventor team), you can:

- Play eight different notes by touching colored buttons on the screen.

- Press a Play button to replay the notes you played earlier.

- Press a Reset button to make the app forget what notes you played earlier so you can enter a new song.

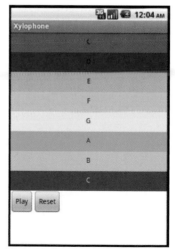

Figure 9-1. The Xylophone app UI

What You'll Learn

This tutorial covers the following concepts:

- Using a single Sound component to play different audio files.

- Using the Clock component to measure and enforce delays between actions.

- Deciding when to create a procedure.

- Creating a procedure that calls itself.

- Advanced use of lists, including adding items, accessing them, and clearing the list.

Getting Started

Connect to the App Inventor website and start a new project. Name it "Xylophone", and also set the screen's title to "Xylophone". Open the Blocks Editor and connect to your phone or emulator.

Designing the Components

This app has 13 different components (8 of which compose the keyboard), listed in Table 9-1. Since there are so many, it would get pretty boring to create all of them before starting to write our program, so we'll break down the app into its functional parts and build them sequentially by going back and forth between the Designer and the Blocks Editor, as we did with the Ladybug Chase app in Chapter 5.

Table 9-1. All of the components for the Xylophone app

Component type	Palette group	What you'll name it	Purpose
Button	Basic	Button1	Play Low C key.
Button	Basic	Button2	Play D key.
Button	Basic	Button3	Play E key.
Button	Basic	Button4	Play F key.
Button	Basic	Button5	Play G key.
Button	Basic	Button6	Play A key.
Button	Basic	Button7	Play B key.
Button	Basic	Button8	Play High C key.
Sound	Media	Sound1	Play the notes.
Button	Basic	PlayButton	Play back the song.
Button	Basic	ResetButton	Reset the song memory.
Horizontal Arrangement	Screen Arrangement	Horizontal Arrangement1	Place the Play and Reset buttons next to each other.
Clock	Basic	Clock1	Keep track of delays between notes.

Creating the Keyboard

Our user interface will include an eight-note keyboard for a pentatonic (seven-note) major scale ranging from Low C to High C. We will create this musical keyboard in this section.

Creating the First Note Buttons

Start by creating the first two xylophone keys, which we will implement as buttons.

1. From the Basic category, drag a Button onto the screen. Leave its name as Button1. We want it to be a long magenta bar, like a key on a xylophone, so set its properties as follows:

    a. Changing its BackgroundColor property to Magenta.

    b. Changing its Text property to "C".

    c. Setting its Width property to "Fill parent" so it goes all the way across the screen.

    d. Setting its Height property to 40 pixels.

2. Repeat for a second Button, named Button2, placing it below Button1. Use Width and Height property values, but set its BackgroundColor property to Red and its Text property to "D".

(Later, we will repeat step 2 for six more note buttons.)

The view in the Component Designer should look something like Figure 9-2.

Figure 9-2. Placing buttons to create a keyboard

The display on your phone should look similar, although there will not be any empty space between the two colored buttons.

Adding the Sound Component

We can't have a xylophone without sounds, so create a Sound component, leaving its name as Sound1. Change the MinimumInterval property from its default value of 500 milliseconds to 0. This allows us to play the sound as often as we want, instead of having to wait half a second (500 milliseconds) between plays. Don't set its Source property, which we will set in the Blocks Editor.

Upload the sound files *1.wav* and *2.wav* from *http://examples.oreilly.com/ 0636920016632/*. Unlike in previous chapters, where it was OK to change the names of media files, it is important to use these exact names for reasons that will soon become clear. You can either upload the remaining six sound files now or wait until directed to later.

Connecting the Sounds to the Buttons

The behavior we need to program is for a sound file to play when the corresponding button is clicked. Specifically, if Button1 is clicked, we'd like to play *1.wav*; if Button2 is clicked, we'd like to play *2.wav*; and so on. We can set this up in the Blocks Editor as shown in Figure 9-3 by doing the following:

1. From the My Blocks tab and Button1 drawer, drag out the **Button1.Click** block.

2. From the Sound1 drawer, drag out the set **Sound1.Source** block, placing it in the **Button1.Click** block.

3. Type "text" to create a text block. (This is quicker than going to the Built-In tab and then the Text drawer, although that would work too.) Set its text value to "1.wav" and place it in the **Sound1.Source** block.

4. Add a **Sound1.Play** block.

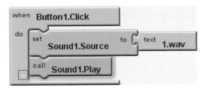

Figure 9-3. Playing a sound when a button is clicked

We could do the same for Button2, as shown in Figure 9-4 (just changing the text value), but the code would be awfully repetitive.

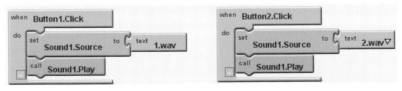

Figure 9-4. Adding more sounds

Repeated code is a good sign that you should create a procedure, which you've already done in Chapter 3's MoleMash game and Chapter 5's Ladybug Chase game. Specifically, we'll create a procedure that takes a number as an argument, sets Sound1's Source to the appropriate file, and plays the sound. This is another example of *refactoring*—improving a program's implementation without changing its behavior, a concept introduced in the MoleMash tutorial. We can use the Text drawer's **join** block (an alternate version of **make text**) to combine the number (e.g., 1) and the text ".wav" to create the proper filename (e.g., "1.wav"). Here are the steps for creating the procedure we need:

1. Under the Built-In tab, go to the Definition drawer and drag out the **to procedure** block.

2. Go back to the Definition drawer and drag a **name** block into the "arg" socket of **to procedure**.

3. Click the rightmost "name" and set the name to "number".

4. Click **procedure** and set the name to "PlayNote".

5. Drag the **Sound1.Source** block from **Button1.Click** into **PlayNote** to the right of the word "do". The **Sound1.Play** block will move with it.

6. Drag the **1.wav** block into the trash can.

7. From the Text drawer, drag the **join** block into **Sound1.Source**'s socket.

8. Type "number" and move it to the left socket of the **join** block (if it is not already there).

9. From the Text drawer, drag the **text** block into the right socket of the **join** block.

10. Change the text value to ".wav". (Remember not to type the quotation marks.)

11. Under the My Blocks tab, go to the My Definitions drawer and drag a **call PlayNote** block into the empty body of **Button1.Click**.

12. Type "1" and put it in the "number" socket.

Now, when Button1 is clicked, the procedure PlayNote will be called, with its number argument having the value 1. It should set Sound1.Source to "1.wav" and play the sound.

Create a similar **Button2.Click** block with a call to PlayNote with an argument of 2. (You can copy the existing **PlayNote** block and move it into the body of **Button2.Click**, making sure to change the argument.) Your program should look like Figure 9-5.

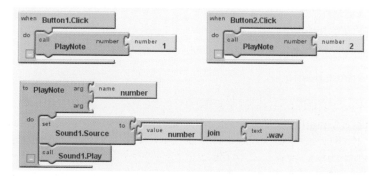

Figure 9-5. Creating a procedure to play a note

Telling Android to Load the Sounds

If you tried out the preceding calls to PlayNote, you may have been disappointed by not hearing the sound you expected or by experiencing an unexpected delay. That's because Android needs to load sounds at runtime, which takes time, before they can be played. This issue didn't come up before, because filenames placed in a Sound component's Source property in the Designer are automatically loaded when the program starts. Since we don't set Sound1.Source until *after* the program has started, that initialization process does not take place. We have to explicitly load the sounds when the program starts up, as shown in Figure 9-6.

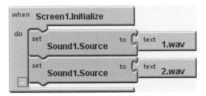

Figure 9-6. Loading sounds when the app launches

 Test your app. *Now if you restart the app by clicking on "Connect to Device…" in the Blocks Editor, the notes should play without delay. (If you don't hear anything, make sure that the media volume on your phone is not set to mute.)*

Implementing the Remaining Notes

Now that we have the first two buttons and notes implemented and working, add the remaining six notes by going back to the Designer and uploading the sound files *3.wav, 4.wav, 5.wav, 6.wav, 7.wav,* and *8.wav.* Then create six new buttons, following the same steps as you did before but setting their Text and BackgroundColor properties as follows:

- Button3 ("E", Pink)
- Button4 ("F", Orange)
- Button5 ("G", Yellow)
- Button6 ("A", Green)
- Button7 ("B", Cyan)
- Button8 ("C", Blue)

You may also want to change Button8's TextColor property to White, as shown in Figure 9-7, so it is more legible.

Figure 9-7. Putting the remaining buttons and sounds in the Component Designer

Back in the Blocks Editor, create **Click** blocks for each of the new buttons with appropriate calls to PlayNote. Similarly, add each new sound file to **Screen.Initialize**, as shown in Figure 9-8.

With your program getting so large, you might find it helpful to click the white minus signs near the bottom of the "container" blocks, such as **PlayNote**, to minimize them and conserve screen space.

Test your app. *You should now have all the buttons, and each one will play a different note when you click it.*

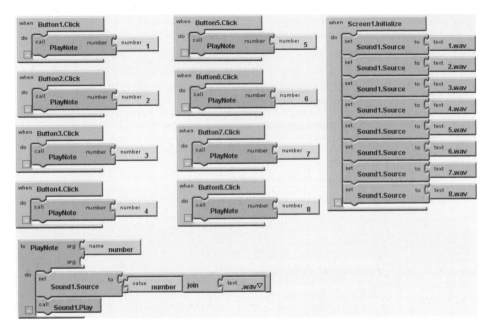

Figure 9-8. Programming the button click events to correspond to all the keyboard keys

Recording and Playing Back Notes

Playing notes by pressing buttons is fun, but being able to record and play back songs is even better. To implement playback, we will need to maintain a record of played notes. In addition to remembering the pitches (sound files) that were played, we must also record the amount of time between notes, or we won't be able to distinguish between two notes played in quick succession and two played with a 10-second silence between them.

Our app will maintain two lists, each of which will have one entry for each note that has been played:

- notes, which will contain the names of the sound files in the order in which they were played

- times, which will record the points in time at which the notes were played

Note. *Before continuing, you may wish to review lists, which we covered in the Presidents Quiz in Chapter 8.*

We can get the timing information from a Clock component, which we will also use to properly time the notes for playback.

Adding the Components

In the Designer, you will need to add a Clock component and Play and Reset buttons, which we will put in a HorizontalArrangement:

1. Drag in a Clock component. It will appear in the "Non-visible components" section. Uncheck its TimerEnabled property because we don't want its timer to go off until we tell it to during playback.

2. Go to the Screen Arrangement category and drag a HorizontalArrangement component beneath the existing button. Set its Width property to "Fill parent."

3. From the Basic category, drag in a Button. Rename it PlayButton and set its Text property to "Play".

4. Drag in another Button, placing it to the right of PlayButton. Rename the new Button to ResetButton and set its Text property to "Reset".

The Designer view should look like Figure 9-9.

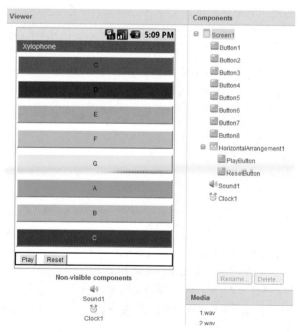

Figure 9-9. Adding components for recording and playing back sounds

Recording Notes and Times

We now need to add the correct behavior in the Blocks Editor. We will need to maintain lists of notes and times and add to the lists whenever the user presses a button.

1. Create a new variable by going to the Built-In tab and dragging out a **def variable** block from the Definition drawer.

2. Click "variable" and change it to "notes".

3. Open the Lists drawer and drag a **make a list** block out, placing it in the socket of **def notes**.

This defines a new variable named "notes" to be an empty list. Repeat the steps for another variable, which you should name "times". These new blocks should look like Figure 9-10.

Figure 9-10. Setting the variables to record notes

How the blocks work

Whenever a note is played, we need to save both the name of the sound file (to the list notes) and the instant in time at which it was played (to the list times). To record the instant in time, we will use the **Clock1.Now** block, which returns the current instant in time (e.g., March 12, 2011, 8:33:14 AM), to the nearest millisecond. These values, obtained through the **Sound1.Source** and **Clock1.Now** blocks, should be added to the lists notes and times, respectively, as shown in Figure 9-11.

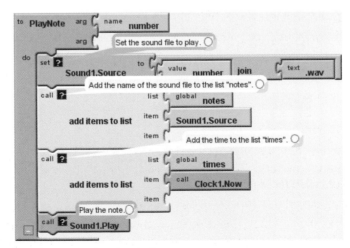

Figure 9-11. Adding the sounds played to the list

For example, if you play "Row, Row, Row Your Boat" [C C C D E], your lists would end up having five entries, which might be:

- notes: *1.wav, 1.wav, 1.wav, 2.wav, 3.wav*

- times [dates omitted]: 12:00:01, 12:00:02, 12:00:03, 12:00:03.5, 12:00:04

When the user presses the Reset button, we want the two lists to go back to their original, empty states. Since the user won't see any change, it's nice to add a small **Sound1.Vibrate** block so he knows that the key click was registered. Figure 9-12 shows the blocks for this behavior.

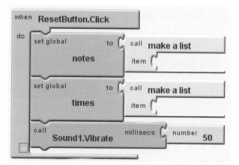

Figure 9-12. Providing feedback when the user resets the app

Playing Back Notes

As a thought experiment, let's first look at how to implement note playback without worrying about timing. We could (but won't) do this by creating these blocks as shown in Figure 9-13:

- A variable count to keep track of which note we're on.

- A new procedure, PlayBackNote, which plays that note and moves on to the next one.

- Code to run when PlayButton is pressed that sets the count to 1 and calls PlayBackNote unless there are no saved notes.

How the blocks work

This may be the first time you've seen a procedure make a call to itself. While at first glance this might seem bogus, it is in fact an important and powerful computer science concept called *recursion*.

To get a better idea of how recursion works, let's step through what happens if a user plays three notes (*1.wav, 3.wav,* and *6.wav*) and then presses the Play button. First, PlayButton.Click starts running. Since the length of the list notes is 3, which is greater than 0, count gets set to 1, and PlayBackNote is called:

1. The first time `PlayBackNote` is called, count = 1:

    a. `Sound1.Source` is set to the first item in notes, which is *1.wav*.

    b. `Sound1.Play` is called, playing this note.

    c. Since count (1) < the length of notes (3),

       count gets incremented to 2.

       `PlayBackNote` gets called again.

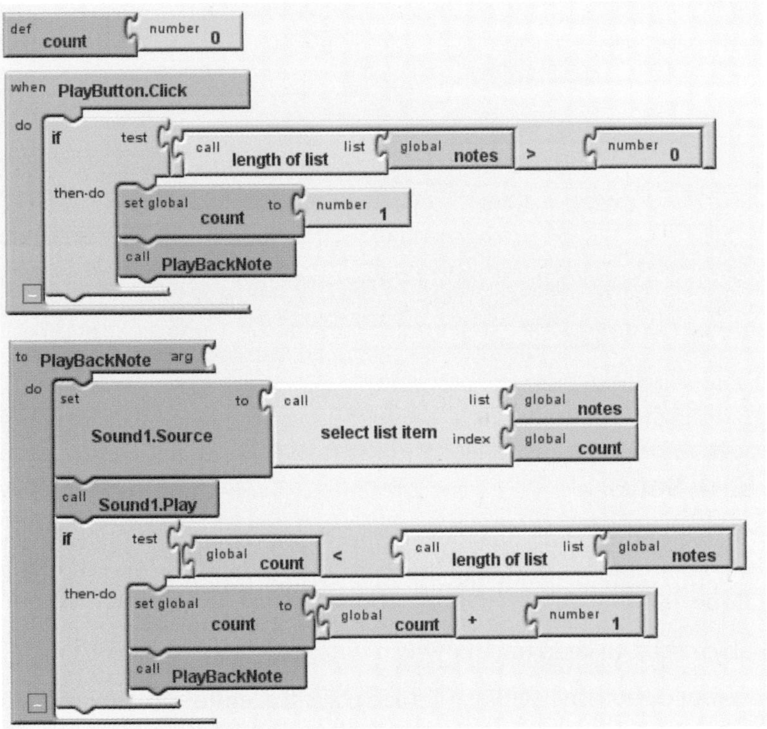

Figure 9-13. Playing back the recorded notes

2. The second time `PlayBackNote` is called, count = 2:

    a. `Sound1.Source` is set to the second item in notes, which is *3.wav*.

    b. `Sound1.Play` is called, playing this note.

    c. Since count (2) < the length of notes (3),

       count gets incremented to 3.

       `PlayBackNote` gets called again.

3. The third time PlayBackNote is called, count = 3:

   a. Sound1.Source is set to the third item in notes, which is *6.wav*.

   b. Sound1.Play is called, playing this note.

   c. Since count (3) is *not* less than the length of notes (3), nothing else happens, and playback is complete.

Note. *Although recursion is powerful, it can also be dangerous. As a thought experiment, ask yourself what would have happened if the programmer forgot to insert the blocks in PlayBackNote that incremented count.*

While the recursion is correct, there is a different problem with the preceding example: almost no time passes between one call to Sound1.Play and the next, so each note gets interrupted by the next note, except for the last one. No note (except for the last) is allowed to complete before Sound1's source is changed and Sound1.Play is called again. To get the correct behavior, we need to implement a delay between calls to PlayBackNote.

Playing Back Notes with Proper Delays

We will implement the delay by setting the timer on the clock to the amount of time between the current note and the next note. For example, if the next note is played 3,000 milliseconds (3 seconds) after the current note, we will set Clock1.TimerInterval to 3,000, after which PlayBackNote should be called again. Make the changes shown in Figure 9-14 to the body of the **if** block in PlayBackNote, and create and fill in the **Clock1.Timer** event handler, which says what should happen when the timer goes off.

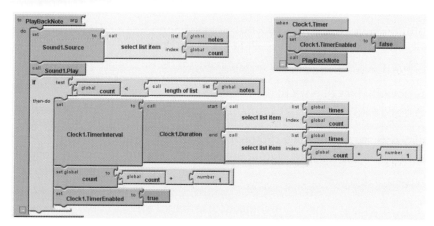

Figure 9-14. Adding delays between the notes

How the blocks work

Let's assume the following contents for the two lists:

- notes: *1.wav*, *3.wav*, *6.wav*
- times: 12:00:00, 12:00:01, 12:00:04

As Figure 9-14 shows, **PlayButton.Click** sets count to 1 and calls **PlayBackNote**.

1. The first time PlayBackNote is called, count = 1:

    a. Sound1.Source is set to the first item in notes, which is "1.wav".

    b. **Sound1.Play** is called, playing this note.

    c. Since count (1) < the length of notes (3),

    Clock1.TimerInterval is set to the amount of time between the first (12:00:00) and second items in times (12:00:01): 1 second.

    count gets incremented to 2.

    Clock1.Timer is enabled and starts counting down.

    Nothing else happens for 1 second, at which time **Clock1.Timer** runs, temporarily disabling the timer and calling **PlayBackNote**.

2. The second time **PlayBackNote** is called, count = 2:

    a. Sound1.Source is set to the second item in notes, which is "3.wav".

    b. **Sound1.Play** is called, playing this note.

    c. Since count (2) < the length of notes (3),

    Clock1.TimerInterval is set to the amount of time between the second (12:00:01) and third items in times (12:00:04): 3 seconds.

    count gets incremented to 3.

    Clock1.Timer is enabled and starts counting down.

    Nothing else happens for 3 seconds, at which time **Clock1.Timer** runs, temporarily disabling the timer and calling **PlayBackNote**.

3. The third time **PlayBackNote** is called, count = 3:

    a. Sound1.Source is set to the third item in notes, which is "6.wav".

    b. **Sound1.Play** is called, playing this note.

    c. Since count (3) is *not* less than the length of notes (3), nothing else happens. Playback is complete.

Variations

Here are some alternative scenarios to explore:

- Currently, there's nothing to stop a user from clicking ResetButton during play-back, which will cause the program to crash. (Can you figure out why?) Modify **PlayButton.Click** so it disables ResetButton. To reenable it when the song is complete, change the **if** block in **PlayButton.Click** into an **ifelse** block, and reenable ResetButton in the "else" portion.

- Similarly, the user can currently click PlayButton while a song is already play-ing. (Can you figure out what will happen if she does so?) Make it so **PlayButton.Click** disables PlayButton and changes its text to "Playing…" You can reenable it and reset the text in an **ifelse** block, as described in the previous bullet.

- Add a button with the name of a song, such as "Für Elise". If the user clicks it, populate the notes and times lists with the corresponding values, set count to 1, and call **PlayBackNote**. To set the appropriate times, you'll find the **Clock1 .MakeInstantFromMillis** block useful.

- If the user presses a note, goes away and does something else, and comes back hours later and presses an additional note, the notes will be part of the same song, which is probably not what the user intended. Improve the program by (1) stopping recording after some reasonable interval of time, such as a minute; or (2) putting a limit on the amount of time used for Clock1.TimerInterval using the **max** block from the Math drawer.

- Visually indicate which note is playing by changing the appearance of the button— for example, by changing its Text, BackgroundColor, or ForegroundColor.

Summary

Here are some of the ideas we've covered in this tutorial:

- You can play different audio files from a single Sound component by changing its Source property. This enabled us to have one Sound component instead of eight. Just be sure to load the sounds at initialization to prevent delays (Figure 9-6).

- Lists can provide a program with memory, with a record of user actions stored in the list and later retrieved and reprocessed. We used this functionality to record and play back a song.

- The Clock component can be used to determine the current time. Subtracting two time values gives us the amount of time between two events.

- The `Clock`'s `TimerInterval` property can be set within the program, such as how we set it to the duration of time between the starts of two notes.

- It is not only possible but sometimes desirable for a procedure to make a call to itself. This is a powerful technique called recursion. When writing a recursive procedure, make sure that there is a base case in which the procedure ends, rather than calling itself, or the program will loop infinitely.

CHAPTER 10

MakeQuiz and TakeQuiz

The Presidents Quiz app in Chapter 8 can be customized to build any quiz, but the customization is restricted to App Inventor programmers. Only you, as the programmer, can modify the questions and answers; there is no way for parents, teachers, or other app users to create their own quizzes or change the quiz questions (unless they too want to learn how to use App Inventor!).

In this chapter, you'll build a MakeQuiz app that lets a "teacher" create quizzes using an input form. The quiz questions and answers will be stored in a web database so that "students" can access a separate TakeQuiz app and take the test. While building these two apps, you'll make yet another significant conceptual leap and learn how to create apps with user-generated data that is shared across apps and among users.

MakeQuiz and TakeQuiz are two apps that work in tandem and allow a "teacher" to create quizzes for a "student." Parents can create fun trivia apps for their children during a long road trip, grade-school teachers can build "Math Blaster" quizzes, and college students can build quizzes to help their study groups prepare for a final. This chapter builds on the Presidents Quiz in Chapter 8, so if you haven't completed that app, you should do so before continuing here.

You'll design two apps, MakeQuiz for the "teacher" (see Figure 10-1) and TakeQuiz for the "student." With MakeQuiz:

- The user enters questions and answers in an input form.

- The entered question-answer pairs are displayed.

Figure 10-1. The MakeQuiz app

- The quiz questions and answers are stored in a database.

TakeQuiz will work similarly to the Presidents Quiz app you've already built. In fact, you'll create it using that app as a starting point. TakeQuiz will differ in that the questions asked will be those that were entered into the database using MakeQuiz.

What You'll Learn

The Presidents Quiz was an example of an app with *static data*: no matter how many times you take the quiz, the questions are always the same because they are written as part of the app (also known as *hardcoded*). News apps, blogs, and social networking apps like Facebook and Twitter work with *dynamic* data, meaning it can change over time. Often, this dynamic information is *user-generated*—the app allows users to enter, modify, and share information. With MakeQuiz and TakeQuiz, you'll learn how to build an app that handles user-generated data.

If you completed the Xylophone app (Chapter 9), you've already been introduced to dynamic lists; in that app, the musical notes the user plays are recorded in lists. Apps with such user-generated data are more complex, and the blocks are more abstract because they don't rely on predefined, static data. You define list variables, but you define them without specific items. As you program your app, you need to envision the lists being populated with data entered by the end user.

This tutorial covers the following App Inventor concepts:

- Input forms for allowing the user to enter information.
- Displaying items from multiple lists.
- Persistent data—MakeQuiz will save the quiz questions and answers in a web database, and TakeQuiz will load them in from the same database.
- Data sharing—you'll store the data in a web database using the TinyWebDB component (instead of the TinyDB component used in previous chapters).

Getting Started

Connect to the App Inventor website and start a new project. Name it "MakeQuiz" and set the screen's title to "Make Quiz". Open the Blocks Editor and connect to your phone.

Designing the Components

Use the Component Designer to create the interface for MakeQuiz. When you finish, it should look something like Figure 10-2 (there are also more detailed instructions after the snapshot).

You can build the user interface shown in Figure 10-2 by dragging out the components listed in Table 10-1. Drag each component from the Palette into the Viewer and name it as specified in the table. Note that you can leave the header label names (Label1 – Label4) as their defaults (you won't use them in the Blocks Editor anyway).

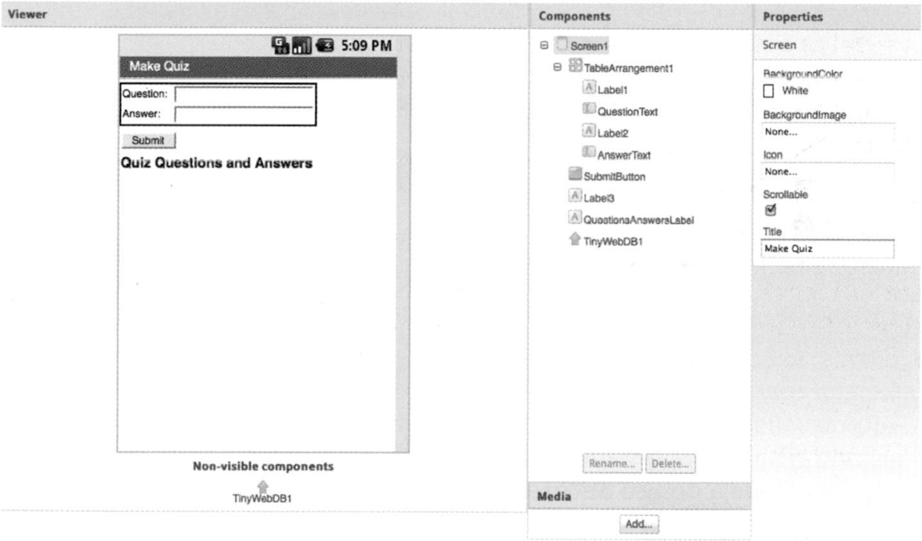

Figure 10-2. MakeQuiz in the Component Designer

Table 10-1. All the components for the MakeQuiz app

Component type	Palette group	What you'll name it	Purpose
TableArrangement	Screen Arrangement	TableArrangement1	Format the form, including the question and answer.
Label	Basic	Label1	The "Question:" prompt.
TextBox	Basic	QuestionText	The user enters questions here.
Label	Basic	Label2	The "Answer:" prompt.
TextBox	Basic	AnswerText	The user enters answers here.
Button	Basic	SubmitButton	The user clicks this to submit a QA pair.
Label	Basic	Label3	Display "Quiz Questions and Answers."
Label	Basic	QuestionsAnswersLabel	Display previously entered QA pairs.
TinyWebDB	Not ready for prime time	TinyWebDB1	Store data to and retrieve data from the database.

Set the properties of the components in the following way:

1. Set the Text of Label1 to "Question", the Text of Label2 to "Answer", and the text of Label3 to "Quiz Questions and Answers".

2. Set the FontSize of Label3 to 18 and check the FontBold box.

3. Set the Hint of QuestionText to "Enter a question" and the Hint of AnswerText to "Enter an answer".

4. Set the Text of SubmitButton to "Submit".

5. Set the Text of QuestionsAnswersLabel to "Questions and Answers".

6. Move the QuestionText, AnswerText, and their associated labels into TableArrangement1.

Adding Behaviors to the Components

As with the Presidents Quiz app, you'll first define some *global variables* for the QuestionList and AnswerList, but this time you won't provide fixed questions and answers. Table 10-2 lists the blocks you'll need to define the lists.

Table 10-2. Blocks for defining the question and answer lists

Block type	Drawer	Purpose
def variable ("Ques-tionList")	Definitions	Define the QuestionList variable (rename it).
def variable ("An-swerList")	Definitions	Define the AnswerList variable (rename it).
make a list	Lists	Set up the QuestionList for new items.
make a list	Lists	Set up the AnswerList for new items.

The blocks should look as shown in Figure 10-3.

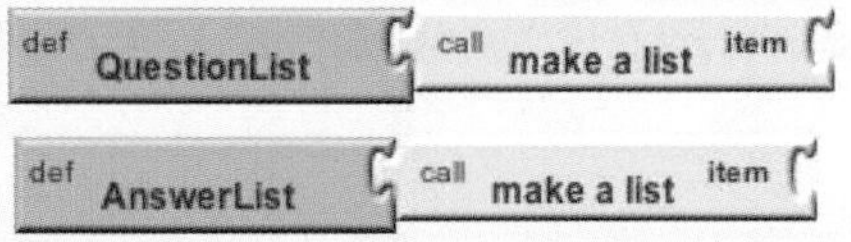

Figure 10-3. The lists for MakeQuiz

Note that, unlike the Presidents Quiz app, the lists are defined without items in the slots. This is because with MakeQuiz and TakeQuiz, all data will be created by the app user (it is *dynamic, user-generated* data).

Recording the User's Entries

The first behavior you'll build is for handling the user's input. Specifically, when the user enters a question and answer and clicks Submit, you'll use **add item to list** blocks to update the QuestionList and AnswerList. Table 10-3 lists the blocks you'll need.

Table 10-3. Blocks for recording the user's entries

Block type	Drawer	Purpose
SubmitButton.Click	SubmitButton	Triggered when the user clicks this button.
add items to list (2)	Lists	Add the data the user enters to the lists.
global QuestionList	My Definitions	Plug this into the "list" slot of the first **add items to list** block.
QuestionText.Text	QuestionText	User's entry; plug this into the "item" slot of the first **add items to list** block.
global AnswerList	My Definitions	Plug this into the "list" slot of the second **add items to list** block.
AnswerText.Text	AnswerText	User's entry; plug this into the "item" slot of the second **add items to list** block.
set QuestionsAnswers Label.Text to	QuestionsAnswersLabel	Display the updated lists.
make text	Text	Build a text object with both lists.
global QuestionList	My Definitions	The questions.
text (:)	Text	Place a colon between lists.
global AnswerList	My Definitions	The answers.

How the blocks work

The **add items to list** block *appends*, or adds, each item to the end of a list. As shown in Figure 10-4, the app takes the text the user has entered in the QuestionText and AnswerText text boxes and appends each to the corresponding list.

The **add items to list** blocks update the QuestionList and AnswerList variables, but these changes are not yet shown to the user. The third row of blocks displays these lists by concatenating them (**make text**) with a colon in between. By default, App Inventor displays lists with surrounding parentheses and spaces between items like this: (item1 item2 item3). Of course, this is not the ideal way to display the lists, but it will allow you to test the app's behavior for now. Later, you'll create a more sophisticated method of displaying the lists that shows each question-answer pair on a separate line.

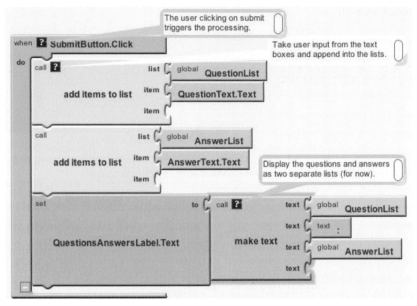

Figure 10-4. Adding the new entries to the lists

Test your app. *On the phone, enter a question and answer and click the* SubmitButton. *The app should display the single entry in the* QuestionList, *a colon, and then the single entry in the* AnswerList. *Add a second question and answer to make sure the lists are being created correctly.*

Blanking Out the Question and Answer

As you'll recall from the Presidents Quiz app, when you moved on to the next question in the list, you needed to blank out the answer results from the previous question. In this app, when a user submits a question-answer pair, you'll want to clear the QuestionText and AnswerText text boxes so they're ready for a new entry instead of showing the previous one. To do this, add the blocks listed in Table 10-4 at the bottom of the **SubmitButton.Click** event handler.

Table 10-4. Blocks for blanking out the question and answer text boxes

Block type	Drawer	Purpose
set QuestionText.Text to	QuestionText	Blank out the question.
set AnswerText.Text to	AnswerText	Blank out the answer.
text (two blank ones)	Text	Replace QuestionText and AnswerText.

How the blocks work

When the user submits a new question and answer, they are added to their respective lists and displayed. At that point, the text in the QuestionText and AnswerText is blanked out with empty text blocks, as shown in Figure 10-5. Note that you can create an empty text block by clicking on the text within the block and pressing Delete.

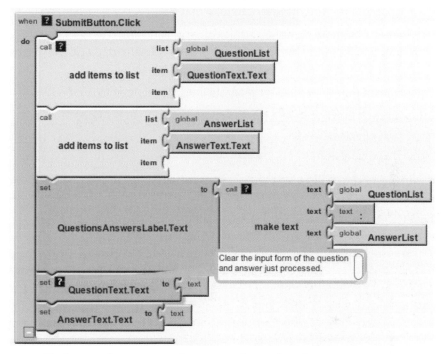

Figure 10-5. Blanking out the question and answer text boxes after submission

Test your app. *Add some questions and answers. Each time you submit a pair, the* QuestionText *and* AnswerText *should be cleared so that only the hint appears (e.g., "Enter a question").*

Displaying Question-Answer Pairs on Multiple Lines

In the app you've built so far, the question and answer lists are displayed separately and with the default list display format for App Inventor. So, if you were making a quiz on state capitals and had entered two pairs of questions and answers, it might appear like so:

    (What is the capital of California? What is the capital of New York? Sacramento Albany)

As you can imagine, if someone is creating a fairly long quiz, that could get pretty messy. A better display would show each question with its corresponding answer, with one question-answer pair per line like this:

```
What is the capital of California?: Sacramento
What is the capital of New York?: Albany
```

The technique for displaying a single list with each item on a separate line is described in Chapter 20—you may want to read that chapter before going on.

The task here is a bit more complicated, as you're dealing with two lists. Because of its complexity, you'll put the blocks for it in a procedure named displayQAs, and call that procedure from the **SubmitButton.Click** event handler.

To display question-answer pairs on separate lines, you'll need to do the following:

- Use a **foreach** block to iterate through each question in the QuestionList.

- Use a variable answerIndex so that you can grab each answer as you iterate through the questions.

- Use **make text** to build a text object with each question and answer pair, and a newline character (\n) separating each pair.

You'll need the blocks listed in Table 10-5.

Table 10-5. Blocks for displaying the question-answer pairs on separate lines

Block type	Drawer	Purpose
to procedure ("displayQAs")	Definition	This is a procedure block enclosing all other blocks.
def var ("answer")	Definition	Temporarily store each answer.
def var ("answerIndex")	Definition	Keep track of which answer (and question) the user is on.
text ("text")	Text	Initialize the variable **answer** to **text**.
number (1)	Math	Initialize the variable answerIndex to 1.
set QuestionsAnswers Label.Text to	My Definitions	Initialize the label to empty.
text ("")	Text	Plug this into **set QuestionsAnswers Label.Text to**.
set global answerIndex to	My Definitions	Reinitialize answerIndex each time **displayQAs** is called.
number (1)	Math	Reinitialize answerIndex to 1.
foreach	Control	Loop through the QuestionList.

Table 10-5. Blocks for displaying the question-answer pairs on separate lines (continued)

Block type	Drawer	Purpose
name question	(Appears as an argument of foreach, default name is var.)	Rename the foreach placeholder variable to question.
global QuestionList	My Definitions	Plug this into in the "list" slot of foreach.
set answer to	My Definitions	Set this variable each time in the foreach.
select list item	Lists	Select from the list AnswerList.
global AnswerList	My Definitions	Plug this into the "list" slot of select list item.
global answerIndex	My Definitions	Plug this into the "index" slot of select list item.
set global answerIndex to	My Definitions	Increment the index on each iteration through the loop.
+	Math	Increment answerIndex.
global answerIndex	My Definitions	Plug this into +.
number (1)	Math	Plug this into +.
set QuestionsAnswers Label.Text to	QuestionsAnswersLabel	Display the QAs.
make text	Text	Build each QA pair.
QuestionsAnswers Label.Text	QuestionsAnswersLabel	As we iterate, add each new pair to the previous ones.
text ("\n")	Text	Place a newline between pairs.
value question	My Definitions	This is the placeholder of the foreach; it's the current question we're processing.
text (":")	Text	Place a colon between the question and answer.
global answer	My Definitions	The current answer.

How the blocks work

The **displayQAs** block encapsulates all of the blocks for displaying the data, as shown in Figure 10-6. By using a procedure, we won't have to have the display blocks more than once in the app, and we can just call **displayQAs** when we need to display the lists.

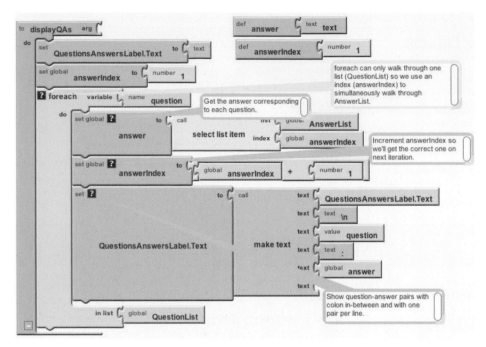

Figure 10-6. The displayQAs procedure

The **foreach** only allows you to iterate through one list. In this case, there are two
lists, and you need to select each answer as you proceed through the questions. To
accomplish this, we'll use an index variable, as we did with the currentQuestion
Index in the Presidents Quiz tutorial in Chapter 8. In this case, the index variable,
answerIndex, is used to track the position in the AnswerList as the **foreach** goes
through the QuestionList.

answerIndex is set to 1 before the **foreach** begins. Within the **foreach**, answerIndex
selects the current answer from the AnswerList, and then it is incremented. On each
iteration of the **foreach**, the current question and answer are concatenated to the
end of the QuestionsAnswersLabel.Text property, with a colon between them.

Calling the new procedure

You now have a procedure for displaying the question-answer pairs, but it won't
help unless you call it when you need it. Modify the **SubmitButton.Click** event
handler by calling **displayQAs** instead of displaying the lists with the simple **set
QuestionsAnswersLabel.Text to** block. The updated blocks should appear as
shown in Figure 10-7.

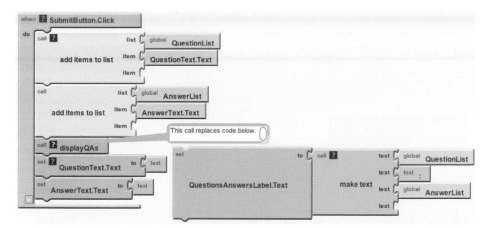

Figure 10-7. Calling the displayQAs procedure from SubmitButton.Click

 Test your app. *On the phone, add some more question-answer pairs. The display should now show each question with its corresponding answer, with each question-answer pair on a separate line.*

Storing the Questions and Answers in a Database

So far, you've created an app that puts the entered questions and answers into a list. But what happens if the quiz maker closes the app? If you've completed the "No Texting While Driving" app (Chapter 4) or the "Android, Where's My Car?" app (Chapter 7), you know that if you don't store the data in a database, it won't be there when the user closes and reopens the app. Storing the data *persistently* will allow the quiz maker to view or edit the latest update of the quiz each time the app is opened. Persistent storage is also necessary because the TakeQuiz app needs access to the data as well.

You're already familiar with using the TinyDB component to store and retrieve data in a database. But in this case, you'll use the TinyWebDB component instead. Whereas TinyDB stores information directly on a phone, TinyWebDB stores data in databases that live on the Web.

What about your app design would merit using an online database instead of one stored on a person's phone? The key issue here is that you're building two apps that both need access to the same data—if the quiz maker stores the questions and answers on her phone, the quiz takers won't have any way of getting to the data for their quiz! Because TinyWebDB stores data on the Web, the quiz taker can access the quiz questions and answers on a different device than the quiz maker's. (Online data storage is often referred to as *the cloud*.)

Here's the general scheme for making list data—like the questions and answers—persistent:

- Store a list to the database each time a new item is added to it.

- When the app launches, load the list from the database into a variable.

Start by storing the QuestionList and AnswerList in the database each time the user enters a new pair. You'll add the blocks shown in Table 10-6 to the **SubmitButton.Click** event handler.

Table 10-6. The blocks for storing the data to the database

Block type	Drawer	Purpose
TinyWebDB1 .StoreValue	TinyWebDB1	Store questions in the database.
text ("questions")	Text	Plug in "questions" as the tag of **StoreValue**.
global Question List	My Definitions	Plug this into the "value" slot of **StoreValue**.
TinyWebDB1 .StoreValue	TinyWebDB1	Store answers in the database.
text ("answers")	Text	Plug in "answers" as the tag of **StoreValue**.
global AnswerList	My Definitions	Plug this into the "value" slot of **StoreValue**.

How the blocks work

The **TinyWebDB1.StoreValue** blocks store data in a web database. **StoreValue** has two arguments: the tag that identifies the data and the value that is the actual data you want to store. As shown in Figure 10-8, the QuestionList is stored with a tag of "questions" while the AnswerList is stored with a tag of "answers."

However, for your app, you should use tags that are more distinctive than "questions" and "answers" (e.g., "DavesQuestions" and "DavesAnswers"). This is important because you're using the default web database for App Inventor, so your data (the list of questions and answers) can be overwritten by others, including other people following this tutorial.

Note that the default web service is shared among programmers and apps, so it is intended only for testing. When you're ready to deploy your app with real users, you'll want to set up your own private database service. Fortunately, doing so is straightforward and requires no programming (see Chapter 22).

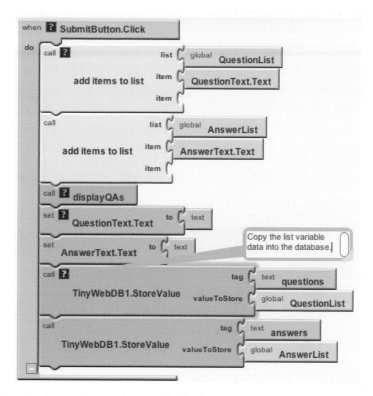

Figure 10-8. Storing the questions and answers in the database

Test your app. *Enter a question and answer and click Submit. To check if your data was stored in the database as desired, open a browser and enter the URL http://appinvtinywebdb.appspot.com in the address bar. The page that appears is the administrative interface to the database and includes a table of tag-value pairs. If you search for the tag you used in the **StoreValue** blocks (e.g., "questions"), you can check the value stored with it. You can also click on the "/getvalue" link and enter your tag to find its value. Does your data appear?*

Loading Data from the Database

One reason we need to store the questions and answers in a database is so the person creating the quiz can close the app and relaunch it at a later time without losing the questions and answers previously entered. (We also do it so the quiz taker can access the questions, but we'll cover that later.) Let's program the blocks for loading the lists back into the app from the web database each time the app is restarted.

As we've covered in earlier chapters, to specify what should happen when an app launches, you program the **Screen.Initialize** event handler. In this case, the app needs to request two lists from the TinyWebDB web database—the questions and the answers—so the **Screen1.Initialize** will make two calls to **TinyWebDB.GetValue**.

You'll need the blocks listed in Table 10-7.

Table 10-7. Screen.Initialize blocks for retrieving database data

Block type	Drawer	Purpose
Screen1.Initialize	Screen1	Triggered when the app begins.
TinyWebDB.Get Value (2)	TinyWebDB	Request the stored QuestionList and AnswerList.
text ("questions")	Text	Instead of "questions," use the tag you used to store the questions.
text ("answers")	Text	Instead of "answers," use the tag you used to store the questions.

How the blocks work

The **TinyWebDB.GetValue** blocks, shown in Figure 10-9, work differently than **TinyDB.GetValue**, which returns a value immediately. **TinyWebDB.GetValue** only *requests* the data from the web database; it doesn't immediately receive a value. Instead, when the data arrives from the web database, a **TinyWebDB.GotValue** event is triggered. You must also program another event handler to process the data that is returned.

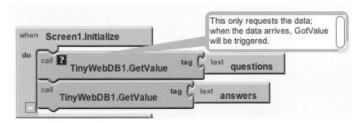

Figure 10-9. Requesting the lists from the database when the app opens

When the **TinyWebDB.GotValue** event occurs, the data requested is contained in an argument named valueFromWebDB. The tag you requested is contained in the argument tagFromWebDB.

In this app, since two different requests are made for the questions and answers, **GotValue** will be triggered twice. To avoid putting questions in your AnswerList or vice versa, your app needs to check the tag to see which request has arrived, and then put the value returned from the database into the corresponding list (QuestionList or AnswerList). Now you're probably realizing how useful those tags really are!

You'll need the blocks listed in Table 10-8 for the **GotValue** event handler.

Table 10-8. Blocks for TinyWebDB.GotValue

Block type	Drawer	Purpose
TinyWebDB.GotValue	TinyWebDB	Triggered when the data arrives.
if	Control	Check if the database has any data.
is a list?	List	If data is a list, it's non-empty.
value valueFrom WebDB	My Definitions	The argument holding the data returned from the database.
ifelse	Control	Ask which GetValue request arrived.
=	Math	Compare tagFromWebDB to "questions."
text ("questions")	Text	This is the tag that was used to store QuestionList.
value tagFromWebDB	My Definitions	An argument of **GotValue**; specifies which request.
set global Question List to	My Definitions	If tagFromWebDB is "questions," this list will be set.
set global Answer List to	My Definitions	If tagFromWebDB is not "questions," this list will be set.
value valueFrom WebDB (2)	My Definitions	Hold the value returned from the database.
if	Control	Check if both the lists are loaded before displaying.
=	Math	Compare the lengths of the lists.
length of list (2)	Lists	Check if the lengths of the lists are the same.
global QuestionList	My Definitions	Plug this into one of the **length of list** blocks.
global AnswerList	My Definitions	Plug this into the other **length of list** block.
call displayQAs	My Definitions	Display the newly loaded questions and answers.

How the blocks work

The app calls **TinyWebDB1.GetValue** twice: once to request the stored QuestionList and once to request the stored AnswerList. When the data arrives from the web database from either request, the **TinyWebDB1.GotValue** event is triggered, as shown in Figure 10-10.

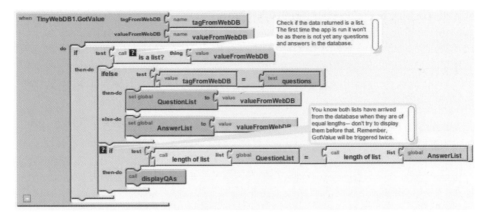

Figure 10-10. GotValue is triggered when the data arrives from the Web

The valueFromWebDB argument of **GotValue** holds the data returned from the database request. We need the outer **if** block in the event handler because the database will return an empty text ("") in valueFromWebDB if it's the first time the app has been used and there aren't yet questions and answers. By asking if the valueFromWebDB **is a list?**, you're making sure there is some data actually returned. If there isn't any data, you'll bypass the blocks for processing it.

If data is returned (**is a list?** is true), the blocks go on to check which request has arrived. The tag identifying the data is in tagFromWebDB: it will be either "questions" or "answers." If the tag is "questions," the valueFromWebDB is put into the variable QuestionList. Otherwise (else), it is placed in the AnswerList. (If you used tags other than "questions" and "answers," check for those instead.)

We only want to display the lists after both have arrived (**GotValue** has been triggered twice). Can you think of how you'd know for sure that you have both lists loaded in from the database? These blocks use an **if** test to check if the lengths of the lists are the same, as this can only be true if both have been returned. If they are, the handy **displayQAs** procedure you wrote earlier is called to display the loaded data.

Test your app. *Restart the app by clicking "Connect to Device…" in the Blocks Editor. When the app initializes, it should display the previously entered questions and answers. If you close the app and restart, the previous quiz should still appear.*

The Complete App: MakeQuiz

Figure 10-11 illustrates the final blocks for the MakeQuiz app.

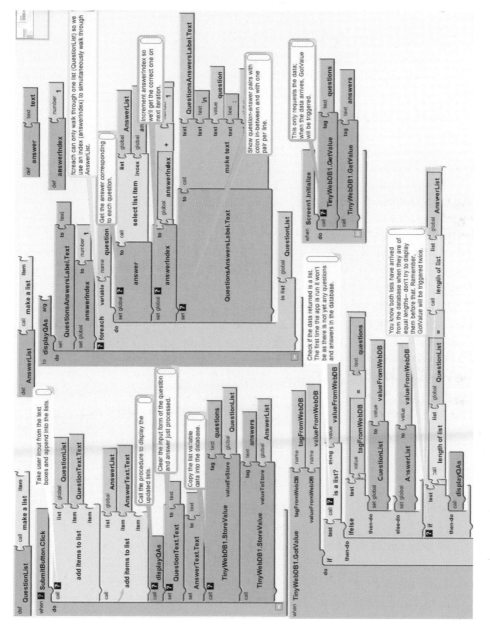

Figure 10-11. The blocks for MakeQuiz

TakeQuiz: An App for Taking the Quiz in the Database

You now have a MakeQuiz app that will store a quiz in a web database. Building TakeQuiz, the app that dynamically loads the quiz, is simpler. It can be built with a few modifications to the Presidents Quiz you completed in Chapter 8 (if you have not completed that tutorial, do so now before continuing).

Begin by opening your Presidents Quiz app, choosing Save As, and naming the new project "TakeQuiz". This will leave your Presidents Quiz app unmodified but allow you to use its blocks as the basis for TakeQuiz.

Then make the following changes in the Designer:

1. This version of MakeQuiz/TakeQuiz does not display images with each question, so first remove the references to images from the TakeQuiz app. In the Component Designer, choose each image from the Media palette and delete it. Then delete the `Image1` component, which will remove all references to it from the Blocks Editor.

2. Since TakeQuiz will work with database data, drag a `TinyWebDB` component into the app.

3. Because you don't want the user to answer or click the `NextButton` until the questions are loaded, uncheck the `Enabled` property of the `AnswerButton` and `NextButton`.

TakeQuiz: Modifying the Blocks to Load the Quiz from the Database

Now modify the blocks so that the quiz given to the user is loaded from the database. First, since there are no fixed questions and answers, remove all the actual question and answer text blocks from the **make a list** blocks within the `QuestionList` and `AnswerList`. The resulting blocks should appear as shown in Figure 10-12.

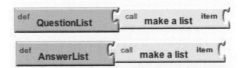

Figure 10-12. The question and answer lists now start empty

You can also completely delete the `PictureList`; this app won't deal with images. Now modify your **Screen1.Initialize** so that it calls **TinyWebDB.GetValue** twice to load the lists, just as you did in MakeQuiz. The blocks should look as they do in Figure 10-13.

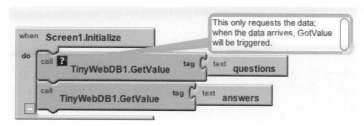

Figure 10-13. Requesting the questions and answers from the web database

Finally, drag out a **TinyWebDB.GotValue** event handler. This event handler should look similar to the one used in MakeQuiz, but here you want to show only the first question and none of the answers. Try making these changes yourself first, and then take a look at the blocks in Figure 10-14 to see if they match your solution.

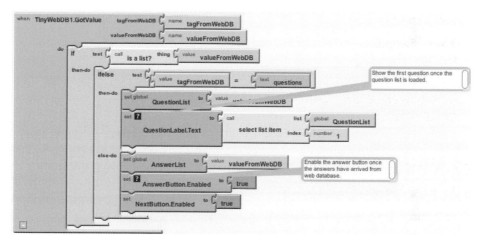

Figure 10-14. GotValue handles the data that arrives from the Web

How the Blocks Work

When the app begins, **Screen1.Initialize** is triggered and the app requests the questions and answers from the web database. When each request arrives, the **TinyWebDB .GotValue** event handler is triggered. The app first checks if there is indeed data in valueFromWebDB using **is a list?**. If it finds data, the app asks which request has come in, using tagFromWebDB, and places the valueFromWebDB into the appropriate list. If the QuestionList is being loaded, the first question is selected from QuestionList and displayed. If the AnswerList is being loaded, the AnswerButton and NextButton are enabled so the user can begin taking the test.

Test your app. *Restart the app by clicking "Connect to Device..." in the Blocks Editor. Does the first question from your MakeQuiz quiz appear? Can you take a quiz just as you did with the Presidents Quiz (except for the pictures)?*

The Complete App: TakeQuiz

Figure 10-15 illustrates the final blocks for TakeQuiz.

Variations

Once you get MakeQuiz and TakeQuiz working, you might want to explore some variations. For example:

- Allow the quiz maker to specify an image for each question. Of course, you (the app developer) can't preload these images, and there is currently no way for an app user to do it. So the images will need to be URLs from the Web, and the quiz maker will need to enter these URLs as a third item in the MakeQuiz form. Note that you can set the Picture property of an Image component to a URL.

- Allow the quiz maker to delete items from the questions and answers. You can let the user choose a question using the ListPicker component, and you can remove an item with the **remove list item** block (remember to remove from both lists and update the database). For help with ListPicker and list deletion, see Chapter 19.

- Let the quiz maker name the quiz. You'll need to store the quiz name under a different tag in the database, and you'll need to load the name along with the quiz in TakeQuiz. Once you've loaded the name, use it to set the Screen.Title property so that it appears when the user takes a quiz.

- Allow multiple, named quizzes to be created. You'll need a list of quizzes, and you can use each quiz name as (part of) the tag for storing its questions and answers.

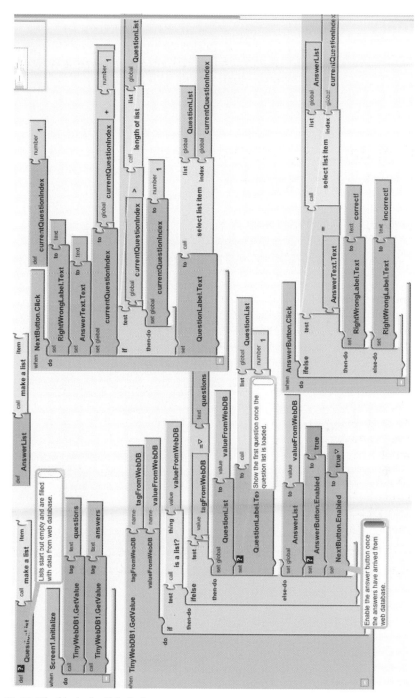

Figure 10-15. The blocks for TakeQuiz

Summary

Here are some of the concepts we've covered in this chapter:

- Dynamic data is information input by the app's user or loaded in from a database. A program that works with dynamic data is more abstract. For more information, see Chapter 19.

- You can store data persistently in a web database with the TinyWebDB component.

- You retrieve data from a TinyWebDB database by requesting it with **TinyWebDB .GetValue**. When the web database returns the data, the **TinyWebDB.GotValue** event is triggered. In the **TinyWebDB.GotValue** event handler, you can put the data in a list or process it in some way.

- TinyWebDB data can be shared among multiple phones and apps. Fore more information on (web) databases, see Chapter 22.

CHAPTER 11

Broadcast Hub

FrontlineSMS (http://www.frontlinesms.com) is a software tool used in developing countries to monitor elections, broadcast weather changes, and connect people who don't have access to the Web but do have phones and mobile connectivity. It is the brainchild of Ken Banks, who has probably done more to help people using mobile technology than any other human alive.

FrontlineSMS runs on a computer with a phone plugged into it. The computer and plugged-in phone serve as a hub for SMS (short message service) text communication within a group. People who don't have Internet access can send in a special code to join the group, after which they receive broadcast messages from the hub. For places with no Internet access, the broadcast hub can serve as a vital connection to the outside world.

With App Inventor, you can create your own SMS-processing app. The cool thing is that the people who use your app don't need to have an Android phone. Your app will run on an Android device, but your app users can interface with it through SMS using any phone, smart or not so smart. Your app will still have a graphical user interface (GUI) as well, but that GUI will be reserved for the administrator who monitors the activity via the Android app you're about to build.

In this chapter, you'll create a hub that works similarly to FrontlineSMS but runs on an Android phone. Having the hub itself on a mobile device means the administrator can be on the move, something that is especially important in controversial situations like election monitoring and healthcare negotiations.

Your broadcast hub will be for the fictitious FlashMob Dance Team (FMDT), a group that uses the hub to organize flash mob dances anywhere, anytime. People will register with the group by texting "joinFMDT" to the hub, and anyone who is registered can broadcast messages to everyone else in the group.

Your app will process received text messages in the following manner:

1. If the text message is sent from someone not yet in the broadcast list, the app responds with a text that invites him to join the broadcast list and lets him know the code.

2. If the text message "joinFMDT" is received, the app adds the sender to the broadcast list.

3. If the text message is sent from a number already in the broadcast list, the message is broadcast to all numbers in the list.

You'll build this app one piece of functionality at a time, starting with the first autoresponse message that invites people to join. By the time you complete this app, you'll have a pretty good idea of how to write apps utilizing SMS text as the user interface.

What You'll Learn

The tutorial covers the following App Inventor concepts, some of which you're likely familiar with by now:

- The Texting component for sending texts and processing received texts.
- List variables—in this case, to keep track of the list of phone numbers.
- The **foreach** block to allow an app to repeat operations on a list of data. In this case, you'll use **foreach** to broadcast messages to the list of phone numbers.
- The TinyDB component to store data persistently. This means that if you close the app and then relaunch it, the list of phone numbers will still be there.

Getting Started

You'll need a phone that can accept and send SMS texts to test this app, as the emulator that comes with App Inventor isn't set up for this. You'll also need to recruit some friends to send you texts in order to fully test the app.

Connect to the App Inventor website and start a new project. Name it "BroadcastHub" and also set the screen's title to "Broadcast Hub". Open the Blocks Editor and connect to the phone.

Designing the Components

Broadcast Hub facilitates communication between mobile phones. Those phones do not need to have the app installed, or even be smartphones. So, in this case, you're not building an interface for your app's users, but instead for the group administrator.

The user interface for the administrator is simple: it displays the current *broadcast list*—that is, the list of phone numbers that have registered for the service—and all of the texts it receives and broadcasts.

To build the interface, add the components listed in Table 11-1.

Table 11-1. User interface components for Broadcast Hub

Component type	Palette group	What you'll name it	Purpose
Label	Basic	Label1	This is the header above the list of phone numbers.
Label	Basic	BroadcastListLabel	Display the phone numbers that are registered.
Label	Basic	Label2	This is the header above the log information.
Label	Basic	LogLabel	Display a log of the texts received and broadcast.
Texting	Social	Texting1	Process the texts.
TinyDB	Basic	TinyDB1	Store the list of registered phone numbers.

As you add the components, set the following properties:

1. Set the Width of each label to "Fill parent" so that it spans the phone horizontally.

2. Set the FontSize of the header labels (Label1 and Label2) to 18 and check their FontBold boxes.

3. Set the Height of BroadcastListLabel and LogLabel to 200 pixels. They'll show multiple lines.

4. Set the Text property of BroadcastListLabel to "Broadcast List...".

5. Set the Text property of LogLabel to blank.

Figure 11-1 shows the app layout in the Component Designer.

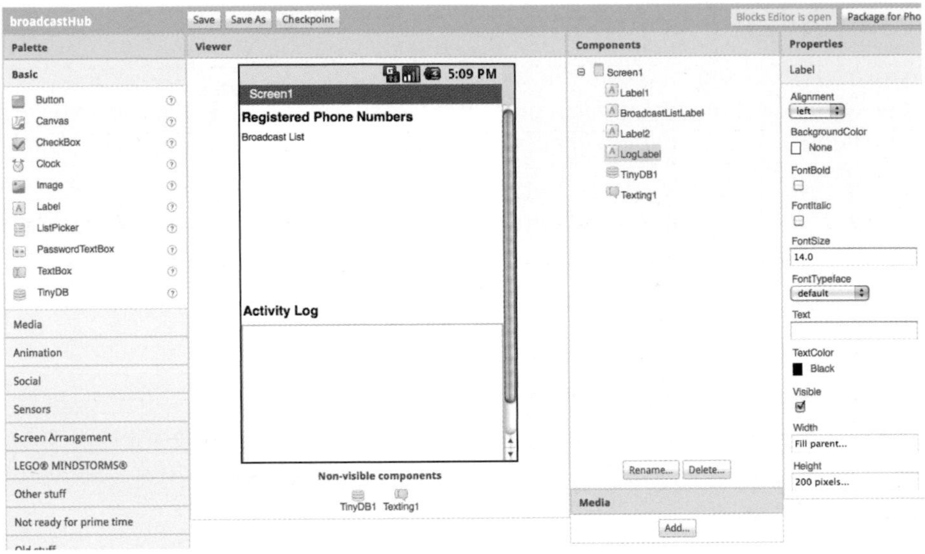

Figure 11-1. Broadcast Hub in the Component Designer

Adding Behaviors to the Components

The activity for Broadcast Hub is not triggered by the user entering information or clicking a button, but rather by texts coming in from other phones. To process these texts and store the phone numbers that sent them in a list, you'll need the following behaviors:

- When the text message is sent from someone not already in the broadcast list, the app responds with a text that invites the sender to join.

- When the text message "joinFMDT" is received, register the sender as part of the broadcast list.

- When the text message is sent from a number already in the broadcast list, the message is broadcast to all numbers in the list.

Let's start by creating the first behavior: when you receive a text, send a message back to the sender inviting her to register by texting "joinFMDT" back to you. You'll need the blocks listed in Table 11-2.

Table 11-2. Blocks for adding the functionality to invite people to the group via text

Block type	Drawer	Purpose
Texting1.Message Received	Texting1	Triggered when the phone receives a text.
set Texting1.Phone Number to	Texting1	Set the number for the return text.
value number	My Definitions	The argument of MessageReceived. This is the phone number of the sender.
set Texting1.Message	Texting1	Set the invite message to send.
text ("To join this broadcast list, text 'joinFMDT' to this number")	Text	The invite message.
Texting1.SendMessage	Texting1	Send it!

How the Blocks Work

Based on the work you did in the No Texting While Driving app in Chapter 4, these blocks should look familiar. **Texting1.MessageReceived** is triggered when the phone receives any text message. As shown in Figure 11-2, the blocks within the event handler set the PhoneNumber and Message of the Texting1 component and then send the message.

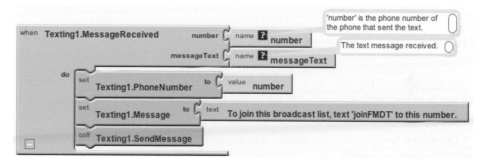

Figure 11-2. Sending the invite message back after receiving a text

Test your app. You'll need a second phone to test this behavior; you don't want to text yourself, as it could loop forever! If you don't have another phone, you can register with Google Voice or a similar service and send SMS texts from that service to your phone. From the second phone, send the text "hello" to the phone running the app. The second phone should then receive a text that invites it to join the group.

Adding Someone to the Broadcast List

Now let's create the blocks for the second behavior: when the text message "joinFMDT" is received, add the sender to the broadcast list. First, you'll need to define a list variable, BroadcastList, to store the phone numbers that register. From Definitions, drag out a **def var** block and name it "BroadcastList". Initialize it to an empty list with a **make a list** block from the Lists drawer, as shown in Figure 11-3 (we'll add the functionality to build this list shortly).

Figure 11-3. The BroadcastList variable for storing the list of registered numbers

Next, modify the **Texting1.MessageReceived** event handler so that it adds the sender's phone number to the BroadcastList if the message received is "joinFMDT." You'll need an **ifelse** block—which you used in MakeQuiz in Chapter 10—within your event handler, and an **add item to list** block to add the new number to the list. The full set of blocks you'll need is listed in Table 11-3. After you add the number to the list, display the new list in the BroadcastListLabel.

Table 11-3. Blocks for checking a text message and adding the sender to the broadcast list

Block type	Drawer	Purpose
ifelse	Control	Depending on the message received, do different things.
=	Math	Determine whether messageText is equal to "joinFMDT."
value messageText	My Definitions	Plug this into the = block.
text ("joinFMDT")	Text	Plug this into the = block.
add items to list	Lists	Add the sender's number to BroadcastList.
global BroadcastList	My Definitions	The list.
value number	My Definitions	Plug this in as an item of **add items to list**.
set BroadcastList Label.Text to	BroadcastListLabel	Display the new list.
global BroadcastList	My Definitions	Plug this in to set the **BroadcastListLabel.Text to** block.
set Texting1.Message to	Texting1	Prepare Texting1 to send a message back to the sender.
text ("Congrats, you…")	Text	Congratulate the sender for joining the group.

How the blocks work

The first row of blocks shown in Figure 11-4 sets Texting1.PhoneNumber to the phone number of the message that was just received; we know we're going to respond to the sender, so this sets that up. The app then asks if the messageText was the special code, "joinFMDT." If so, the sender's phone number is added to the

BroadcastList, and a congratulations message is sent. If the messageText is some thing other than "joinFMDT," the reply message repeats the invitation message. After the **ifelse** block, the reply message is sent (bottom row of the blocks).

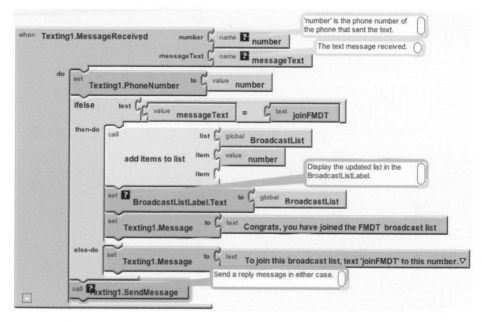

Figure 11-4. If the incoming message is "joinFMDT", add the sender to BroadcastList

Test your app. *From a second phone, send the text message "joinFMDT" to the phone running the app. You should see the phone number listed in the user interface under "Registered Phone Numbers." The second phone should also receive the Congrats message. Try sending a message other than "joinFMDT" as well to check if the invite message is still sent correctly.*

Broadcasting Messages

Next, you'll add the behavior so that the app broadcasts received messages to the numbers in BroadcastList, but only if the message arrives from a number already stored in that list. This additional complexity will require more control blocks, including another **ifelse** and a **foreach**. You'll need an additional **ifelse** block to check if the number is in the list, and a **foreach** block to broadcast the message to each number in the list. You'll also need to move the **ifelse** blocks from the previous behavior and slot them into the "else" part of the new **ifelse**. All the additional blocks you'll need are listed in Table 11-4.

Table 11-4. Blocks for checking if the sender is in the group already

Block type	Drawer	Purpose
ifelse	Control	Depending on whether the sender is already in the list, do different things.
is in list?	Lists	Check to see if something is in a list.
global BroadcastList	My Definitions	Plug this into the "list" slot of **is in list?**.
value number	My Definitions	Plug this into the "thing" slot of **is in list?**.
foreach	Control	Repeatedly send out a message to all members in the list.
global BroadcastList	My Definitions	Plug this into the "list" slot of **foreach**.
set Texting1.Message to	Texting1	Set the message.
value messageText	My Definitions	The message that was received and will be broadcast.
set Texting1.Phone-Number to	Texting1	Set the phone number.
value var	My Definitions	Hold the current item of the BroadcastList; it's a (phone) number.

How the blocks work

The app has become complex enough that it requires a *nested* **ifelse** block, as shown in Figure 11-5. A nested **ifelse** block is one slotted within the "if" or "else" part of another, outer **ifelse**. In this case, the outer **ifelse** branch checks whether the phone number of the received message is already in the list. If it is, the message is relayed to everyone in the list. If the number is not in the list, then the *nested* test is performed: the blocks check if the messageText is equal to "joinFMDT" and branches one of two ways based on the answer.

In general, **if** and **ifelse** blocks can be nested to arbitrary levels, giving you the power to program increasingly complex behaviors (see Chapter 18 for more information on conditional blocks).

The message is broadcast using a **foreach** (within the outer then clause). The **foreach** loops through and sends the message to each item in the BroadcastList. As the **foreach** repeats, each succeeding phone number from the BroadcastList is stored in var (var is a variable placeholder for the current item being processed in the **foreach**). The blocks within the **foreach** set Texting.PhoneNumber to the current item var and then send the message. For more information on how **foreach** works, see Chapter 20.

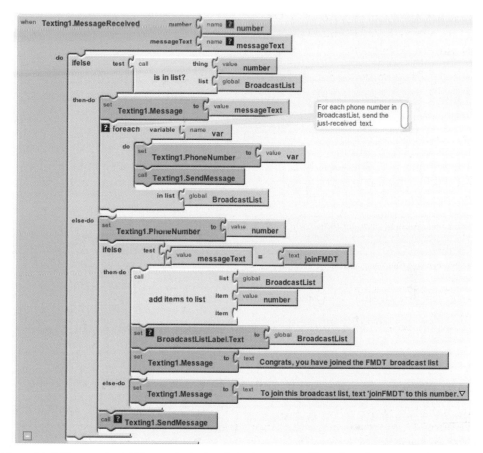

Figure 11-5. Now we check if the sender is already in the group and broadcast the message if so

 Test your app. First, have two different phones register by texting *"joinFMDT"* to the phone running the app. Then, text another message from one of the phones. Both phones should receive the text (including the one that sent it).

Cleaning Up Your List Display

The app can now broadcast messages, but the user interface for the app administrator needs some work. First, the list of phone numbers is displayed in an inelegant way. Specifically, when you place a list variable into a label, it displays the list with spaces between the items, fitting as much as possible on each line. So the `BroadcastListLabel` might show the `BroadcastList` like this:

    (+1415111-1111   +1415222-2222   +1415333-3333 +1415444-4444)

To improve this formatting, create a procedure displayBroadcastList using the blocks listed in Table 11-5. This procedure displays the list with each phone number on a separate line. Be sure to call the procedure from below the **add items to list** block so that the updated list is displayed.

Table 11-5. Blocks to clean up the display of phone numbers in your list

Block type	Drawer	Purpose
to procedure ("displayBroadcast List")	Definitions	Create the procedure (do not choose **procedure WithResult**).
set BroadcastListLabel .Text to	BroadcastListLabel	Display the list here.
text ("")	Text	Click **text** and then click Delete to create an empty text object.
foreach	Control	Iterate through the numbers.
name pnumber	in the **foreach**	Name the **foreach** variable "pnumber". This is the current item as iteration proceeds.
global BroadcastList	My Definitions	Plug this into the "in list" slot of **foreach**.
set BroadcastListLabel .Text to	BroadcastListLabel	Modify this with each of the numbers.
make text	Text	Build a text object from multiple parts.
BroadcastListLabel.Text	BroadcastListLabel	Add this to the label on each iteration of **foreach**.
text ("\n")	Text	Add a newline character so that the next number is on the next line.
value pnumber	My Definitions	The current number from the list.

How the blocks work

The **foreach** in displayBroadcastList successively adds a phone number to the end of the label, as shown in Figure 11-6, placing a newline character (\n) between each item to place each number on a new line.

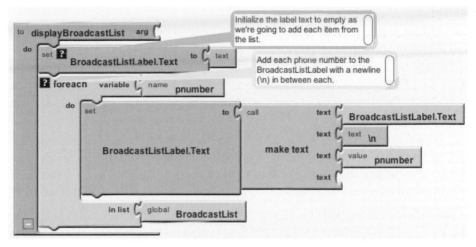

Figure 11-6. Displaying the phone numbers with a newline between each

Of course, this displayBroadcastList procedure will not do anything unless you call it. Place a call to it in the **Texting1.MessageReceived** event handler, right below the call to **add item to list**. The call should replace the blocks that simply set the BroadcastListLabel.Text to BroadcastList. The **call displayBroadcastList** block can be found in My Definitions.

Figure 11-7 shows how the relevant blocks within the **Texting1.MessageReceived** event handler should look.

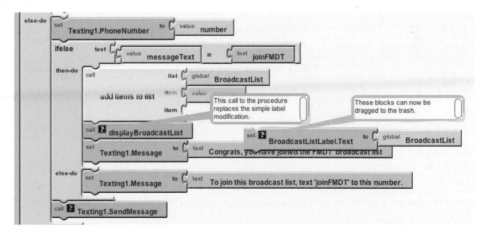

Figure 11-7. Calling the displayBroadcastList procedure

For more information on using **foreach** to display a list, see Chapter 20. For more information about creating and calling procedures, see Chapter 21.

Test your app. *Restart the app to clear the list and then have at least two different phones register (again). Do the phone numbers appear on separate lines?*

Logging the Broadcasted Texts

When a text is received and broadcast to the other phones, the app should log that occurrence so the administrator can monitor the activity. In the Component Designer, you added the label LogLabel to the user interface for this purpose. Now, you'll code some blocks that change LogLabel each time a new text arrives.

You need to build a text that says something like "message from +1415111–2222 was broadcast." The number +1415111–2222 is not fixed data—instead, it is the value of the argument number that comes with the **MessageReceived** event. So, to build the text, you'll concatenate the first part, "message from", with a **value number** block and finally with the last part of the message, the text "broadcast."

As you've done in previous chapters, use **make text** to concatenate the parts using the blocks listed in Table 11-6.

Table 11-6. Blocks to build your log of broadcasted messages

Block type	Drawer	Purpose
set LogLabel .Text to	LogLabel	Display the log here.
make text	Text	Build a text object out of multiple parts.
text ("message from")	Text	This is the report message.
value number	My Definitions	The sender's phone number.
text ("broadcast\n")	Text	Add the last part of "message from 111–2222 broadcast" and include newline.
LogLabel.Text	LogLabel	Add a new log to the previous ones.

How the blocks work

After broadcasting the received message to all of the numbers in BroadcastList, the app now modifies the LogLabel to add a report of the just-broadcasted text, as shown in Figure 11-8. Note that now we add the message to the beginning of the list instead of the end, so the more recent message sent to the group shows up at the top.

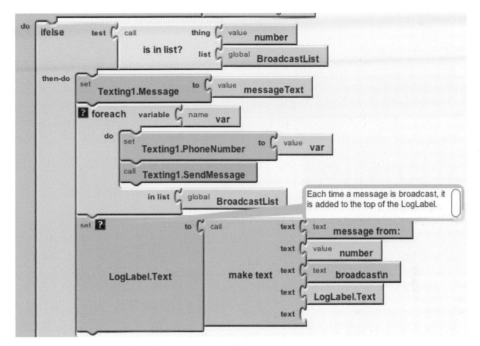

Figure 11-8. Adding a new broadcast message to the log

The **make text** block creates new entries of the form:

```
message from: 111-2222 broadcast
```

Each time a text is broadcast, the log entry is *prepended to* (added to the front of) the LogLabel.Text so that the most recent entries will appear on top. The way you organize the **make text** block determines the ordering of the entries. In this case, the new message is added with the top three slots of **make text**, and LogLabel.Text—which holds the existing entries—is plugged into the last slot.

The "\n" in the text "broadcast\n" is the newline character that displays each log entry on a separate line:

```
message from: 1112222 broadcast
message from: 555-6666 broadcast
```

For more information about using **foreach** to display a list, see Chapter 20.

Storing the BroadcastList in a Database

The app works great so far, but if you've completed some of the earlier tutorials, you've probably guessed that there's a problem: if the administrator closes the app and relaunches it, the broadcast list will be lost and everyone will have to reregister. To fix this, you'll use the TinyDB component to store and retrieve the BroadcastList to and from a database.

You'll use a similar scheme to the one we used in the MakeQuiz app (Chapter 10):

- Store the list to the database each time a new item is added.

- When the app launches, load the list from the database into a variable.

Start by coding the blocks listed in Table 11-7 to store the list in the database. With the TinyDB component, a tag is used to identify the data and distinguish it from other data stored in the database. In this case, you can tag the data as "broadcastList." You'll add the blocks in the **Texting1.MessageReceived** event, under the **add items to list** block.

Table 11-7. Blocks to store the list with TinyDB

Block type	Drawer	Purpose
TinyDB1.Store Value	TinyDB1	Store the data in the database.
text ("broadcastList")	Text	Plug this into the "tag" slot of **Store Value**.
global Broadcast List	My Definitions	Plug this into the "value" slot of **Store Value**.

How the blocks work

When a "joinFMDT" text comes in and the new member's phone number is added to the list, **TinyDB1.StoreValue** is called to store the BroadcastList to the database. The tag (a text object named "broadcastList") is used so that you can later retrieve the data. As shown in Figure 11-9, the value that gets called by **StoreValue** is the variable BroadcastList.

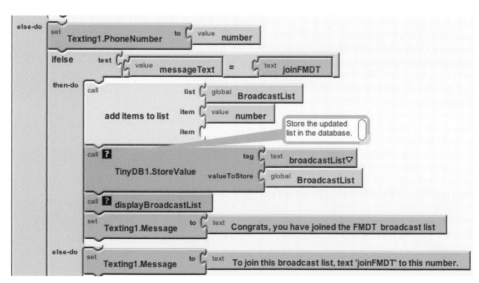

Figure 11-9. Calling TinyDB to store the BroadcastList

Loading the BroadcastList from a Database

Now add the blocks listed in Table 11-8 for loading the list back in each time the app launches. When the app begins, the **Screen1.Initialize** event is triggered, so your blocks will go in that event handler. You'll call **TinyDB.GetValue**, using the same tag you used to store the list ("broadcastList"). At this point, as we've done in previous chapters that work with databases, we have to check if there is actually any data being returned. In this case, we'll check if the returned value is a list, because it won't be if there isn't any data in the list yet.

How the blocks work

When the app begins, the **Screen1.Initialize** event is triggered. The blocks shown in Figure 11-10 first request the data from the database with **TinyDB1.GetValue**. The returned data is placed in the variable valueFromDB, a variable defined to temporarily hold it.

Table 11-8. Blocks to load the broadcast list back into the app when it launches

Block type	Drawer	Purpose
def variable ("value-FromDB")	Definition	A temporary variable for holding database data and checking it.
text ("text")	Text	An initial value for valueFromDB.
Screen1.Initialize	Screen1	Triggered when the app launches.
set global valueFrom DB to	My Definitions	Put the returned value here temporarily.
TinyDB1.GetValue	TinyDB1	Request the data from the database.
text ("broadcastList")	Text	Plug this into the "tag" slot of **GetValue**.
if	Control	Check if the database had the data.
is a list?	List	If the data returned is a list, we know it wasn't empty.
global valueFromDB	My Definitions	Plug this into is a list?.
set global Broadcast List to	My Definitions	Set this to the value returned from the database.
call displayBroadcast List	My Definitions	After loading data, display it.

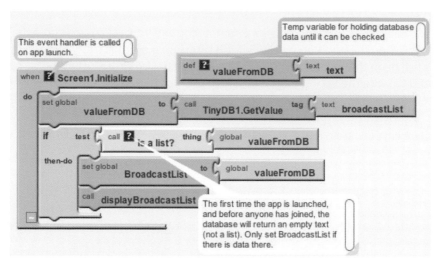

Figure 11-10. Loading the BroadcastList from the database

We need the **if** block in the event handler because the database will return an empty text ("") if it's the first time the app has been used and there isn't yet a broadcast list. By asking if the valueFromDB is a list, you're making sure there is some data actually returned. If there isn't, you'll bypass the blocks that transfer the returned data (valueFromDB) into the variable BroadcastList and the blocks to display that data.

Test your app. *You can't use live testing for apps that modify the database because each time you click "Connect to Device," the database starts out empty. So, to test the database storage and the* **Screen .Initialize** *event handler, you'll need to package and download the app to a phone (you can download an app by choosing "Package for Phone"→"Download to Connected Phone" in the Component Designer). Once you've downloaded your app, use your second and third test phones to send a text to join the group and then close the app on your original phone. If the numbers are still listed when you relaunch the app, then the database part is working.*

The Complete App: Broadcast Hub

Figure 11-11 illustrates the blocks in the completed Broadcast Hub app.

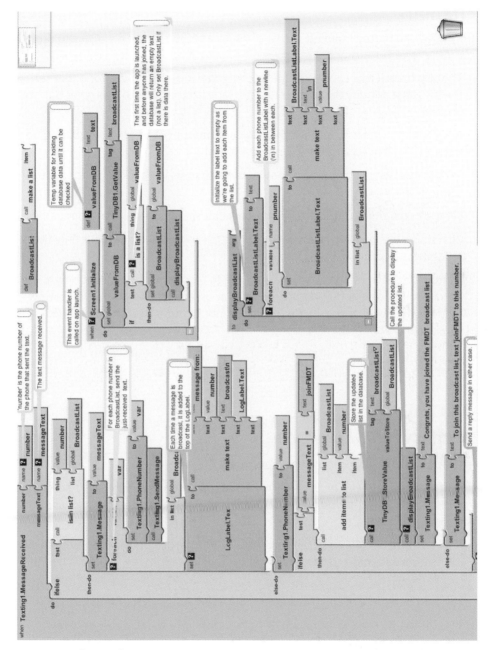

Figure 11-11. The complete app

Variations

After you've celebrated building such a complex app, you might want to explore some variations. For example:

- The app broadcasts each message to everyone, including the phone that sent the message. Modify this so that the message is broadcast to everyone but the sender.

- Allow client phones to remove themselves from the list by texting "quitabc" to the app. You'll need a **remove from list** block.

- Let the hub administrator add and remove numbers from the broadcast list through the user interface.

- Let the hub administrator specify numbers that should not be allowed into the list.

- Customize the app so that anyone can join to receive messages, but only the administrator can broadcast messages.

- Customize the app so that anyone can join to receive messages, but only a fixed list of phone numbers can broadcast messages to the group (this is how the Helsinki event app worked; see *http://appinventorblog.com/2010/08/25/ success-story-from-helsinki/*).

- The app stores the broadcast list persistently, but not the log. Each time you close the app and reopen it, the log starts over. Change this so that the log is persistent.

Summary

Here are some of the concepts we've covered in this tutorial:

- Apps can react to events that are not initiated by the app user, like a text being received. That means you can build apps in which your users are on a different phone.

- Nested **ifelse** and **foreach** blocks can be used to code complex behaviors. For more information on conditionals and **foreach** iteration, see Chapters 18 and 20, respectively.

- The **make text** block can be used to build a text object out of multiple parts.

- TinyDB can be used to store and retrieve data from a database. A general scheme is to call **StoreValue** to update the database whenever the data changes and call **GetValue** to retrieve the database data when the app begins.

CHAPTER 12

NXT Remote Control

In this chapter, you'll create an app that turns your Android phone into a remote control for a LEGO MINDSTORMS NXT robot. The app will have buttons for driving the robot forward and backward, turning left and right, and stopping. You'll program it so the robot automatically stops if it detects an obstacle. The app will use the Bluetooth capabilities of the phone to communicate with the robot.

LEGO MINDSTORMS robots are fun to play with, but they are also educational. After-school programs use robots to teach elementary- and middle-school children problem-solving skills and introduce them to engineering and computer programming. NXT robots are also used by kids aged 9–14 in FIRST Lego League robotics competitions.

The NXT programmable robotics kit includes a main unit called the NXT Intelligent Brick. It can control three motors and four input sensors. You can assemble a robot from LEGO building elements, gears, wheels, motors, and sensors. The kit comes with its own software to program the robot, but now you can use App Inventor to create Android applications to control an NXT using Bluetooth connectivity.

The application in this chapter is designed to work with a robot that has wheels and an ultrasonic sensor, such as the Shooterbot robot pictured here. The Shooterbot is often the first robot that people build with the LEGO MINDSTORMS NXT 2.0 set. It has left wheels connected to output port C, right wheels connected to output port B, a color sensor connected to input port 3, and an ultrasonic sensor connected to input port 4.

What You'll Learn

This chapter uses the following components and concepts:

- The BluetoothClient component for connecting to the NXT.
- The ListPicker component to provide a user interface for connecting to the NXT.
- The NxtDrive component for driving the robot's wheels.
- The NxtUltrasonicSensor component for using the robot's ultrasonic sensor to detect obstacles.
- The Notifier component for displaying error messages.

Getting Started

You'll need Android version 2.0 or higher to use the application in this chapter. Also, for security reasons, Bluetooth devices must be paired before they can connect to each other. Before you get started building the app, you'll need to pair your Android with your NXT by following these steps:

1. On the NXT, click the right arrow until it says Bluetooth and then press the orange square.
2. Click the right arrow until it says Visibility and then press the orange square.
3. If the Visibility value is already Visible, continue to step 4. If not, click the left or right arrow to set the value to Visible.
4. On the Android, go to Settings→Wireless & Networks.
5. Make sure the Bluetooth checkbox is checked.
6. Click "Bluetooth settings" and "Scan for devices."
7. Under "Bluetooth devices," look for a device named "NXT."

 Note. If you've ever changed your robot's name, look for a device name that matches your robot's name instead of "NXT."

8. If you see "Paired but not connected" under your robot's name, you're finished! Otherwise, continue to step 9.
9. If you see "Pair with this device" under your robot's name, click it.
10. On the NXT, it should ask for a passkey. Press the orange square to accept 1234.

11. On the Android, it should ask for the PIN. Enter 1234 and press OK.

12. You should now see "Paired but not connected." You're finished!

Connect to the App Inventor website and start a new project. Name it "NXTRemoteControl" and set the screen's title to "NXT Remote Control". Open the Blocks Editor and connect to the phone.

Designing the Components

For this app, we'll need to create and define behaviors for both non-visible and visible components.

Non-Visible Components

Before creating the user interface components, you'll create some non-visible components, listed in Table 12-1 and illustrated in Figure 12-1, to control the NXT.

Table 12-1. Non-visible components for the Robot NXT controller app

Component type	Palette group	What you'll name it	Purpose
BluetoothClient	Other stuff	BluetoothClient1	Connect to the NXT.
NxtDrive	LEGO MINDSTORMS	NxtDrive1	Drive the robot's wheels.
NxtUltrasonicSensor	LEGO MINDSTORMS	NxtUltrasonicSensor1	Detect obstacles.
Notifier	Other stuff	Notifier1	Display error messages.

BluetoothClient1 NxtDrive1 NxtUltrasonicSensor1 Notifier1

Figure 12-1. The non-visible components displayed at the bottom of the Component Designer

Set the properties of the components in the following way:

1. Set the BluetoothClient property of NxtDrive1 and NxtUltrasonicSensor1 to BluetoothClient1.

2. Check BelowRangeEventEnabled on NxtUltrasonicSensor1.

3. Set the DriveMotors property of NxtDrive1:

   - If your robot has the left wheel's motor connected to output port C and the right wheel's motor connected to output port B, then the default setting of "CB" doesn't need to be changed.

   - If your robot is configured differently, set the DriveMotors property to a two-letter text value where the first letter is the output port connected to the left wheel's motor and the second letter is the output port connected to the right wheel's motor.

4. Set the `SensorPort` property of `NxtUltrasonicSensor1`.

  - If your robot's ultrasonic sensor is connected to input port 4, then the default setting of "4" doesn't need to be changed.

  - If your robot is configured differently, set the `SensorPort` property to the input port connected to the ultrasonic sensor.

Visible Components

Now let's create the user interface components shown in Figure 12-2.

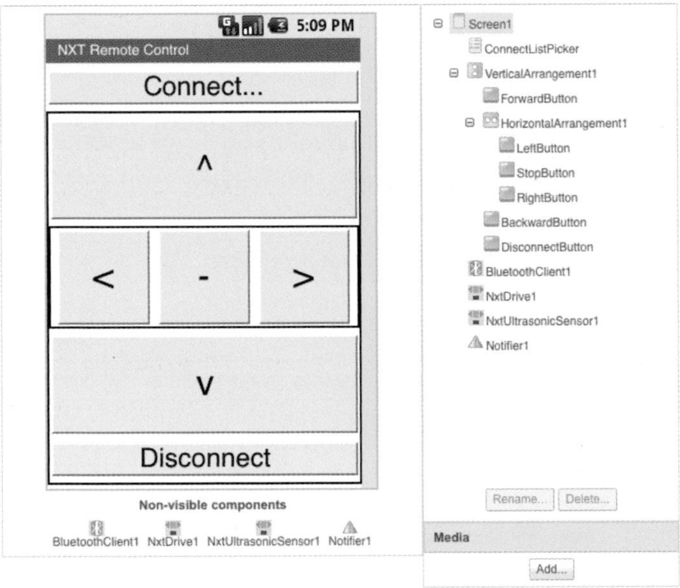

Figure 12-2. The app in the Component Designer

To make the Bluetooth connection, you'll need the unique Bluetooth address of the NXT. Unfortunately, Bluetooth addresses consist of eight 2-digit hexadecimal numbers (a way of representing binary values) separated by colons, making them very cumbersome to type. You won't want to type in the address on your phone every time you run the app. So, to avoid that, you'll use a `ListPicker` that displays a list of the robots that have been paired with your phone and lets you choose one.

You'll use buttons for driving forward and backward, turning left and right, stopping, and disconnecting. You can use a `VerticalArrangement` to lay out everything except for the `ListPicker`, and a `HorizontalArrangement` to contain the buttons for turning left, stopping, and turning right.

You can build the interface shown in Figure 12-2 by dragging out the components listed in Table 12-2.

Table 12-2. Visible components for the Robot NXT controller app

Component type	Palette group	What you'll name it	Purpose
ListPicker	Basic	ConnectListPicker	Choose the robot to connect to.
VerticalArrangement	Screen Arrangement	VerticalArrangement1	A visual container.
Button	Basic	ForwardButton	Drive forward.
HorizonalArrangement	Screen Arrangement	HorizontalArrangement1	A visual container.
Button	Basic	LeftButton	Turn left.
Button	Basic	StopButton	Stop.
Button	Basic	RightButton	Turn right.
Button	Basic	BackwardButton	Drive backward.
Button	Basic	DisconnectButton	Disconnect from the NXT.

To arrange the visual layout as shown in Figure 12-2, place LeftButton, StopButton, and RightButton inside HorizontalArrangement1, and place ForwardButton, HorizontalArrangement1, BackwardButton, and DisconnectButton inside VerticalArrangement1.

Set the properties of the components in the following way:

1. Uncheck Scrollable on Screen1.

2. Set the Width of ConnectListPicker and DisconnectButton to "Fill parent."

3. Set the Width and Height of VerticalArrangement1, ForwardButton, HorizontalArrangement1, LeftButton, StopButton, RightButton, and BackwardButton to "Fill parent."

4. Set the Text of ConnectListPicker to "Connect…".

5. Set the Text of ForwardButton to "∧".

6. Set the Text of LeftButton to "<".

7. Set the Text of StopButton to " ".

8. Set the Text of RightButton to ">".

9. Set the Text of BackwardButton to "v".

10. Set the Text of DisconnectButton to "Disconnect".

11. Set the FontSize of ConnectListPicker and DisconnectButton to 30.

12. Set the FontSize of ForwardButton, LeftButton, StopButton, RightButton, and BackwardButton to 40.

In this application, it makes sense to hide most of the user interface until the Bluetooth is connected to the NXT. To accomplish this, uncheck the Visible property of VerticalArrangement1. Don't worry—in a moment, we'll make the application reveal the user interface after it connects to the NXT.

Adding Behaviors to the Components

In this section, you'll program the behavior of the app, including:

- Letting the user connect the app to a robot by choosing it from a list.
- Letting the user disconnect the app from a robot.
- Letting the user drive the robot using the control buttons.
- Forcing the robot to stop when it senses an obstacle.

Connecting to the NXT

The first behavior you'll add is connecting to the NXT. When you click ConnectListPicker, it will show a list of the paired robots. When you choose a robot, the app will make a Bluetooth connection to that robot.

Displaying the List of Robots

To display the list of robots, you'll use ConnectListPicker. A ListPicker looks like a button, but when it's clicked, it displays a list of items and lets you choose one.

You'll use the **BluetoothClient1.AddressesAndNames** block to provide a list of the addresses and names of Bluetooth devices that have been paired with the Android. Because BluetoothClient1 is used with NXT components, it automatically limits the devices included in the AddressesAndNames property to those that are robots, so you won't see other kinds of Bluetooth devices (like headsets) in the list. Table 12-3 lists the blocks you'll need for this step.

Table 12-3. Blocks to add a ListPicker to the app

Block type	Drawer	Purpose
ConnectListPicker .BeforePicking	ConnectListPicker	Triggered when ConnectListPicker is clicked.
set ConnectListPicker .Elements to	ConnectListPicker	Set the choices that will appear.
BluetoothClient1 .AddressesAndNames	BluetoothClient1	The addresses and names of robots that have been paired with the Android.

How the blocks work

When ConnectListPicker is clicked, the **ConnectListPicker.BeforePicking** event is triggered before the list of choices is displayed, as shown in Figure 12-3. To specify the items that will be listed, set the **ConnectListPicker.Elements** property to the **BluetoothClient1.AddressesAndNames** block. ConnectListPicker will list the robots that have been paired with the Android.

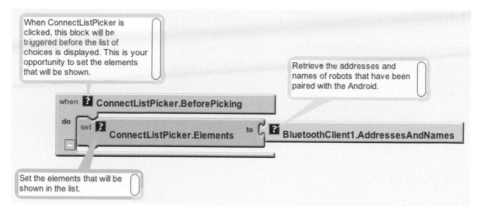

Figure 12-3. Displaying the list of robots

 Test your app. *On your phone, click "Connect..." and see what happens. You should see a list of all the robots your phone has been paired with.*

If you just see a black screen, your phone hasn't been paired with any robots. If you see addresses and names of other Bluetooth devices, such as a Bluetooth headset, the BluetoothClient *property of* NxtDrive1 *and* NxtUltrasonicSensor1 *has not been set properly.*

Making the Bluetooth Connection

After you choose a robot from the list, the app will connect to that robot via Bluetooth. If the connection is successful, the user interface will change. ConnectListPicker will be hidden, and the rest of the user interface components will appear. If the robot is not turned on, the connection will fail and an error message will pop up.

You'll use the **BluetoothClient1.Connect** block to make the connection. The **ConnectListPicker.Selection** property provides the address and name of the chosen robot.

You'll use an **ifelse** block to test whether the connection was successful or not. The **ifelse** block has three different areas where blocks are connected: "test," "then-do," and "else-do." The "test" area will contain the **BluetoothClient1.Connect** block. The "then-do" area will contain the blocks to be executed if the connection is successful. The "else-do" area will contain the blocks to be executed if the connection fails.

If the connection is successful, you will use the `Visible` property to hide `ConnectListPicker` and show `VerticalArrangement1`, which contains the rest of the user interface components. If the connection fails, you will use the **Notifier1 .ShowAlert** block to display an error message. Table 12-4 lists the blocks you'll need for this behavior.

Table 12-4. Blocks for using Bluetooth to connect with the robot

Block type	Drawer	Purpose
ConnectListPicker.AfterPicking	ConnectListPicker	Triggered when a robot is chosen from `ConnectListPicker`.
ifelse	Control	Test whether the Bluetooth connection is successful.
BluetoothClient1.Connect	BluetoothClient1	Connect to the robot.
ConnectListPicker.Selection	ConnectListPicker	The address and name of the chosen robot.
set ConnectListPicker.Visible to	ConnectListPicker	Hide `ConnectListPicker`.
false	Logic	Plug into **set ConnectListPicker. Visible to**.
set VerticalArrangement1.Visible to	VerticalArrangement1	Show the rest of the user interface.
true	Logic	Plug into **set VerticalArrangement1 .Visible to**.
Notifier1.ShowAlert	Notifier1	Show an error message.
text ("Unable to make a Bluetooth connec-tion.")	Text	The error message.

How the blocks work

After a robot is picked, the **ConnectListPicker.AfterPicking** event is triggered, as shown in Figure 12-4. The **BluetoothClient1.Connect** block makes the Bluetooth connection to the selected robot. If the connection is successful, the "then-do" blocks are executed: the **ConnectListPicker.Visible** property is set to false to hide `ConnectListPicker`, and the **VerticalArrangement1.Visible** property is set to true to show `VerticalArrangement1`. If the connection fails, the "else-do" blocks are executed: the **Notifier1.ShowAlert** block displays an error message.

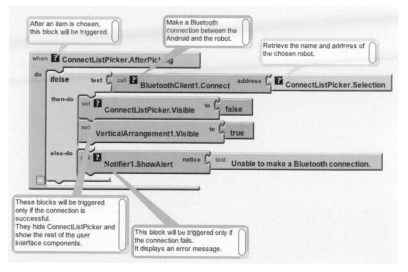

Figure 12-4. Making the Bluetooth connection

Disconnecting from the NXT

You're probably excited about connecting your Android to your NXT, but before you do that, let's do one more thing: add the behavior for disconnecting. That way, you'll be able to test both connecting and disconnecting.

When `DisconnectButton` is clicked, the app will close the Bluetooth connection and the user interface will change. `ConnectListPicker` will reappear, and the rest of the user interface components will be hidden.

Use the blocks listed in Table 12-5 to build the **BluetoothClient1.Disconnect** block that closes the Bluetooth connection. You will use the `Visible` property to show `ConnectListPicker` and hide `VerticalArrangement1`, which contains the rest of the user interface components.

Table 12-5. Blocks for disconnecting from the robot

Block type	Drawer	Purpose
DisconnectButton.Click	DisconnectButton	Triggered when `DisconnectButton` is clicked.
BluetoothClient1. Disconnect	BluetoothClient1	Disconnect from the robot.
set ConnectListPicker. Visible to	ConnectListPicker	Show `ConnectListPicker`.
true	Logic	Plug into **set ConnectListPicker.Visible to**.
set VerticalArrangement 1.Visible to	VerticalArrangement1	Hide the rest of the user interface.
false	Logic	Plug into **set VerticalArrangement1.Visible to**.

How the blocks work

When `DisconnectButton` is clicked, the **DisconnectButton.Clicked** event is triggered, as shown in Figure 12-5. The **BluetoothClient1.Disconnect** block closes the Bluetooth connection. The **ConnectListPicker.Visible** property is set to true to show `ConnectListPicker`, and the **VerticalArrangement1.Visible** property is set to false to hide `VerticalArrangement1`.

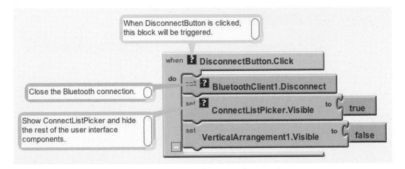

Figure 12-5. Disconnecting from the robot

Test your app. *Make sure your robot is turned on and then, on your phone, click "Connect…" and choose the robot you want to connect to. It will take a moment to make the Bluetooth connection. Once the robot connects, you should see the buttons for controlling the robot, as well as the Disconnect button.*

Click the Disconnect button. The buttons for controlling the robot should disappear, and the Connect button should reappear.

Driving the NXT

Let's get to the really fun part: adding behavior for driving forward and backward, turning left and right, and stopping. Don't forget about stopping—if you do, you'll have an out-of-control robot on your hands!

The `NxtDrive` component provides five blocks for driving the robot's motors:

- **MoveForwardIndefinitely** drives both motors forward.

- **MoveBackwardIndefinitely** drives both motors backward.

- **TurnCounterClockwiseIndefinitely** turns the robot to the left by driving the right motor forward and the left motor backward.

- **TurnClockwiseIndefinitely** turns the robot to the right by driving the left motor forward and the right motor backward.

- **Stop** stops both motors.

The **Move…** and **Turn…** blocks each have a parameter called Power. You'll use a **number** block, along with all the other items listed in Table 12-6, to specify the amount of power the robot should use to turn the motors. The value can range from 0 to 100. However, if you specify too little power, the motors will make a whining sound but not turn. In this application, you'll use 90 (percent).

Table 12-6. Blocks for controlling the robot

Block type	Drawer	Purpose
ForwardButton.Click	ForwardButton	Triggered when ForwardButton is clicked.
NxtDrive1.MoveForward Indefinitely	NxtDrive1	Drive the robot forward.
number (90)	Math	The amount of power.
BackwardButton.Click	BackwardButton	Triggered when BackwardButton is clicked.
NxtDrive1.MoveBackward Indefinitely	NxtDrive1	Drive the robot backward.
number (90)	Math	The amount of power.
LeftButton.Click	LeftButton	Triggered when LeftButton is clicked.
NxtDrive1.TurnCounterClock- wiseIndefinitely	NxtDrive1	Turn the robot counterclockwise.
number (90)	Math	The amount of power.
RightButton.Click	RightButton	Triggered when RightButton is clicked.
NxtDrive1.TurnClock- wiseIndefinitely	NxtDrive1	Turn the robot clockwise.
number (90)	Math	The amount of power.
StopButton.Click	StopButton	Triggered when StopButton is clicked.
NxtDrive1.Stop	NxtDrive1	Stop the robot.

How the blocks work

When ForwardButton is clicked, the **ForwardButton.Clicked** event is triggered. The **NxtDrive1.MoveForwardIndefinitely** block shown in Figure 12-6 is used to move the robot forward at 90% power. The remaining events function similarly for the other buttons, each powering the robot backward, left, and right.

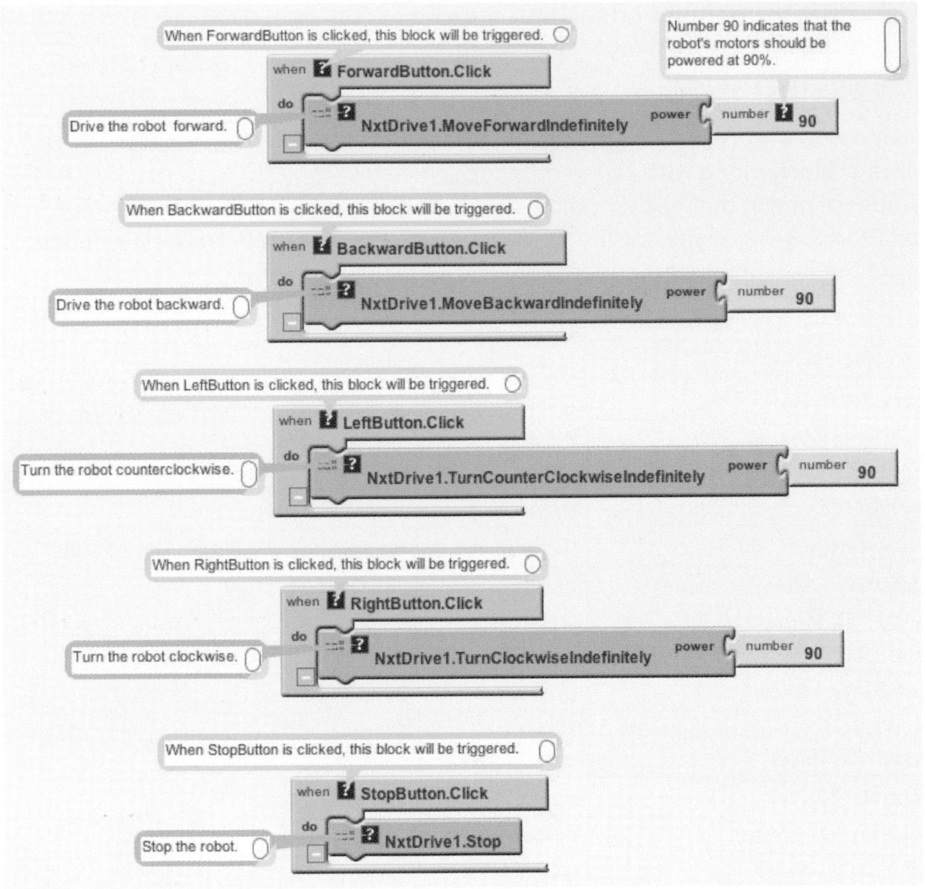

When FowardButton is clicked, this block will be triggered. ◯

Number 90 indicates that the robot's motors should be powered at 90%.

when 🎴 ForwardButton.Click

do

Drive the robot forward. ◯   NxtDrive1.MoveForwardIndefinitely   power [number 🎴 90

When BackwardButton is clicked, this block will be triggered. ◯

when 🎴 BackwardButton.Click

do

Drive the robot backward. ◯   NxtDrive1.MoveBackwardIndefinitely   power [number 90

When LeftButton is clicked, this block will be triggered. ◯

when 🎴 LeftButton.Click

do

Turn the robot counterclockwise. ◯   NxtDrive1.TurnCounterClockwiseIndefinitely   power [number 90

When RightButton is clicked, this block will be triggered. ◯

when 🎴 RightButton.Click

do

Turn the robot clockwise. ◯   NxtDrive1.TurnClockwiseIndefinitely   power [number 90

When StopButton is clicked, this block will be triggered. ◯

when 🎴 StopButton.Click

do

Stop the robot. ◯   NxtDrive1.Stop

Figure 12-6. Driving the robot

When StopButton is clicked, the **StopButton.Clicked** event is triggered. The **NxtDrive1.Stop** block is used to stop the robot.

Test your app. *Follow the instructions in the previous "Test your app" section to connect to the NXT. Make sure the robot is not on a table where it could fall, and then test its behavior as follows:*

1. *Click the forward button. The robot should move forward.*

2. *Click the backward button. The robot should move backward.*

3. *Click the left button. The robot should turn counterclockwise.*

4. *Click the right button. The robot should turn clockwise.*

5. *Click the stop button. The robot should stop.*

If your robot doesn't move, but you can hear a whining sound, you may need to increase the power. You can use 100 for maximum power.

Using the Ultrasonic Sensor to Detect Obstacles

Using the ultrasonic sensor, the robot will stop if it encounters an obstacle, like the culprit shown in Figure 12-7, within 30 centimeters.

Figure 12-7. A common household obstacle for your NXT robot

The NxtUltrasonicSensor component can be used to detect obstacles. It has two properties named BottomOfRange and TopOfRange that define the detection range in centimeters. By default, the BottomOfRange property is set to 30 centimeters and TopOfRange is set to 90 centimeters.

The NxtUltrasonicSensor component also has three events called BelowRange, WithinRange, and AboveRange. The BelowRange event will be triggered when an obstacle is detected at a distance below BottomOfRange. The WithinRange event will be triggered when an obstacle is detected at a distance between BottomOfRange and TopOfRange. The AboveRange event will be triggered when an obstacle is detected at a distance above TopOfRange.

You'll use the **NxtUltrasonicSensor1.BelowRange** event block, shown in Table 12-7, to detect an obstacle within 30 centimeters. If you want to detect an obstacle within a different distance, you can adjust the BottomOfRange property. You'll use the **NxtDrive1.Stop** block to stop the robot.

Table 12-7. Blocks for using the NxtUltrasonicSensor

Block type	Drawer	Purpose
NxtUltrasonicSensor1 .BelowRange	NxtUltrasonicSensor1	Triggered when the ultrasonic sensor detects an obstacle at a distance below 30 centimeters.
NxtDrive1.Stop	NxtDrive1	Stop the robot.

How the blocks work

When the robot's ultrasonic sensor detects an obstacle at a distance below 30 centimeters, the **NxtUltrasonicSensor1.BelowRange** event is triggered, as shown in Figure 12-8. The **NxtDrive1.Stop** block stops the robot.

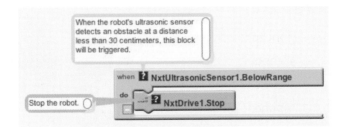

Figure 12-8. Detecting an obstacle

Test your app. *Follow the instructions in the previous "Test your app" section to connect to the NXT. Using the navigation buttons, drive your robot toward an obstacle, such as a cat. The robot should stop when it gets within 30 centimeters of the cat.*

If the robot doesn't stop, the cat may have moved away from the robot before it got within 30 centimeters. You may need to test your app with an inanimate obstacle.

Variations

After you get this application working—and you've spent enough time actually playing with your NXT robot—you might want to try:

- Varying the amount of power when driving the robot.

    - You can do this by changing the numeric value that you plug into the **MoveForwardIndefinitely**, **MoveBackwardIndefinitely**, **TurnCounterclockwiseIndefinitely**, and **TurnClockwiseIndefinitely** blocks.

- Using the NxtColorSensor to shine a red light when an obstacle is detected.

    - You can use an NxtColorSensor component and its GenerateColor property.

    - You'll need to set the DetectColor property to false (or uncheck it in the Component Designer) because the color sensor cannot detect and generate color at the same time.

- Using an OrientationSensor to control the robot.

- Using LEGO building elements to physically attach your phone to the robot. Create applications that make the robot autonomous.

Summary

Here are some of the concepts we've covered in this tutorial:

- The ListPicker component allows you to choose from a list of paired robots.

- The BluetoothClient component makes the connection to the robot.

- The Notifier component displays an error message.

- The Visible property is used to hide or show user interface components.

- The NxtDrive component can drive, turn, and stop the robot.

- The NxtUltrasonicSensor component is used to detect obstacles.

CHAPTER 13

Amazon at the Bookstore

Say you're browsing books at your favorite book-store and want to know how much a book costs on Amazon.com. With the "Amazon at the Bookstore" app, you can scan a book or enter an ISBN, and the app will tell you the current lowest price of the book at Amazon.com. You can also search for books on a particular topic.

"Amazon at the Bookstore" demonstrates how App Inventor can be used to create apps that talk to web services (aka APIs, or application programming inter-faces). This app will get data from a web service created by one of this book's authors. By the end of this chapter, you'll be able to create your own custom app for talking to Amazon.

The application has a simple user interface that lets the user enter keywords or a book's ISBN (international standard book number—a 10- or 13-digit code that uniquely identi-fies a book) and then lists the title, ISBN, and lowest price for a new copy at Amazon. It also uses the BarcodeScanner *component so the user can scan a book to trigger a search instead of entering text (technically, the scanner just inputs the book's ISBN for you!).*

What You'll Learn

In this app (shown in Figure 13-1), you'll learn:

- How to use a barcode scanner within an app.

- How to access a web information source (Amazon's API) through the TinyWebDB component.

- How to process complex data returned from that web information source. In particular, you'll learn how to process a list of books in which each book is itself a list of three items (title, price, and ISBN).

You'll also be introduced to source code that you can use to create your own web service API with the Python programming language and Google's App Engine.

Figure 13-1. "Amazon at the Bookstore" running in the emulator

What Is an API?

Before we start designing our components and programming the app, let's take a closer look at what an *application programmer interface* (*API*) is and how one works. An API is like a website, but instead of communicating with humans, it communicates with other computer programs. APIs are often called "server" programs because they typically serve information to "client" programs that actually interface with humans— like an App Inventor app. If you've ever used a Facebook app on your phone, you're using a client program that communicates with the Facebook API server.

In this chapter, you'll create an Android client app that communicates with an Amazon API. Your app will request book and ISBN information from the Amazon API, and the API will return up-to-date listings to your app. Your app will then present the book data to the user.

The Amazon API you'll use is specially configured for use with App Inventor. We won't get into the gory details here, but it's useful to know that, because of this configuration, you can use the TinyWebDB component to communicate with Amazon. The good news is, you already know how to do that! You'll call **TinyWebDB.GetValue** to request information and then process the information returned in the **TinyWebDB .GotValue** event handler, just as you do when you use a web database. (You can go back to the MakeText app in Chapter 10 to refresh your memory if needed.)

Before creating the app, you'll need to understand the Amazon API's *protocol*, which specifies the format for your request and the format of the data returned. Just as different cultures have different protocols (when you meet someone, do you shake hands, bow, or nod your head?), computers talking to one another have protocols as well.

The Amazon API you'll be using here provides a web interface for exploring how the API works before you start using it. While the API is designed to talk to other computers, this web interface allows you to see just how that communication will happen. Following these steps, you can try out what particular **GetValue** calls will return via the website, and know that the API interface will behave exactly the same when you ask it for data via the TinyWebDB component in App Inventor:

1. Open a browser and go to *http://aiamazonapi.appspot.com/*. You'll see the website shown in Figure 13-2.

Figure 13-2. The web interface for the App Inventor Amazon API

2. The page allows you to try the one function you can call with this API: getvalue. Enter a term (e.g., "baseball") in the Tag field and then click "Get value." The web page will display a listing of the top five books returned from Amazon, as shown in Figure 13-3.

Figure 13-3. Making a call to the Amazon API to search for books related to the tag (or keyword) "baseball"

The value returned is a list of books, each one enclosed in brackets [like this] and providing the title, cost, and ISBN. If you look closely, you'll see that each book is in fact represented as a sublist of another main list. The main list (about baseball) is enclosed in brackets, and each sublist (or book) is enclosed in its own set of brackets within the main brackets. So the return value from this API is actually a *list of lists*, with each sublist providing the information for one book. Let's look at this a bit more closely.

Each left bracket ([) in the data denotes the beginning of a list. The first left bracket of the result denotes the beginning of the outer list (the list of books). To its immediate right is the beginning of the first sublist, the first book:

```
["The Baseball Codes: Beanballs, Sign Stealing, and Bench-Clearing Brawls: The
Unwritten Rules of America\'s Pastime", '$12.98', '0375424695']
```

The sublist has three parts: a title, the lowest current price for the book at Amazon, and the book's ISBN. When you get this information into your App Inventor app, you'll be able to access each part using **select list item**, with index 1 for the title, index 2 for the price, and index 3 for the ISBN. (To refresh your memory on working with an index and lists, revisit the MakeQuiz app in Chapter 10.)

3. Instead of searching by keyword, you can search for a book by entering an ISBN. To perform such a search, you enter a tag of the form "isbn:xxxxxxxxxxxxx," as shown in Figure 13-4.

The double brackets ([[) in the result [['"App Inventor"', '$21.93', '1449397484']] denote that a list of lists is still returned, even though there is only one book. It may seem a bit strange now, but this will be important when we access the information for our app.

Returned as value to TinyWebDB component:
[['"App Inventor"', '$21.93', '1449397484']]

Figure 13-4. Querying the Amazon API by ISBN instead of keyword

Designing the Components

The user interface for our Amazon book app is relatively simple: give it a Textbox for entering keywords or ISBNs, two buttons for starting the two types of searches (keyword or ISBN), and a third button for letting the user scan a book (we'll get to that in a bit). Then, add a heading label and another label for listing the results that the Amazon API will return, and finally two non-visible components: TinyWebDB and a BarcodeScanner. Check your results against Figure 13-5.

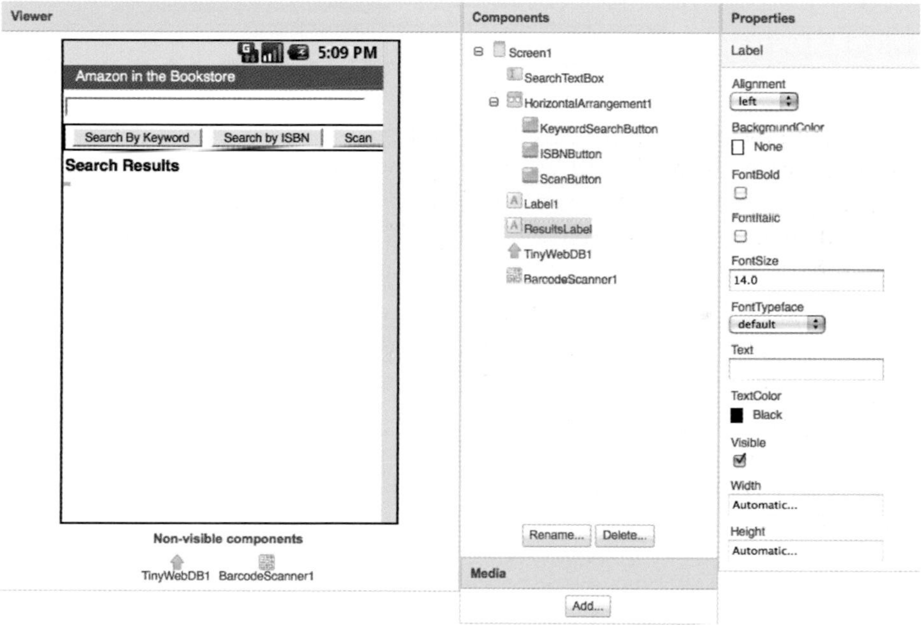

Figure 13-5. The Amazon at the Bookstore user interface shown in the Designer

Table 13-1 lists all the components you'll need to build the UI shown in Figure 13-5.

Table 13-1. Component list for the "Amazon at the Bookstore" app

Component type	Palette group	What you'll name it	Purpose
Textbox	Basic	SearchTextBox	The user enters keywords or ISBN here.
HorizontalArrangement	Screen Arrangements	HorizontalArrangement1	Arrange the buttons in a line.
Button	Basic	KeywordSearchButton	Click to search by keyword.
Button	Basic	ISBNButton	Click to search by ISBN.
Button	Basic	ScanButton	Click to scan an ISBN from a book.
Label	Basic	Label1	The header "Search Results."
Label	Basic	ResultsLabel	Where you'll display the results.
TinyWebDB	Not ready for prime time	TinyWebDB1	Talk to Amazon.com.
BarcodeScanner	Other stuff	BarcodeScanner1	Scan barcodes.

Set the properties of the components in the following way:

1. Set the Hint of the SearchTextBox to "Enter keywords or ISBN".

2. Set the Text properties of the buttons and labels as shown in Figure 13-5.

3. Set the ServiceURL property of the TinyWebDB component to *http://aiamazonapi. appspot.com/*.

Designing the Behavior

For this app, you'll specify the following behaviors in the Blocks Editor:

Searching by keyword
> The user enters some terms and clicks the KeywordSearchButton to invoke an Amazon search. You'll call **TinyWebDB.GetValue** to make it happen.

Searching by ISBN
> The user enters an ISBN and clicks the ISBNButton. You'll package the prefix "isbn:" with the number entered and run the Amazon search.

Barcode scanning
> The user clicks a button and the scanner is launched. When the user scans an ISBN from a book, your app will start the Amazon search.

Processing the list of books
> At first, your app will display the data returned from Amazon in a rudimentary way. Later, you'll modify the blocks so that the app extracts the title, price, and ISBN from each book returned and displays them in an organized way.

Searching by Keyword

When the user clicks the KeywordSearchButton, you want to grab the text from the SearchTextbox and send it as the tag in your request to the Amazon API. You'll use the **TinyWebDB.GetValue** block to request the Amazon search.

When the results come back from Amazon, the **TinyWebDB.GotValue** event handler will be triggered. For now, let's just display the result that is returned directly into the ResultsLabel, as shown in Figure 13-6. Later, after you see that the data is indeed being retrieved, you can display the data in a more sophisticated fashion.

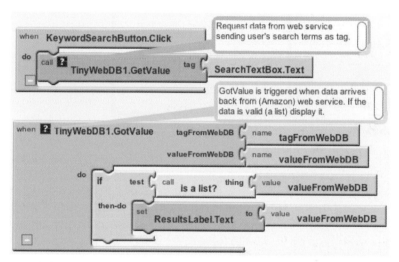

Figure 13-6. Send the search request to the API and put results in the ResultsLabel

How the blocks work

When the user clicks the KeywordSearchButton, the **TinyWebDB1.GetValue** request is made. The tag sent with the request is the information the user entered in the SearchTextBox.

If you completed the MakeQuiz app (Chapter 10), you know that **TinyWebDB .GetValue** requests are not answered immediately. Instead, when the data arrives from the API, **TinyWebDB1.GotValue** is triggered. In **GotValue**, the blocks check the value returned to see if it's a list (it won't be if the Amazon API is offline or there is no data for the keywords). If it is a list, the data is placed into the ResultsLabel.

Test your app. *Enter a term in the search box and click Search By Keyword. You should get a listing similar to what is shown in Figure 13-7. (It's not terribly nice-looking, but we'll deal with that shortly.)*

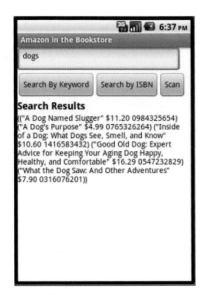

Figure 13-7. Keyword search result for "dogs"

Searching by ISBN

The code for searching by ISBN is similar, but in this case the Amazon API expects the tag to be in the form "isbn:xxxxxxxxxxxx" (this is the *protocol* the API expects for searching by ISBN). You don't want to force the user to know this protocol; the user should just be able to enter the ISBN in the text box and click Search by ISBN, and the app will add the "isbn:" prefix behind the scenes with **make text**. Figure 13-8 shows the blocks to do that.

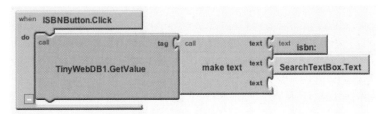

Figure 13-8. Using make text to add the isbn: prefix

How the blocks work

The **make text** block concatenates the "isbn:" prefix with the information the user has input in the SearchTextBox and sends the result as the tag to **TinyWebDB. GetValue**.

Just as with keyword search, the API sends back a list result for an ISBN search—in this case, a list of just the one item whose ISBN matches the user's input exactly. Because the **TinyWebDB.GotValue** event handler is already set up to process a list of books (even a list with only one item), you won't have to change your event handler to make this work.

 Test your app. *Enter an ISBN (e.g., 9781449397487) in the* SearchTextBox *and click the* ISBNButton. *Does the book information appear?*

Don't Leave Your Users Hanging

As we've seen in earlier chapters that work with TinyWebDB, when you call a web service (API) with **TinyWebDB.GetValue**, there can be a delay before the data arrives and **TinyWebDB.GotValue** is triggered. It is generally a good idea to let users know the request is being processed so they don't worry that the app has hung. For this app, you can place a message in the ResultsLabel each time you make the call to **TinyWebDB.GetValue**, as shown in Figure 13-9.

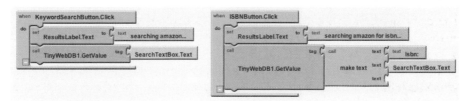

Figure 13-9. Adding a message to let the user know what is happening

How the blocks work

For both the keyword and ISBN searches, a "Searching Amazon…" message is placed in ResultsLabel when the data is requested. Note that when **GotValue** is triggered, this message is overwritten with the actual results from Amazon.

Scanning a Book

Let's face it: typing on a cell phone isn't always the easiest thing, and you tend to make a mistake here and there. It would certainly be easier (and result in fewer mistakes) if a user could just launch your app and scan the barcode of the book she is interested in. This is another great built-in Android phone feature you can tap into easily with App Inventor.

The function **BarcodeScanner.DoScan** starts up the scanner. You'll want to call this when the ScanButton is clicked. The event handler **BarcodeScanner.AfterScan** is triggered once something has been scanned. It has an argument, result, which contains the information that was scanned. In this case, you want to initiate an ISBN search using that result, as shown in Figure 13-10.

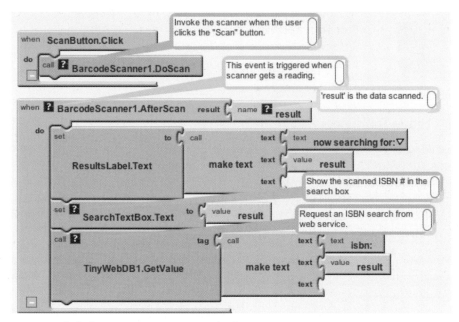

Figure 13-10. Blocks for initiating an ISBN search after a user scans

How the blocks work

When the user clicks the ScanButton, **DoScan** launches the scanner. When something has been scanned, **AfterScan** is triggered. The argument result holds the result of the scan—in this case, a book's ISBN. The user is notified that a request has been made, the result (the ISBN scanned) is placed in the SearchTextBox, and **TinyWebDB.GetValue** is called to initiate the search. Once again, the **TinyWebDB .GotValue** event handler will process the book information returned.

Test your app. *Click the* ScanButton *and scan the barcode of a book. Does the app display the book information?*

Improving the Display

A client app like the one you're creating can do whatever it wants with the data it receives—you could compare the price information with that of other online stores, or use the title information to search for similar books from another library.

Almost always, you'll want to get the API information loaded into variables that you can then process further. In the **TinyWebDB.GotValue** event handler you have so far, you just place all the information returned from Amazon into the ResultsLabel.

Instead, let's *process* (or do something to) the data by (1) putting the title, price, and ISBN of each book returned into separate variables, and (2) displaying those items in an orderly fashion. By now, you're really getting the hang of creating variables and using them in your display, so try building out the variables you think you'll need and the blocks to display each search result on its own separate line. Then compare what you've done with Figure 13-11.

How the blocks work

Four variables—resultList, title, cost, and isbn—are defined to hold each piece of data as it is returned from the API. The result from the API, valueFromWebDB, is placed into the variable resultList. This app could have processed the argument valueFromWebDB directly, but in general, you'll put it in a variable in case you want to process the data outside the event handler. (Event arguments like valueFromWebDB hold their value only within the event handler.)

A **foreach** loop is used to iterate through each item of the result. Recall that the data returned from Amazon is a list of lists, with each sublist representing the information for a book. So the placeholder of the **foreach** is named bookitem, and it holds the current book information, a list, on each iteration.

Now we have to deal with the fact that the variable bookitem is a list—the first item is the title, the second, the price; and the third, the ISBN. Thus, **select list item** blocks are used to extract these items and place them into their respective variables (title, price, and isbn).

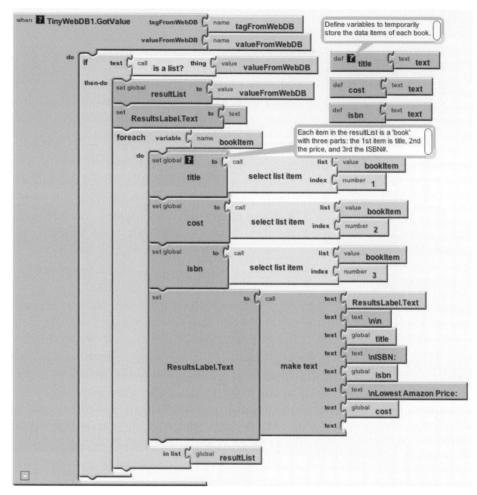

Figure 13-11. Extracting the title, cost, and ISBN of each book, then displaying them on separate lines

Once the data has been organized this way, you can process it however you'd like. This app just uses the variables as part of a **make text** block that displays the title, price, and ISBN on separate lines.

Test your app. *Try another search and check out how the book information is displayed. It should look similar to Figure 13-12.*

Figure 13-12. The search listing displayed in a more sophisticated fashion

Customizing the API

The API you connected to, *http://aiamazonapi.appspot.com*, was created with the programming language Python and Google's App Engine. App Engine lets you create and deploy websites and services (APIs) that live on Google's servers. You only pay for App Engine if your site or API becomes very popular (meaning you're using up a lot more of Google's servers for it).

The API service used here provides only partial access to the full Amazon API and returns a maximum of five books for any search. If you'd like to provide more flexibility—for example, have it search for items other than books—you can download the source code from *http://appinventorapi.com/amazon/* and customize it.

Such customization does require knowledge of Python programming, so beware! But if you've been completing the App Inventor apps in this book, you might just be ready for the challenge. To get started learning Python, check out the online text *How to Think Like a Computer Scientist: Learning with Python* (*http://openbookproject .net//thinkCSpy/*) and check out the section on App Inventor API building in Chapter 24 of this book.

Variations

Once you get the app working, you might want to explore some variations. For example,

- As is, the app hangs if the search doesn't return any books (for instance, when the user enters an invalid ISBN). Modify the blocks so that the app reports when there are no results.

- Modify the app so that it only displays books under $10.

- Modify the app so that after you scan a book, its lowest Amazon price is spoken out loud (use the TextToSpeech component discussed in the "Android, Where's My Car?" app in Chapter 7).

- Download the *http://aiamazonapi.appspot.com* API code from *http://examples .oreilly.com/0636920016632/* and modify it so that it returns more information. For example, you might have it return the Amazon URL of each book, display the URL along with each listed book, and let the user click the URL to open that page. As mentioned earlier, modifying the API requires Python programming and some knowledge of Google's App Engine. For more information, check out Chapter 24.

Summary

Here are some of the concepts we've covered with this app:

- You can access the Web from an app using TinyWebDB and specially constructed APIs. You set the ServiceURL of the TinyWebDB component to the API URL and then call **TinyWebDB.GetValue** to request the information. The data isn't immediately returned but can instead be accessed within the **TinyWebDB.GotValue** event handler.

- The **BarcodeScanner.DoScan** function launches the scan. When the user scans a barcode, the **BarcodeScanner.AfterScan** event is triggered and the scanned data is placed in the argument result.

- In App Inventor, complex data is represented with lists and lists of lists. If you know the format of the data returned from an API, you can use **foreach** and **select list item** to extract the separate pieces of information into variables, and then perform whatever processing or display you'd like using those variables.

PART II
Inventor's Manual

This section is organized by concept, like a traditional programming textbook. You'll get an overview of app architecture, then delve into programming topics, including variables, animation, conditional statements, lists, iteration, procedures, databases, sensors, APIs, and software engineering and debugging. You can refer to these chapters as needed during your app building, or use them for conceptual study as you ride the bus or relax at night.

CHAPTER 14

Understanding an App's Architecture

This chapter examines the structure of an app from a programmer's perspective. It begins with the traditional analogy that an app is like a recipe and then proceeds to reconceptualize an app as a set of components that respond to events. The chapter also examines how apps can ask questions, repeat, remember, and talk to the Web, all of which will be described in more detail in later chapters.

Many people can tell you what an app is from a user's perspective, but understanding what it is from a programmer's perspective is more complicated. Apps have an internal structure that we must fully understand in order to create them effectively.

One way to describe an app's internals is to break it into two parts, its *components* and its *behaviors*. Roughly, these correspond to the two main windows you use in App Inventor: you use the Component Designer to specify the objects (components) of the app, and you use the Blocks Editor to program how the app responds to user and external events (the app's behavior).

Figure 14-1 provides an overview of this app architecture. In this chapter, we'll explore this architecture in detail.

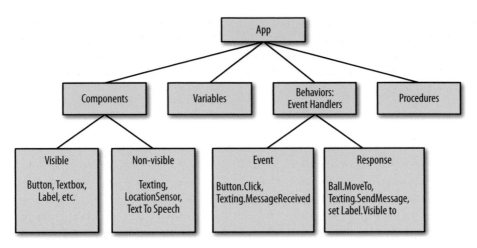

Figure 14-1. The internal architecture of an App Inventor app

Components

There are two main types of components in an app: visible and non-visible. The app's visible components are the ones you can see when the app is launched—things like buttons, text boxes, and labels. These are often referred to as the app's *user interface*.

Non-visible components are those you can't see, so they're not part of the user interface. Instead, they provide access to the built-in functionality of the device; for example, the Texting component sends and processes SMS texts, the LocationSensor component determines the device's location, and the TextToSpeech component talks. The non-visible components are the technology within the device—little people that do jobs for your app.

Both visible and non-visible components are defined by a set of *properties*. Properties are memory slots for storing information about the component. Visible components, for instance, have properties like Width, Height, and Alignment, which together define how the component looks. So a button that looks like the Submit button in Figure 14-2 to the end user is defined in the Component Designer with a set of properties, including those shown in Table 14-1.

Table 14-1. Button properties

Width	Height	Alignment	Text
50	30	center	Submit

Submit

Figure 14-2. Submit button

You can think of properties as something like the cells you see in a spreadsheet. You modify them in the Component Designer to define the *initial* appearance of a component. If you change the number in the Width slot from 50 to 70, the button will appear wider, both in the Designer and in the app. Note that the end user of the app doesn't see the 70; he just sees the button's width change.

Behavior

An app's components are generally straightforward to understand: a text box is for entering information, a button is for clicking, and so on. An app's behavior, on the other hand, is conceptually difficult and often complex. The behavior defines how the app should respond to events, both user initiated (e.g., a button click) and external (e.g., an SMS text arriving to the phone). The difficulty of specifying such interactive behavior is why programming is so challenging.

Fortunately, App Inventor provides a visual "blocks" language perfectly suited for specifying behaviors. This section provides a model for understanding it.

An App As a Recipe

Traditionally, software has often been compared to a recipe. Like a recipe, a traditional app follows a linear sequence of instructions, such as those shown in Figure 14-3, that the computer (chef) should perform.

A typical app might start a bank transaction (A), perform some computations and modify a customer's account (B), and then print out the new balance on the screen (C).

Figure 14-3. Traditional software follows a linear sequence of instructions

An App As a Set of Event Handlers

However, most apps today, whether they're for mobile phones, the Web, or desktop computers, don't fit the recipe paradigm anymore. They don't perform a bunch of instructions in a predetermined order; instead, they *react to events*—most commonly, events initiated by the app's end user. For example, if the user clicks a button, the app responds by performing some operation (e.g., sending a text message). For touchscreen phones and devices, the act of dragging your finger across the screen is another event. The app might respond to that event by drawing a line from the point of your original touch to the point where you lifted your finger.

These types of apps are better conceptualized as a set of components that respond to events. The apps do include "recipes"—sequences of instructions—but each recipe is only performed in response to some event, as shown in Figure 14-4.

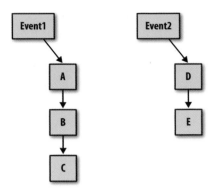

Figure 14-4. An app as multiple recipes hooked to events

So, as events occur, the app reacts by calling a sequence of *functions*. Functions are things you can do to or with a component—operations like sending an SMS text, or property-changing operations such as changing the text in a label of the user inter-face. To *call* a function means to *invoke* it, to make it happen. We call an event and the set of functions performed in response to it an *event handler*.

Many events are initiated by the end user, but some are not. An app can react to events that happen within the phone, such as changes to its orientation sensor and the clock (i.e., the passing of time), and events created by things outside the phone, such as other phones or data arriving from the Web, as shown in Figure 14-5.

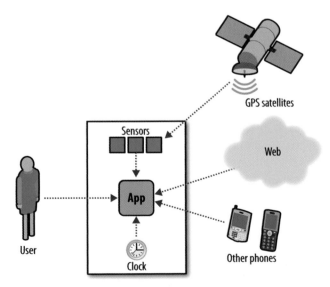

Figure 14-5. An app can respond to both internal and external events

One reason App Inventor programming is intuitive is that it's based directly on this event-response paradigm; event handlers are primary "words" in the language (in many languages, this is not the case). You begin defining a behavior by dragging out an *event block*, which has the form, "When <event> do". For example, consider an app, SpeakIt, that responds to button clicks by speaking the text the user has entered aloud. This application could be programmed with a single event handler, shown in Figure 14-6.

Figure 14-6. An event handler for a SpeakIt app

These blocks specify that when the user clicks the button named SpeakItButton, the TextToSpeech component should speak the words the user has entered in the text box named TextBox1. The response is the call to the function **TextToSpeech1.Speak**. The event is **SpeakItButton.Click**. The event handler includes all the blocks in Figure 14-6.

With App Inventor, all activity occurs in response to an event. Your app shouldn't contain blocks outside of an event's "when-do" block. For instance, the blocks in Figure 14-7 don't make sense floating alone.

Figure 14-7. Floating blocks won't do anything outside an event handler

Event Types

The events that can trigger activity fall into the categories listed in Table 14-2.

Table 14-2. Events that can trigger activity

Event type	Example
User-initiated event	*When* the user clicks button1, *do*...
Initialization event	*When* the app launches, *do*...
Timer event	*When* 20 milliseconds passes, *do*...
Animation event	*When* two objects collide, *do*...
External event	*When* the phone receives a text, *do*...

User-initiated events

User-initiated events are the most common type of event. With input forms, it is typically the button click event that triggers a response from the app. More graphical apps respond to touches and drags.

Initialization events

Sometimes your app needs to perform certain functions right when the app begins, not in response to any end-user activity or other event. How does this fit into the event-handling paradigm?

Event-handling languages like App Inventor consider the app's launch as an event. If you want specific functions to be performed immediately when the app opens, you drag out a **Screen1.Initialize** event block and place some function call blocks within it.

For instance, in the game MoleMash (Chapter 3), the MoveMole procedure is called at the start of the app to randomly place the mole, as shown in Figure 14-8.

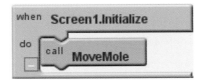

Figure 14-8. Using a Screen1.Initialize event block to move the mole when the app begins

Timer events

Some activity in an app is triggered by the passing of time. You can think of an animation as an object that moves when triggered by a *timer event*. App Inventor has a Clock component that can be used to trigger timer events. For instance, if you wanted a ball on the screen to move 10 pixels horizontally at a set time interval, your blocks would look like Figure 14-9.

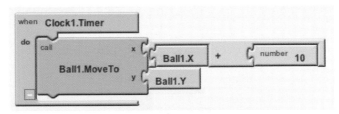

Figure 14-9. Using a timer event block to move a ball whenever Clock1.Timer fires

Animation events

Activity involving graphical objects (sprites) within canvases will trigger events. So you can program games and other interactive animations by specifying what should occur when two objects collide or when an object reaches the edge of the canvas. For more information, see Chapter 17.

External events

When your phone receives location information from GPS satellites, an event is triggered. Likewise, when your phone receives a text, an event is triggered (Figure 14-10).

Such external inputs to the device are considered events, just like the user clicking a button.

So every app you create will be a set of event handlers: one to initialize things, some to respond to the end user's input, some triggered by time, and some triggered by external events. Your job is to conceptualize your app in this way and then design the response to each event handler.

Figure 14-10. The Texting1.MessageReceived event is triggered whenever a text is received

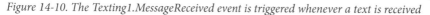

Event Handlers Can Ask Questions

The responses to events are not always linear recipes; they can ask questions and repeat operations. "Asking questions" means to query the data the app has stored and determine its course (branch) based on the answers. We say that such apps have *conditional branches*, as illustrated in Figure 14-11.

In the diagram, when the event occurs, the app performs operation A and then checks a condition. Function B1 is performed if the condition is true. If the condition is false, the app instead performs B2. In either case, the app continues on to perform function C.

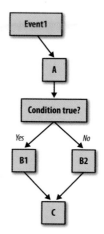

Figure 14-11. An event handler can branch based on the answer to a conditional question

Conditional tests are questions such as "Has the score reached 100?" or "Did the text I just received come from Joe?" Tests can also be more complex formulas including multiple relational operators (less than, greater than, equal to) and logical operators (and, or, not).

You specify conditional behaviors in App Inventor with the **if** and **ifelse** blocks. For instance, the block in Figure 14-12 would report "You Win!" if the player scored 100 points.

Conditional blocks are discussed in detail in Chapter 18.

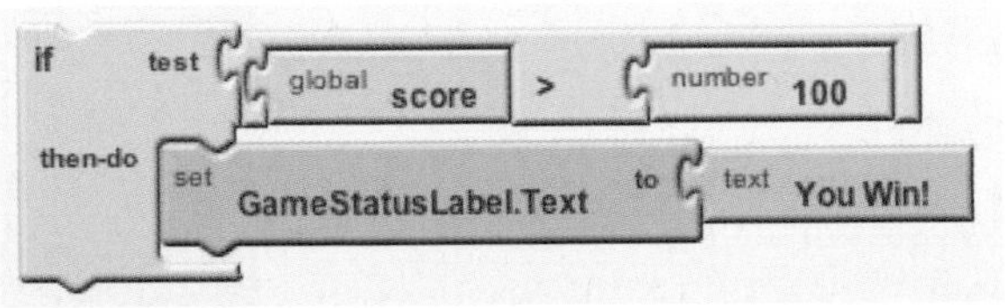

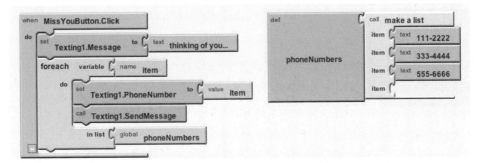

Figure 14-12. Using an if block to report a win once the player reaches 100 points

Event Handlers Can Repeat Blocks

In addition to asking questions and branching based on the answer, your app can also repeat operations multiple times. App Inventor provides two blocks for repeating, the **foreach** and the **while do**. Both enclose other blocks. All the blocks within **foreach** are performed once for each item in a list. For instance, if you wanted to text the same message to a list of phone numbers, you could use the blocks in Figure 14-13.

Figure 14-13. The blocks within the foreach block are repeated for each item in the list

The blocks within the **foreach** block are repeated—in this case, three times, because the list **PhoneNumbers** has three items. So the message "thinking of you…" is sent to all three numbers. Repeating blocks are discussed in detail in Chapter 20.

Event Handlers Can Remember Things

Because an event handler executes blocks, it often needs to keep track of information. Information can be stored in memory slots called *variables*, which you define in the Blocks Editor. Variables are like component properties, but they're not associated with any particular component. In a game app, for example, you can define a variable called "score" and your event handlers would modify its value when the user does something accordingly. Variables store data temporarily while an app is running; when you close the app, the data is no longer available.

Sometimes your app needs to remember things not just while it runs, but even when it is closed and then reopened. If you tracked a high score for the history of a game, for example, you'd need to store this data long-term so it is available the next time someone plays the game. Data that is retained even after an app is closed is called *persistent data*, and it's stored in some type of a database.

We'll explore the use of both short-term memory (variables) and long-term memory (database data) in Chapters 16 and 22, respectively.

Event Handlers Can Talk to the Web

Some apps use only the information within the phone or device. But many apps communicate with the Web by sending requests to *web service APIs* (*application programming interfaces*). Such apps are said to be "web-enabled."

Twitter is an example of a web service to which an App Inventor app can talk. You can write apps that request and display your friend's previous tweets and also update your Twitter status. Apps that talk to more than one web service are called *mashups*. We'll explore web-enabled apps in Chapter 24.

Summary

An app creator must view his app both from an end-user perspective and from the inside-out perspective of a programmer. With App Inventor, you design how an app looks and then you design its behavior—the set of event handlers that make an app behave as you want. You build these event handlers by assembling and configuring blocks representing events, functions, conditional branches, repeat loops, web calls, database operations, and more, and then test your work by actually running the app on your phone. After you write a few programs, the mapping between the internal structure of an app and its physical appearance becomes clear. When that happens, you're a programmer!

CHAPTER 15

Engineering and Debugging an App

HelloPurr, MoleMash, and the other apps covered in this book's early chapters are relatively small software projects and don't really require what people often refer to as engineering. That term is co-opted from other industries; think about building a scale model of a house from a premade kit versus designing and building your own real home. That's a slightly exaggerated example, but in general, the process of building something extremely complex that requires a significant  *amount of forethought, planning, and technique falls under the umbrella of engineering. As soon as you take on a more complicated project, you'll realize that the difficulty of building software increases rapidly for each bit of complexity you add—it is not anywhere close to a linear relationship. For most of us, it takes a few hard knocks before we realize this fact. At that point, you'll be ready to learn some software engineering principles and debugging techniques. If you're already at that point, or if you're one of those few people who want to learn a few techniques in the hope of avoiding some of those growing pains, this chapter is for you.*

Software Engineering Principles

Here are some basic principles that we'll cover in this chapter:

- Involve your prospective users in the process as early and as often as possible.
- Build an initial, simpler prototype and then add to it incrementally.
- Code and test in small increments—never more than a few blocks at a time.
- Design the logic for your app before beginning to code.
- Divide, layer, and conquer.
- Comment your blocks so others (and you) can understand them.
- Learn to trace blocks with pencil and paper so that you understand their mechanics.

If you follow this advice, you will save yourself time and frustration and build better software. But you probably won't follow it every time! Some of this advice may seem counterintuitive. Your natural inclination is to think of an idea, assume you know what your users want, and then start piecing together blocks until you think you've finished the app. Let's go back to the first principle and look at how to understand what your users want before you start building anything.

Design for Real People with Real Problems

In the movie *Field of Dreams*, the character Ray hears a voice whisper, "If you build it, [they] will come." Ray listens to the whisper, builds a baseball field in the middle of his Iowa corn patch, and indeed, the 1919 White Sox and thousands of fans show up.

You should know right now that the whisperer's advice does not apply to software. In fact, it's the opposite of what you should do. The history of software is littered with great solutions *for which there is no problem* ("Let's write an app that will tell people how long it takes to drive their car to the moon!"). Solving a *real* problem is what makes for an amazing (and hopefully, in most cases, profitable) app. And to know what the problem is, you've got to talk to the people who have it. This is often referred to as *user-centered* design, and it will help you build better apps.

If you meet some programmers, ask them what percentage of the programs they have written have actually been deployed with real users. You'll be surprised at how low the percentage is, even for great programmers. Most software projects run into so many issues that they don't even see the light of day.

User-centered design means thinking and talking to prospective users early and often. This should really start even before you decide what to build. Most successful software was built to solve a particular person's pain point, and then—and only then—generalized into the next big thing.

Build a Quick Prototype and Show It to Your Prospective Users

Most prospective users won't react too well if you ask them to read a document that specifies what the app will do and give their feedback based on that. What *does* work is to show them an interactive model for the app you're going to create—a *prototype*. A prototype is an incomplete, unrefined version of the app. When you build it, don't worry about details or completeness or having a beautiful graphical interface; build it so that it does just enough to illustrate the core value-add of the app. Then, show it to your prospective users, be quiet, and listen.

Incremental Development

When you begin your first significantly sized app, your natural inclination might be to add all of the components and blocks you'll need in one grand effort and then download the app to your phone to see if it works. Take, for instance, a quiz app. Without guidance, most beginning programmers will add blocks with a long list of the questions and answers, blocks to handle the quiz navigation, blocks to handle checking the user's answer, and blocks for every detail of the app's logic, all before testing to see if any of it works. In software engineering, this is called the *Big Bang approach*.

Just about every beginning programmer uses this approach. In my classes at USF, I will often ask a student, "How's it going?" as he's working on an app.

"I think I'm done," he'll reply.

"Splendid. Can I see it?"

"Ummm, not yet; I don't have my phone with me."

"So you haven't run the app at all?" I ask.

"No…."

I'll look over his shoulder at an amazing, colorful configuration of 30 or so blocks. But he hasn't tested a single piece of functionality.

It's easy to get mesmerized and drawn into building your UI and creating all the behavior you need in the Blocks Editor. A beautiful arrangement of perfectly interconnected blocks becomes the programmer's focus instead of a complete, tested app that someone else can use. It sounds like a shampoo commercial, but the best advice I can give my students—and aspiring programmers everywhere—is this:

> *Code a little, test a little, repeat.*

Build your app one piece at a time, testing as you go. Soon enough, even this process will become surprisingly satisfying, because you'll see results sooner (and have fewer big, nasty bugs) when you follow it.

Design Before Coding

There are two parts to programming: understanding the logic of the app, and then translating that logic into some form of programming language. Before you tackle the translation, spend some time on the logic. Specify what should happen both for the user and internally in the app. Nail down the logic of each event handler before moving on to translating that logic into blocks.

Entire books have been written on various program design methodologies. Some people use diagrams like flowcharts or structure charts for design, while others prefer handwritten text and sketches. Some believe that all "design" should end up directly alongside your code as annotation (comments), not in a separate document.

The key for beginning programmers is to understand that there is a logic to all programs that has nothing to do with a particular programming language. Simultaneously
tackling both that logic and its translation into a language, no matter how intuitive the
language, can be overwhelming. So, throughout the process, get away from the computer and think about your app, make sure you're clear on what you want it to do, and
document what you come up with in some way. Then be sure and hook that "design
documentation" to your app so others can benefit from it. We'll cover this next.

Comment Your Code

If you've completed a few of the tutorials in this book, you've probably seen the
yellow boxes that appear in some block samples (see Figure 15-1). These are called
comments. In App Inventor, you can add comments to any block by right-clicking it
and choosing Add Comment. Comments are just annotation; they don't affect the
app's execution at all.

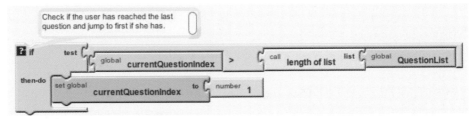

Figure 15-1. Using a comment on the if block to describe what it does in plain English

Why comment then? Well, if your app is successful, it will live a long life. Even after
spending only a week away from your app, you will forget what you were thinking
at the time and not have a clue what some of the blocks do. For this reason, even if
nobody else will ever see your blocks, you should add comments to them.

And if your app is successful, it will undoubtedly pass through many hands. People
will want to understand it, customize it, extend it. As soon as you have the wonderful
experience of starting a project with someone's uncommented code, you'll understand completely why comments are essential.

Commenting a program is not intuitive, and I've never met a beginning programmer
who thought it was important. But I've also never met an experienced programmer
who didn't do it.

Divide, Layer, and Conquer

Problems become overwhelming when they're too big. The key is to break a problem down. There are two main ways to do this. The one we're most familiar with is
to break a problem down into parts (A, B, C) and tackle each one individually. The

second, less common way is to break a problem into layers from simple to complex. Add a few blocks for some simple behavior, test the software to make sure it behaves as you want, add another layer of complexity, and so on.

Let's use the MakeQuiz app in Chapter 10 as an example for evaluating these two methods. That app lets the user navigate through the questions by clicking a Next button. It also checks the user's answers to see if she's correct. So, in designing this app, you might break it into two parts—question navigation and answer checking—and program each separately.

But within each of those two parts, you could also break down the process from simple to complex. So, for question navigation, start by creating the code to display only the first question in the list of questions, and test it to make sure it works. Then build the code for getting to the next question, but ignore the issue of what happens when you get to the last question. Once you've tested that the quiz will take you to the end, add the blocks to handle the "special case" of the user reaching the last question.

It's not an either/or case of whether you should break a problem down into parts or into layers of complexity, but it's worth considering which approach might help you more based on what you're actually building.

Understand Your Language: Tracing with Pen and Paper

When an app is in action, it is only partially visible. The end user of an app sees only its outward face—the images and data that are displayed in the user interface. The inner workings of software are hidden to the outside world, just like the internal mechanisms of the human brain (thankfully!). As an app executes, we don't see the instructions (blocks), we don't see the program counter that tracks which instruction is currently being executed, and we don't see the software's internal memory cells (its variables and properties). In the end, this is how we want it: the end user should see only what the program explicitly displays. But while you are developing and testing software, you want to see *everything* that is happening.

You as the programmer see the code during development, but only a static view of it. Thus, you must *imagine* the software in action: events occurring, the program counter moving to and executing the next block, the values in the memory cells changing, and so on.

Programming requires a shift between two different views. You begin with the static model—the code blocks—and try to envision how the program will actually behave. When you are ready, you shift to testing mode: playing the role of the end user and testing the software to see if it behaves as you expect. If it does not, you must shift back to the static view, tweak your model, and test again. Through this back and forth process, you move toward an acceptable solution.

When you begin programming, you have only a partial model of how a computer program works—the entire process seems almost magical. You begin with some simple apps: clicking a button causes a cat to meow! You then move on to more complex apps, step through some tutorials, and maybe make a few changes to customize them. The beginner partially understands the inner workings of the apps but certainly does not feel in control of the process. The beginner will often say, "*it's* not working," or "*it's* not doing what it's supposed to do." The key is to learn how things work to the point that you think more subjectively about the program and instead say things such as, "*My* program is doing this," and "*My* logic is causing the program to…."

One way to learn how programs work is to trace the execution of some simple app, representing *on paper* exactly what happens inside the device when each block is performed. Envision the user triggering some event handler and then step through and show the effect of each block: how the variables and properties in the app change, how the components in the user interface change. Like a "close reading" in a literature class, this step-by-step *tracing* forces you to examine the elements of the language—in this case, App Inventor blocks.

The complexity of the sample you trace is almost immaterial; the key is that you slow down your thought process and examine the cause and effect of each block. You'll gradually begin to understand that the rules governing the whole process are not as overwhelming as you originally thought.

For example, consider these slightly altered blocks, shown in Figures 15-2 and 15-3, from the Presidents Quiz app (Chapter 8).

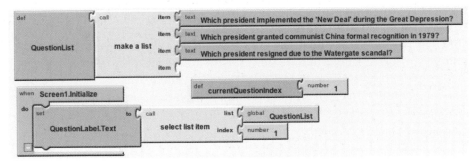

Figure 15-2. Setting the Text in QuestionLabel to the first item in QuestionList when the app begins

Do you understand this code? Can you trace it and show exactly what happens in each step?

You start tracing by first drawing memory cell boxes for all pertinent variables and properties. In this case, you need boxes for the currentQuestionIndex and the QuestionLabel.Text, as shown in Table 15-1.

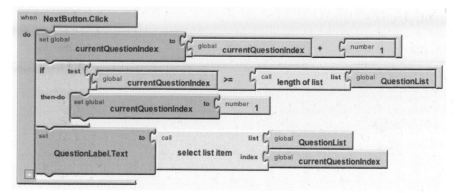

Figure 15-3. This block is executed when the user clicks the NextButton

Table 15-1. Boxes to hold the changing text and index values

QuestionLabel.Text	currentQuestionIndex

Next, think about what happens when an app begins—not from a user's perspective, but internally within the app when it initializes. If you've completed some of the tutorials, you probably know this, but perhaps you haven't thought about it in mechanical terms. When an app begins:

1. All the component properties are set based on their initial values in the Component Designer.

2. All variable definitions and initializations are performed.

3. The blocks in the **Screen.Initialize** event handler are performed.

Tracing a program helps you understand these mechanics. So what should go in the boxes after the initialization phase?

As shown in Table 15-2, the 1 is in currentQuestionIndex because the variable definition is executed when the app begins, and it initializes it to 1. The first question is in QuestionLabel.Text because **Screen.Initialize** selects the first item from QuestionList and puts it there.

Table 15-2. The values after the Presidents Quiz app initializes

QuestionLabel.Text	currentQuestionIndex
Which president implemented the "New Deal" during the Great Depression?	1

Next, trace what happens when the user clicks the Next button. Examine each block one by one. First, the currentQuestionIndex is incremented. At an even more detailed level, the current value of the variable (1) is added to 1, and the result (2) is placed in `currentQuestionIndex`. The **if** statement is false because the value of `currentQuestionIndex` (2) is less than the length of `QuestionList` (3). So the second item is selected and put into `QuestionLabel.Text`, as illustrated in Table 15-3.

Table 15-3. The values after NextButton is clicked

QuestionLabel.Text	currentQuestionIndex
Which president granted communist China formal recognition in 1979?	2

Trace what happens on the second click. Now `currentQuestionIndex` is incremented and becomes 3. What happens with the **if**? Before reading ahead, examine it very closely and see if you can trace it correctly.

On the **if** test, the value of `currentQuestionIndex` (3) is indeed greater than or equal to the length of `QuestionList`. So the `currentQuestionIndex` is set to 1 and the first question is placed into the label, as shown in Table 15-4.

Table 15-4. The values after NextButton is clicked a second time

QuestionLabel.Text	currentQuestionIndex
Which president implemented the "New Deal" during the Great Depression?	1

Our trace has uncovered a bug: the last question in the list never appears!

It is through discoveries like this that you become a programmer, an engineer. You begin to understand the mechanics of the programming language, absorbing sentences and words in the code instead of vaguely grasping paragraphs. Yes, the programming language is complex, but each "word" has a definite and straightforward interpretation by the machine. If you understand how each block maps to some variable or property changing, you can figure out how to write or fix your app. You realize that *you* are in complete control.

Now if you tell your friends, "I'm learning how to let a user click a Next button to get to the next question; it's really tough," they'd think you were crazy. But such programming *is* very difficult, not because the concepts are so complex, but because you have to slow down your brain to figure out how it, or a computer, processes each and every step, including those things your brain does subconsciously.

Debugging an App

Tracing an app step by step is one way to understand programming; it's also a time-tested method of debugging an app when it has problems.

Tools like App Inventor (which are often referred to as *interactive development environments*, or *IDEs*) provide the high-tech version of pen-and-paper tracing through debugging tools that automate some of the process. Such tools improve the app development process by providing an illuminated view of an app *in action*. These tools allow the programmer to:

- Pause an app at any point and examine its variables and properties.
- Perform individual instructions (blocks) to examine their effects.

Watching Variables

Probably the most important capability a debugger can provide is to let you examine the value of variables and properties as an app executes—in essence, making the internal memory of the computer visible to the software developer.

App Inventor lets you do just that with its Watch mechanism, shown in Figure 15-4. (The variable definition block hidden from view is for currentQuestionIndex.) As you are live testing on the phone or emulator, you simply right-click any variable definition block within the Blocks Editor and choose Watch.

Figure 15-4. Using the Watch mechanism to view variable values as the app runs

A box appears that's connected to the "watched" variable, showing its current value. If you then play the role of the end user and initiate some events in the app, you'll see the variable's value change in the Blocks Editor as the user interface changes.

For example, if you were testing the NextButton behavior of a quiz app, you could watch the currentQuestionIndex variable, as shown in Figure 15-5. When the app starts, the variable should contain the value 1.

If you then click the NextButton in the user interface (on either the emulator or phone), the **NextButton.Click** event handler will be triggered, and the watch box will change when the variable is incremented, as shown in Figure 15-6.

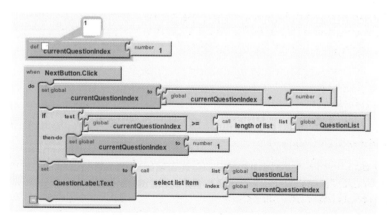

Figure 15-5. Testing the NextButton behavior by watching the currentQuestionIndex variable

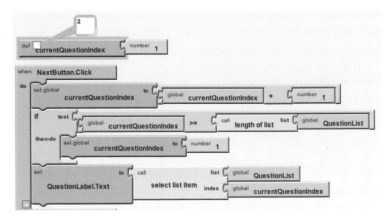

Figure 15-6. The watch box changes as the variable is incremented

Note that the value in the white watch box is the dynamic value of the variable as the app runs. The **number 1** block slotted into the variable definition never changes unless the programmer changes it; it is the initialization value, the value at which the variable will begin if you relaunch the app.

You could continue in this way, clicking the NextButton to test that the event handler works even when the boundary condition (arriving at the last question) is met. For our buggy blocks, you'd see that the index switched to 1 a step too early.

In essence, the Watch mechanism performs the pen-and-paper trace for you and lets you see the "hidden" memory of the app as it runs. It's a great way to really understand your app and discover bugs!

Testing Individual Blocks

While the Watch mechanism allows you to examine variables during an app's execution, another tool called Do It lets you try out individual blocks *outside* the ordinary execution sequence. Right-click any block and choose Do It, and the block will be performed. If the block is an expression that returns a value, App Inventor will show that value in a box above the block.

Do It is very useful in debugging logic problems in your blocks. Consider the quiz's **NextButton.Click** event handler again, and suppose it has a logic problem in which you don't navigate through all the questions. You could test the program by clicking Next in the user interface and checking to see if the appropriate question appears each time. You might even watch the currentQuestionIndex to see how each click changes it.

But this type of testing only allows you to examine the effect of entire event handlers. The app will perform all the blocks in the event handler for the button click before allowing you to examine your watch variables or the user interface.

The Do It tool lets you slow down the testing process and examine the state of the app after any block. The general scheme is to initiate user interface events until you get to the problem point in the app. After discovering that the third question wasn't appearing in the quiz app, you might click the NextButton once to get to the second question. Then, instead of clicking the NextButton again and having the entire event handler performed in one swoop, you could use Do It to perform the blocks within the **NextButton.Click** event handler one at a time. You'd start by right-clicking the top row of blocks (the increment of currentQuestionIndex) and choosing Do It, as illustrated in Figure 15-7.

This would change the index to 3. App execution would then stop—Do It causes only the chosen block and any subordinate blocks to be performed. This allows you, the tester, to examine the watched variables and the user interface. When you're ready, you can choose the next row of blocks (the **if** test) and select Do It so that it's performed. At every step of the way, you can see the effect of each block.

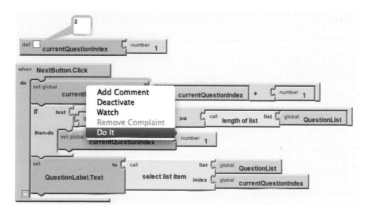

Figure 15-7. Using the Do It tool to perform the blocks one at a time

Incremental Development with Do It

It's important to note that performing individual blocks is not just for debugging. It can also be used during development to test blocks as you go. For instance, if you were creating a long formula to compute the distance in miles between two GPS coordinates, you might test the formula at each step to verify that the blocks make sense.

Activating and Deactivating Blocks

Another way to help you debug and test your app incrementally is to activate and deactivate blocks. This allows you to leave problematic or untested blocks in an app but tell the system to ignore them temporarily as the app runs. You can then test the activated blocks and get them to work fully without worrying about the problematic ones.

You can deactivate any block by right-clicking it and choosing Deactivate. The block will be grayed out, and when you run the app it will be ignored. When you're ready, you can activate the block by right-clicking it again and choosing Activate.

Summary

The great thing about App Inventor is how easy it is—its visual nature gets you started building an app right away, and you don't have to worry about a lot of low-level details. But the reality is that App Inventor can't figure out what your app should do for you, much less exactly *how* to do it. Even though it's tempting to just jump right into the Designer and Blocks Editor and start building an app, it's important to spend some time thinking about and planning in detail what exactly your app will do. It sounds a bit painful, but if you listen to your users, prototype, test, and trace the logic of your app, you'll be building better apps in no time.

CHAPTER 16

Programming Your App's Memory

Just as people need to remember things, so do apps. This chapter examines how you can program an app to remember information.

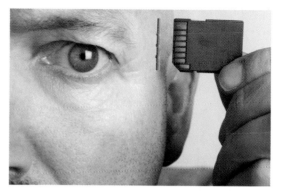

When someone tells you the phone number of a pizza place for a one-time immediate call, your brain stores it in a memory slot. If someone calls out some numbers for you to add, you also store the immediate results in a memory slot. In such cases, you are not fully conscious of how your brain stores information or recalls it.

An app has a memory as well, but its inner workings are far less mysterious than those of your brain. In this chapter, you'll learn how to set up an app's memory, how to store information in it, and how to retrieve that information at a later time.

Named Memory Slots

An app's memory consists of a set of *named memory slots.* Some of these memory slots are created when you drag a component into your app; these slots are called *properties.* You can also define named memory slots that are not associated with a particular component; these are called *variables.* Whereas properties are typically associated with what is visible in an app, variables can be thought of as the app's hidden "scratch" memory.

Properties

Components—at least the visible ones like Button, TextBox, and Canvas—are part of the user interface. But to the app, each component is completely defined by a set of properties. The values stored in the memory slots of each property determine how the component appears.

You can modify property memory slots directly in the Component Designer, as shown in Figure 16-1.

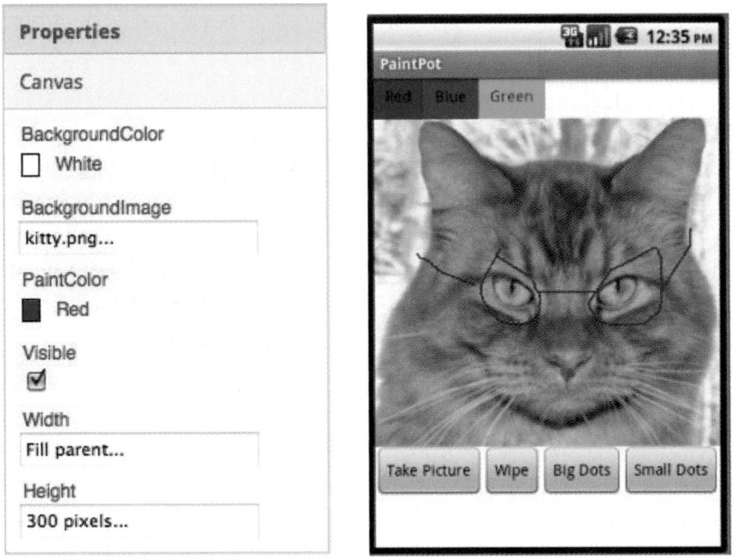

Figure 16-1. Modifying the memory slots in the property form to change the app's appearance

The Canvas component of Figure 16-1 has six properties. The BackgroundColor and PaintColor are memory slots that hold a color. The BackgroundImage holds a filename (*kitty.png*). The Visible property holds a *Boolean* value (true or false, depending on whether the box is checked). The Width and Height slots hold a number or a special designation (e.g., "Fill parent").

When you change a property in the Component Designer, you are specifying how the app should appear when it's launched. Someone using the app (the end user) never sees that there is a memory slot named Height containing a value of 300. The end user only sees the user interface with a component that is 300 pixels tall.

Defining Variables

Like properties, variables are named memory slots, but they are not associated with a particular component. You define a variable when your app needs to remember something that is not being stored within a component property. For example, a game app might need to remember what level the user has reached. If the level number were going to appear in a Label component, you might not need a variable, because you could just store the level in the Text property of the Label component. But if the level number is not something the user will see, you'd define a variable to store it.

The Presidents Quiz (Chapter 8) is another example of an app that needs a variable. In that app, only one question of the quiz should appear at a time in the user interface, while the rest of the questions are kept hidden from the user. Thus, you need to define a variable to store the list of questions.

Whereas properties are created automatically when you drag a component into the Component Designer, you define a new variable explicitly in the Blocks Editor by dragging out a **def variable** block. You can name the variable by clicking the text "variable" within the block, and you can specify an initial value by dragging out a **number**, **text**, **color**, or **make a list** block and plugging it in. Here are the steps you'd follow to create a variable called score with an initial value of 0:

1. Drag the **def variable** block (Figure 16-2) from the Definitions folder in the Built-In blocks.

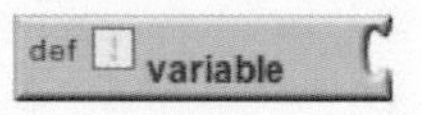

Figure 16-2. A def variable block

2. Change the name of the variable by clicking on the text "variable" and typing "score", as illustrated in Figure 16-3.

Figure 16-3. Changing the variable name

3. Set the initial value to a number by dragging out the **number** block and plugging it into the variable definition (Figure 16-4).

Figure 16-4. Setting the value to a number

4. Change the initial value from the default number (123) to 0 (Figure 16-5).

Figure 16-5. Setting the initial value to 0

When you define a variable, you tell the app to set up a named memory slot for storing a value. These slots, as with properties, are not visible to the user.

The initialization block you plug in specifies the value that should be placed in the slot when the app begins. Besides initializing with numbers or text, you can also place a **make a list** block into the **def var** block. This tells the app that the variable names a list of memory slots instead of a single value. To learn more about lists, see Chapter 19.

Setting and Getting a Variable

When you define a variable, App Inventor creates two blocks for it, both of which appear in the My Definitions drawer, shown in Figure 16-6.

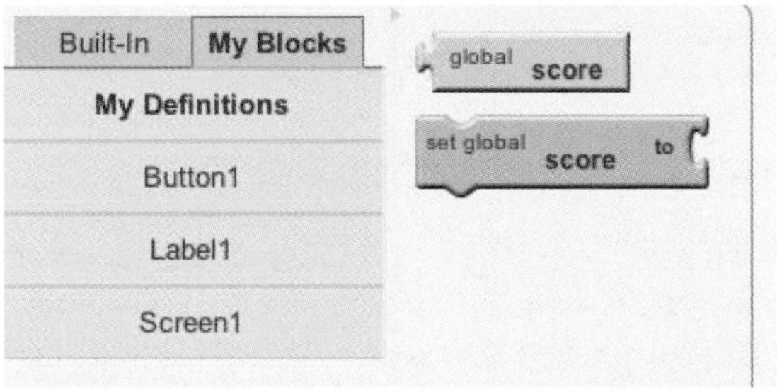

Figure 16-6. The My Definitions drawer contains set and get blocks for your variable

The **set global to** block lets you modify (set) the value stored in the variable. For instance, the blocks in Figure 16-7 place a 5 in the variable **score**. The term "global" in the **set global score to** block refers to the fact that the variable can be used in all of the program's event handlers (globally). Some programming languages allow you to define variables that are "local" to a particular part of the program; App Inventor does not.

Figure 16-7. Placing a number 5 into the variable score

The block labeled **global score** helps you retrieve (get) the value of a variable. For instance, if you wanted to check if the score was 100 or greater, you'd plug the **global score** block into an **if** test, as demonstrated in Figure 16-8.

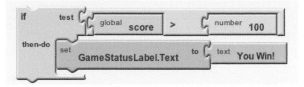

Figure 16-8. Using the global score block to get the value stored in the variable

Setting a Variable to an Expression

You can put simple values like 5 into a variable, but often you'll set the variable to a more complex *expression* (expression is the computer science term for a formula). For example, when the user clicks Next to get to the next question in a quiz app, you'll need to set the `currentQuestion` variable to *one more than its current value*. When someone does something bad in a game app, you might modify the `score` variable to *10 less than its current value*. In a game like MoleMash (Chapter 3), you change the horizontal (*x*) location of the mole to *a random position within a canvas*. You'll build such expressions with a set of blocks that plug into a **set global to** block.

Incrementing a Variable

Perhaps the most common expression is for *incrementing* a variable, or setting a variable based on its own current value. For instance, in a game, when the player scores a point, the variable `score` can be incremented by 1. Figure 16-9 shows the blocks to implement this behavior.

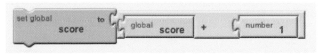

Figure 16-9. Incrementing the variable score by 1

If you can understand these kinds of blocks, you're well on your way to becoming a programmer. You read these blocks as "set the score to one more than it already is," which is another way to say *increment* your variable. The way it works is that the blocks are interpreted inside out, not left to right. So the innermost blocks—the **global score** and the **number 1** block—are evaluated first. Then the + block is performed and the result is "set" into the variable `score`.

Supposing there were a 5 in the memory slot for score before these blocks, the app would perform the following steps:

1. Retrieve the 5 from score's memory slot.

2. Add 1 to it to get 6.

3. Place the 6 into score's memory slot (replacing the 5).

For more on incrementing, see Chapter 19.

Building Complex Expressions

In the Math drawer of the Built-In blocks (Figure 16-10), App Inventor provides a wide range of mathematical functions similar to those you'd find in a spreadsheet or calculator.

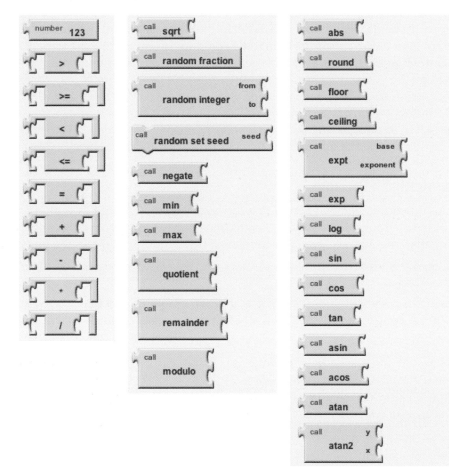

Figure 16-10. The blocks contained in the Math drawer

You can use these blocks to build a complex expression and then plug them in as the *righthand-side expression* of a **set variable to** block. For example, to move an image sprite to a random column within the bounds of a canvas, you'd configure an expression consisting of a * (multiply) block, a – (subtract) block, a Canvas.Width property, and a **random fraction** function, as illustrated in Figure 16-11.

Figure 16-11. You can use math blocks to build complex expressions like this one

As with the increment example in the previous section, the blocks are interpreted by the app in an inside-out fashion. Supposing the Canvas has a Width of 300 and the ImageSprite has a Width of 50, the app would perform the following steps:

1. Retrieve the 300 and the 50 from the memory slots for **Canvas1.Width** and **ImageSprite.Width**, respectively.

2. Subtract: 300 – 50 = 250.

3. Call the **random fraction** function to get a number between 0 and 1 (say, .5).

4. Multiply: 250 * .5 = 125.

5. Place the 125 into the memory slot for the ImageSprite1.X property.

Displaying Variables

When you modify a component property, as in the preceding example, the user interface is directly affected. This is not true for variables; changing a variable has no direct effect on the app's appearance. If you just incremented a variable score but didn't modify the user interface in some other way, the user would never know there was a change. It's like the proverbial tree falling in the forest: if nobody was there to hear it, did it really happen?

Sometimes you do not want to immediately manifest a change to the user interface when a variable changes. For instance, in a game you might track statistics (e.g., missed shots) that will only appear when the game ends.

This is one of the advantages of storing data in a variable as opposed to a component property: it allows you to show just the data you want when you want to show it. It also allows you to separate the computational part of your app from the user interface, making it easier to change that user interface later.

For example, with a game you could store the score directly in a Label or in a variable. If you store it in a Label, you'd increment the Label's Text property when points were scored, and the user would see the change directly. If you stored the score in a variable and incremented the variable when points were scored, you'd need to include blocks to also move the value of the variable into a label.

However, if you decided to change the app to display the score in a different manner, the variable solution would be easier to change. You wouldn't need to find all the places that change the score; those blocks would be unmodified. You'd only need to modify the display blocks.

The solution using the Label and no variable would be harder to change, as you'd need to replace all the increment changes with, say, modifications to the Width of the label.

Summary

When an app is launched, it begins executing its operations and responding to events that occur. When responding to events, the app sometimes needs to remember things. For a game, this might be each player's score or the direction in which an object is moving.

Your app remembers things within component properties, but when you need additional memory slots not associated with a component, you can define variables. You can store values into a variable and retrieve the current value, just like you do with properties.

As with property values, variable values are not visible to the end user. If you want the end user to see the information stored in a variable, you add blocks that display that information in a label or another user interface component.

CHAPTER 17

Creating Animated Apps

This chapter discusses methods for creating apps with simple animations—objects that move. You'll learn the basics of creating two-dimensional games with App Inventor and become comfortable with image sprites and handling events like two objects colliding.

When you see an object moving smoothly along the computer screen, what you're really seeing is a quick succession of images with the object in a slightly different place each time. It's an illusion not much different from "flipbooks," in which you see a moving picture by flipping quickly through the pages (and it's also how far more sophisticated animated films are made!).

With App Inventor, you'll define animation by placing objects within a Canvas component and moving those objects around the Canvas over time. In this chapter, you'll learn how the Canvas coordinate system works, how the **Clock.Timer** event can be used to trigger movement, how to control the speed of objects, and how to respond to events such as two objects colliding.

Adding a Canvas Component to Your App

You can drag a Canvas component into your app from the Basic palette. After dragging it out, specify the Canvas's Width and Height. Often, you'll want the Canvas to span the width of the device screen. To do this, choose "Fill parent" when specifying the Width, as shown in Figure 17-1.

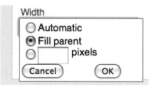

Figure 17-1. Setting the Canvas's Width to span the screen

You can do the same for the Height, but generally you'll set it to some number (e.g., 300 pixels) to leave room for other components above and below the Canvas.

The Canvas Coordinate System

A drawing on a canvas is really a table of *pixels*, where a pixel is the tiniest possible dot of color that can appear on the phone (or other device). Each pixel has a location (or table cell) on the canvas, which is defined by an *x–y* coordinate system, as illustrated in Figure 17-2. In this coordinate system, *x* defines a location on the horizontal plane (left to right), and *y* defines a location on the vertical plane (up and down).

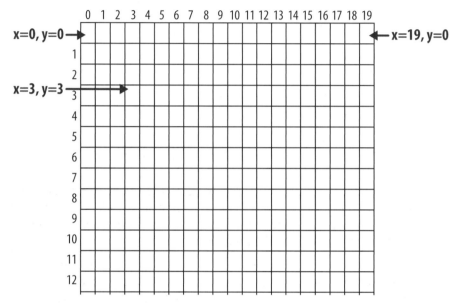

Figure 17-2. The Canvas coordinate system

It might seem a bit counterintuitive, but the top-left cell in a Canvas starts with 0 for both coordinates, so this position is represented as (*x*=0,*y*=0). (This is different than the index you use in App Inventor for lists, which starts at the seemingly more normal value of 1.) As you move right, the *x* coordinate gets larger; as you move down, the *y* coordinate gets larger. The cell to the immediate right of the top-left corner is (*x*=1,*y*=0). The top-right corner has an *x* coordinate equal to the width of the canvas minus 1. Most phone screens have a width close to 300, but for the sample canvas shown here, the Width is 20, so the top-right corner is the coordinate (*x*=19,*y*=0).

You can change the appearance of the canvas in two ways: (1) by painting on it, or (2) by placing and moving objects within it. This chapter will focus primarily on the latter, but let's first discuss how you "paint" and how to create animation by painting (this is also the topic of the PaintPot app in Chapter 2).

Each cell of the canvas holds a pixel defining the color that should appear there. The Canvas component provides the **Canvas.DrawLine** and **Canvas.DrawCircle** blocks for painting pixels on it. You first set the Canvas.PaintColor property to the color you want and then call one of the Draw blocks to draw in that color. With **DrawCircle**, you can paint circles of any radius, but if you set the radius to 1, as shown in Figure 17-3, you'll paint an individual pixel.

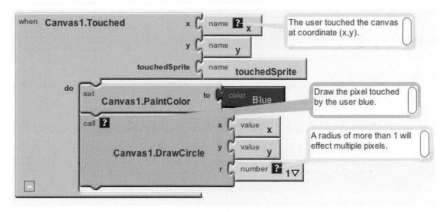

Figure 17-3. DrawCircle with radius 1 paints an individual pixel with each touch

App Inventor provides a palette of 14 basic colors that you can use to paint pixels (or component backgrounds). You can access a wider range of colors by using the color numbering scheme explained in the App Inventor documentation at *http://appinventor .googlelabs.com/learn/reference/blocks/colors.html*.

The second way to modify the appearance of a canvas is to place Ball and ImageSprite components on it. A *sprite* is a graphical object placed within a larger scene—in this case, a canvas. Both the Ball and ImageSprite components are sprites; they are different only in appearance. A Ball is a circle whose appearance can only be modified by changing its color or radius, whereas an ImageSprite can take on any appearance as defined by an image file you upload. Image Sprites and Balls can only be added within a Canvas; you can't drag them into the user interface outside of one.

Animating Objects with Timer Events

One way to specify animation in App Inventor is to change an object in response to a timer event. Most commonly, you'll move sprites to different locations on the canvas at set time intervals. Using timer events is the most general method of defining those set time intervals. Later, we'll also discuss an alternative method of programming animation using the ImageSprite and Ball components' Speed and Heading properties.

Button clicks and other user-initiated events are simple to understand: the user does something, and the app responds by performing some operations. Timer events are different: they aren't triggered by the end user but instead by the passing of time. You have to conceptualize the phone's clock triggering events in the app instead of a user doing something.

To define a timer event, you first drag a Clock component into your app within the Component Designer. The Clock component has a TimerInterval property associated with it. The interval is defined in terms of milliseconds (1/1,000 of a second). If you set the TimerInterval to 500, that means a timer event will be triggered every half-second. The smaller the TimerInterval, the faster your object will move.

After adding a Clock and setting a TimerInterval in the Designer, you can drag out a **Clock.Timer** event in the Blocks Editor. You can put any blocks you like in this event, and they'll be performed every time interval.

Creating Movement

To show a sprite moving over time, you'll use the **MoveTo** function found in both the ImageSprite and Ball components. For example, to move a ball *horizontally* across the screen, you'd use the blocks in Figure 17-4.

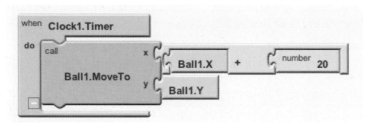

Figure 17-4. Moving the ball horizontally across the screen

MoveTo moves an object to an *absolute* location on the canvas, not a relative amount. So, to move an object some amount, you set the **MoveTo** arguments to the object's current location plus an offset. Since we're moving horizontally, the x argument is set to the current *x* location (**Ball1.X**) plus the offset 20, while the y argument is set to stay at its current setting (**Ball1.Y**).

If you wanted to move the ball diagonally, you'd add an offset to both the *x* and *y* coordinates, as shown in Figure 17-5.

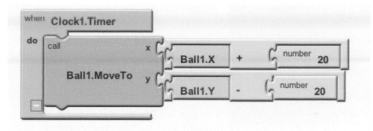

Figure 17-5. Offsetting both the x and y coordinates to move the ball diagonally

Speed

How fast is the ball moving in the preceding example? The speed depends on both the Clock's TimerInterval property and the parameters you specify in the **MoveTo** function. If the interval is set to 1,000 milliseconds, that means an event will be triggered every second. For the horizontal example shown in Figure 17-4, the ball will move 20 pixels per second.

But a TimerInterval of 1,000 milliseconds doesn't provide very smooth animation; the ball will only move every second, and this will appear jerky. To get smoother movement, you need a smaller interval. If the TimerInterval was set instead to 100 milliseconds, the ball would move 20 pixels every tenth of a second, or 200 pixels per second—a rate that will appear much smoother to anyone using your app. There's another way to change the speed instead of changing the timer interval—can you think of what that is? (*Hint:* Speed is a function of how often you move the ball and how far you move it each time.) You could also alter speed by keeping a timer interval of 1,000 milliseconds and instead changing the **MoveTo** operation so the ball only moves 2 pixels every time interval—2 pixels/100ms is still 20 pixels/second.

High-Level Animation Functions

The ability to move an object across the screen is useful for things like animated ads that slide in and out, but to build games and other animated apps, you need more complex functionality. Fortunately, App Inventor provides some high-level blocks for dealing with animation events such as an object reaching the screen's edge or two objects colliding.

In this context, *high-level block* means that App Inventor takes care of the *lower-level* details of determining events like when two sprites collide. You could check for such occurrences yourself using **Clock.Timer** events and checking the X,Y, Height, and Width properties of the sprites. Such programming would require some fairly complex logic, however. Because these events are common to many games and other apps, App Inventor provides them for you.

EdgeReached

Consider again the animation in which the object is moving diagonally from the top left to the bottom right of the canvas. As we programmed it, the object would move diagonally and then stop when it reached the right or bottom edge of the canvas (the system won't move an object past the canvas boundaries).

If you instead wanted the object to reappear at the top-left corner after it reaches the bottom right, you could define a response to the **Ball.EdgeReached** event shown in Figure 17-6.

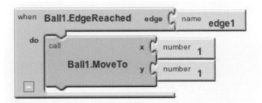

Figure 17-6. Making the ball reappear at the top-left corner when it reaches an edge

EdgeReached (an event that is applicable only for sprites and balls) is triggered when the `Ball` hits any edge of the canvas. This event handler, combined with the diagonal movement specified with the previously described timer event, will cause the ball to move diagonally from top left to bottom right, pop back up to the top left when it reaches the edge, and then do it all over again, forever (or until you tell it otherwise).

Note that there is an argument, `edge1`, with the **EdgeReached** event. The argument specifies which edge the ball reached, using the following directional numbering scheme:

- North = 1
- Northeast = 2
- East = 3
- Southeast = 4
- South = –1
- Southwest = –2
- West = –3
- Northwest = –4

CollidingWith and NoLongerCollidingWith

Shooting games, sports, and other animated apps often rely on activity occurring when two or more objects collide (e.g., a bullet hitting a target).

Consider a game, for instance, in which an object changes colors and plays an explosion sound when it hits another object. Figure 17-7 shows the blocks for such an event handler.

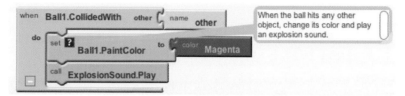

Figure 17-7. Making the ball change color and play an explosion sound when it hits another object

NoLongerCollidingWith provides the opposite event of **CollidedWith**. It is triggered only when two objects have come together and then separated. So, for your game, you might include blocks as shown in Figure 17-8.

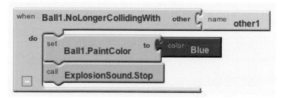

Figure 17-8. Changing the color back and stopping the explosion noise when the objects separate

Note that both **CollidedWith** and **NoLongerCollidingWith** have an argument, other. other specifies the particular object you collided with (or separated from). This allows you to perform operations only when the object (e.g., Ball1) interacts with a particular other object, as shown in Figure 17-9.

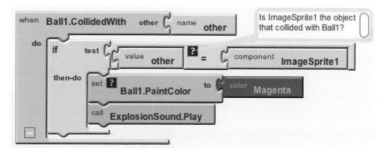

Figure 17-9. Only perform the response if Ball1 hit ImageSprite1

The **component ImageSprite1** block is one we haven't yet discussed. When you need to compare components (to know which ones have collided), as in this example, you must have some way to refer to a specific component. For this reason, each component has a special block that refers to itself. So, in the drawer for ImageSprite1, you'll find the **component ImageSprite1** block.

Interactive Animation

In the animated behaviors we've discussed so far, the end user isn't involved. Of course, games are interactive, with the end user playing a central role. Often, the end user controls the speed or direction of an object with buttons or other user interface objects.

As an example, let's update the diagonal animation by allowing the user to stop and start the diagonal movement. You can do this by programming a **Button.Click** event handler to disable and reenable the timer event of the clock component.

By default, the Clock component's timerEnabled property is checked. You can disable it dynamically by setting it to false in an event handler. The event handler in Figure 17-10, for example, would stop the activity of a Clock timer on the first click.

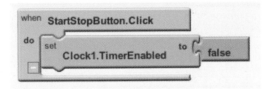

Figure 17-10. Stopping the timer the first time the button is clicked

After the Clock1.TimerEnabled property is set to false, the **Clock1.Timer** event will no longer trigger, and the ball will stop moving.

Of course, stopping the movement on the first click isn't too interesting. Instead, you could "toggle" the movement of the ball by adding an **ifelse** in the event handler that either enables or disables the timer, as shown in Figure 17-11.

This event handler stops the timer on first click, and resets the button so that it says "Start" instead of "Stop." The second time the user clicks the button, the TimerEnabled is false, so the "else" part is executed. In this case, the timer is enabled, which gets the object moving again, and the button text is switched back to "Stop." For more information about **ifelse** blocks, see Chapter 18, and for examples of interactive animations that use the orientation sensor, see Chapters 5 and 23.

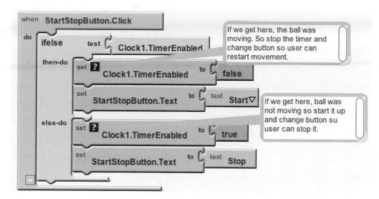

Figure 17-11. Adding an ifelse so that clicking the button starts and stops the movement of the ball

Specifying Sprite Animation Without a Clock Timer

The animation samples described so far use a Clock component and specify that an object should move each time the Clock's timer event is triggered. The **Clock.Timer** event scheme is the most general method of specifying animation; other than moving an object, you could also have it change an object's color over time, change some text (to appear as though the app is typing), or have the app speak words at a certain pace.

For object movement, App Inventor provides an alternative that doesn't require the use of a Clock component. As you may have noticed, the ImageSprite and Ball components have properties for Heading, Speed, and Interval. Instead of defining a **Clock.Timer** event handler, you can set these properties in the Component Designer or Blocks Editor to control how a sprite moves.

To illustrate, let's reconsider the example that moved a ball diagonally. The Heading property of a sprite or ball has a range of 360 degrees, as seen in Figure 17-12.

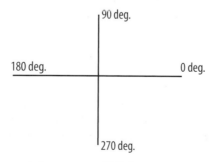

Figure 17-12. The Heading property has a range of 360 degrees

If you set the Heading to 0, the ball will move left to right. If you set it to 90, it will move bottom to top. If you set it to 180, it will move right to left. If you set it to 270, it will move top to bottom.

Of course, you can set it to any number between 0 and 360. To move a ball diagonally from top left to bottom right, you'd set the Heading to 315. You also need to set the Speed property to a value other than 0. The Speed property works the same way as moving objects with **MoveTo**: it specifies the number of pixels the object will move per time interval, where the interval is defined by the object's Interval property.

To try out these properties, create a test app with a Canvas and Ball and click "Connect to Phone" to see your app. Then modify the Heading, Speed, and Interval properties of the ball to see how it moves.

If you wanted the program to continually move from top left to bottom right and then back, you'd initialize the ball's Heading property to 315 in the Component Designer. You'd then add the **Ball1.EdgeReached** event handler, shown in Figure 17-13, to change the ball's direction when it reaches either edge.

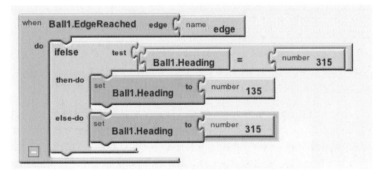

Figure 17-13. Changing the ball's direction when it reaches either edge

Summary

Animation is an object being moved or otherwise transformed over time, and App Inventor provides some high-level components and functionality to facilitate it. By programming the Clock component's Timer event, you can specify any type of animation, including object movement—the fundamental activity in almost any type of game.

The Canvas component allows you to define a subarea of the device's screen in which objects can move around and interact. You can put only two types of components, ImageSprites and Balls, within a Canvas. These components provide high-level functionality for handling events such as collisions and reaching a Canvas edge. They also have properties—Heading, Speed and Interval—that provide an alternative method of movement.

CHAPTER 18

Programming Your App to Make Decisions: Conditional Blocks

Computers, even small ones like the phone in your pocket, are good at performing thousands of operations in just a few seconds. Even more impressively, they can also make decisions based on the data in their memory banks and logic specified by the programmer. This decision-making capability is probably the key ingredient of what people think of as artificial intelligence—and it's definitely a very important part of creating smart, interesting apps! In this chapter, we'll explore how to build decision-making logic into your apps.

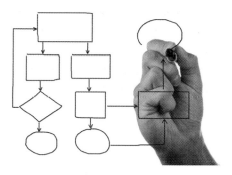

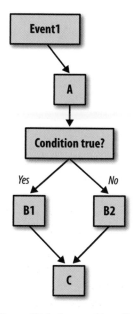

Figure 18-1. An event handler that tests for a condition and branches accordingly

As we discussed in Chapter 14, an app's behavior is defined by a set of event handlers. Each event handler executes specific functions in response to a particular event. The response need not be a linear sequence of functions, however; you can specify that some functions be performed only under certain conditions. A game app might check if the score has reached 100. A location-aware app might ask if the phone is within the boundaries of some building. Your app can ask such questions and, depending on the answer, proceed down a certain program *branch* (or direction).

Figure 18-1 depicts a flowchart of an event handler with a conditional check.

When the event occurs, function A is performed no matter what. Then a decision test is performed. If the test is true, B1 is performed. If it is false, B2 is performed. In either case, the rest of the event handler (C) is completed.

Because decision diagrams like the one in Figure 18-1 look something like trees, it is common to say that the app "branches" one way or the other depending on the test result. So, in this instance, you'd say, "If the test is true, the branch containing B1 is performed."

Testing Conditions with if and ifelse Blocks

App Inventor provides two types of conditional blocks (Figure 18-2): **if** and **ifelse**, both of which are found in the Control drawer of the Built-In palette.

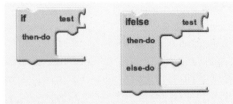

Figure 18-2. The if and ifelse conditional blocks

You can plug any *Boolean expression* into the "test" slot of these blocks. A Boolean expression is a mathematical equation that returns a result of either true or false. The expression tests the value of properties and variables using relational and logical operators such as the ones shown in Figure 18-3.

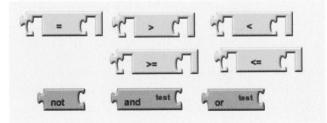

Figure 18-3. Relational and logical operator blocks used in conditional tests

For both **if** and **ifelse**, the blocks you put within the "then-do" slot will only be executed if the test is true. For an **if** block, if the test is false, the app moves on to the blocks below it. If the **ifelse** test is false, the blocks within the "else-do" slot are performed.

So, for a game, you might plug in a Boolean expression concerning the score, as shown in Figure 18-4.

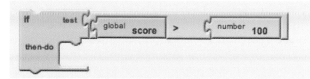

Figure 18-4. A Boolean expression used to test the score value

In this example, a sound file is played if the score goes over 100. Note that if the test is false, no blocks are executed. If you want a false test to trigger an action, you can use an **ifelse** block.

Programming an Either/Or Decision

Consider an app you could use when you're bored: you press a button on your phone, and it calls a random friend. In Figure 18-5, we use a **random integer** block to generate a random number and then an **ifelse** block to call a particular phone number based on that random number.

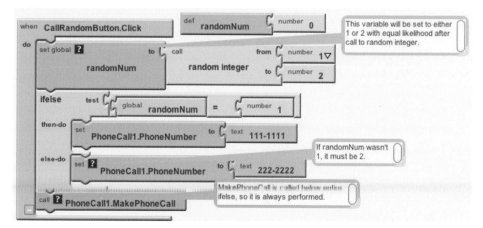

Figure 18-5. This ifelse block calls one of two numbers based on the randomly generated integer

In this example, **random integer** is called with arguments 1 and 2, meaning that the returned random number will be 1 or 2 with equal likelihood. The variable RandomNum stores the random number returned.

After setting RandomNum, the blocks compare it to the number 1 in the **ifelse** test. If the value of RandomNum is 1, the app takes the first branch (then-do), and the phone number is set to 111–1111. If the value is not 1, the test is false, so the app takes the second branch (else-do), and the phone number is set to 222–2222. The app makes the phone call either way because the call to **MakePhoneCall** is below the entire **ifelse** block.

Programming Conditions Within Conditions

Many decision situations are not *binomial*—that is, they don't have just two out-comes to choose from. For example, you might want to choose between more than two friends in your Random Call program. To do this, you could place an **ifelse** within the original else-do clause, as shown in Figure 18-6.

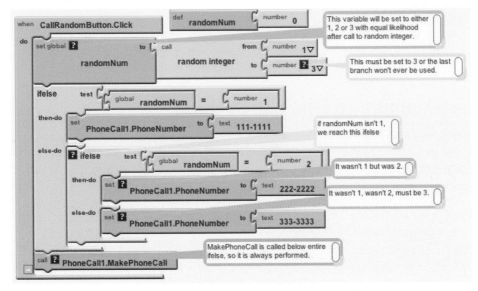

Figure 18-6. An ifelse condition is placed within the else-do of an outer condition

With these blocks, if the first test is true, the app executes the first then-do branch and calls the number 111–1111. If the first test is false, the outer else-do branch is executed, which immediately runs another test. So, if the first test (RandomNum=1) is false, and the second (RandomNum=2) is true, the second then-do is executed, and 222–2222 is called. If both tests are false, the inner else-do branch at the bottom is executed, and the third number (333–3333) is called.

Note that this modification only works because the to parameter of the **random integer** call was changed to 3 so that 1, 2, or 3 is called with equal likelihood.

Placing one control construct within another is called *nesting*. In this case, you'd say the blocks had a "nested if-else." You can use such nested logic to provide more choices in your Random Call app, and in general, to add arbitrary complexity to any app.

Programming Complex Conditions

Besides nesting questions, you can also specify tests that are more complex than a simple equality test. For example, consider an app that vibrates when you (and your phone) leave a building or some boundary. Such an app might be used by a person on probation to warn him when he strays too far from his legal boundaries, or by parents to monitor their children's whereabouts. A teacher might use it to automatically take roll (if all her students have an Android phone!).

For this example, let's ask this question: is the phone within the boundary of Harney Science Center at the University of San Francisco? Such an app would require a complex test consisting of four different questions:

- Is the phone's latitude less than the maximum latitude (37.78034) of the boundary?

- Is the phone's longitude less than the maximum longitude (–122.45027) of the boundary?

- Is the phone's latitude more than the minimum latitude (37.78016) of the boundary?

- Is the phone's longitude more than the minimum longitude (–122.45059) of the boundary?

We'll be using the LocationSensor component for this example. You should be able to follow along here even if you haven't been exposed to LocationSensor, but you can learn more about it in Chapter 23.

You can build complex tests using the logical operators **and**, **or**, and **not**, which are found in the Logic drawer. In this case, you'd start by dragging out an **if** block and an **and** block and then placing the **and** block within the "test" slot of the **if**, as illustrated in Figure 18-7.

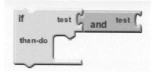

Figure 18-7. An and block is placed within the "test" slot of the if block

You'd then drag out blocks for the first question and place them into the **and** block's "test" slot, as shown in Figure 18-8.

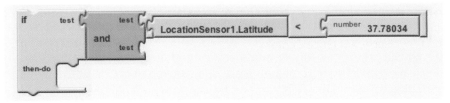

Figure 18-8. *When the blocks for the first test are placed into the and block, a new test slot opens*

Note that as you fill a (sub-)test of the **and** block, a new test slot opens. If you fill these slots with the other tests and place the entire **ifelse** within a **LocationSensor.LocationChanged** event, you'll have an event handler that checks the boundary, as shown in Figure 18-9.

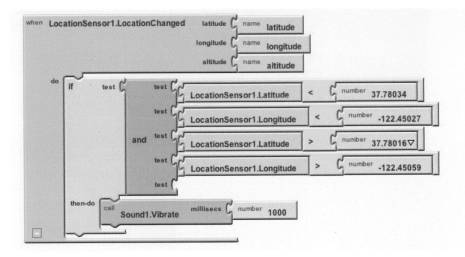

Figure 18-9. *This event handler checks the boundary each time the location changes*

With these blocks, each time the LocationSensor gets a new reading and its location is within the boundary, the phone vibrates.

OK, so far this is pretty cool, but now let's try something even more complicated to give you an idea of the full extent of the app's decision-making powers. What if you wanted the phone to vibrate only when the boundary was crossed from inside to outside? Before moving ahead, think about how you might program such a condition.

Our solution is to define a variable withinBoundary that remembers whether the *previous* sensor reading was within the boundary or not, and then compares that to each successive sensor reading. withinBoundary is an example of a *Boolean variable*—instead of storing a number or text, it stores true or false. For this example, you'd initialize it as false, as shown in Figure 18-10, meaning that the device is not within USF's Harney Science Center.

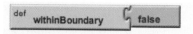

Figure 18-10. withinBoundary is initialized as false

The blocks can now be modified so that the withinBoundary variable is set on each location change, and so that the phone vibrates only when it moves from inside to outside the boundary. To put that in terms we can use for blocks, the phone should vibrate when (1) the variable withinBoundary is true, meaning the previous reading was inside the boundary, and (2) the new location sensor reading is outside the boundary. Figure 18-11 shows the updated blocks.

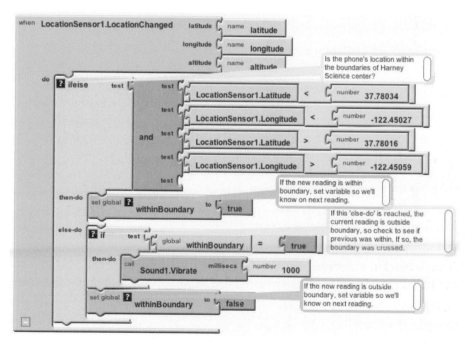

Figure 18-11. These blocks cause the phone to vibrate only when it moves from within the boundary to outside the boundary

Let's examine these blocks more closely. When the LocationSensor gets a reading, it first checks if the new reading is within the boundary. If it is, LocationSensor sets the withinBoundary variable to true. Since we want the phone to vibrate only when we are outside the boundary, no vibration takes place in this first branch.

If we get to the else-do, we know that the new reading is outside the boundary. At that point, we have to check the previous reading: if we're outside the boundary, we want the phone to vibrate only if the previous reading was *inside* the boundary. withinBoundary tells us the previous reading, so we can check that. If it is true, we vibrate the phone.

There's one more thing we need to do once we've confirmed that the phone has moved from inside to outside the boundary—can you think of what it is? We also need to reset withinBoundary to false so the phone won't vibrate again on the next sensor reading.

One last note on Boolean variables: check out the two **if** tests in Figure 18-12. Are they equivalent?

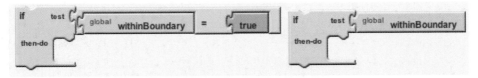

Figure 18-12. Can you tell whether these two if tests are equivalent?

The answer is "yes!" The only difference is that the test on the right is actually the more sophisticated way of asking the question. The test on the left compares the value of a Boolean variable with true. If withinBoundary contains true, you compare true to true, which is true. If the variable contains false, you compare false to true, which is false. However, just testing the value of withinBoundary, as in the test on the right, gives the same result and is easier to code.

Summary

Is your head spinning? That last behavior was quite complex! But it's the type of decision making that sophisticated apps need to perform. If you build such behaviors part by part (or branch by branch) and test as you go, you'll find that specifying complex logic—even, dare we say, *artificial intelligence*—is doable. It will make your head hurt and exercise the logical side of your brain quite a bit, but it can also be lots of fun.

CHAPTER 19

Programming Lists of Data

As you've already seen, apps handle events and make decisions; such processing is fundamental to computing. But the other fundamental part of an app is its data—the information it processes. An app's data is rarely restricted to single memory slots such as the score of a game. More often, it consists of complex, interrelated items that must be organized just as carefully as the app's functionality.

In this chapter, we'll examine the way App Inventor handles data. You'll learn the fundamentals of programming both static lists (in which the data doesn't change) and dynamic lists (in which the data is user-generated). Then you'll learn how to deal with even more complex data involving lists whose items are also lists.

Many apps process lists of data. For example, Facebook processes your list of friends. A quiz app works with a list of questions and answers. A game might have a list of characters or all-time high scores.

List variables work like text and number variables you've worked with, but instead of the variable representing a single named memory cell, it represents a related set of memory cells. Consider, for example, the list of phone numbers in Table 19-1.

Table 19-1. A list variable represents a set of memory cells

111–2222
333–4444
555–6666

The elements of a list are accessed using an *index*. An index is a position in a list, so index 1 of the list in Table 19-1 refers to 111–2222, index 2 refers to 333–4444, and index 3 refers to 555–6666.

App Inventor provides blocks for creating lists, adding elements to lists, selecting a particular item from a list, and applying operations to an entire list. Let's start with how we create a list.

Creating a List Variable

You create a list variable in the Blocks Editor using a **def variable** block and a **make a list** block. For example, suppose you were writing an app to text a list of phone numbers with one click. You create the phone numbers list in the following manner:

1. From the Built-In Palette, drag a **def variable** block (Figure 19-1) into the program area.

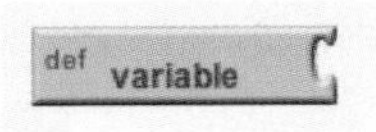

Figure 19-1. A def variable block

2. Click the text "variable" and change the name to "phoneNumbers", as shown in Figure 19-2.

Figure 19-2. Renaming the variable to phoneNumbers

3. From the Lists palette, drag out a **make a list** block and plug it into the definition block, as shown in Figure 19-3. This tells App Inventor that the variable will store a list of data as opposed to a single value.

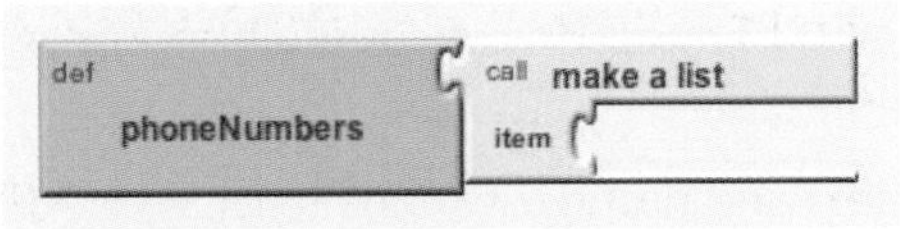

Figure 19-3. Defining phoneNumbers as a list using the make a list block

4. Finally, drag in some **text** blocks, enter the desired phone numbers, and plug them into the "item" slots in the **make a list** block. Note that a new "item" slot opens up at the bottom of **make a list** each time you add a new element to the list, as shown in Figure 19-4.

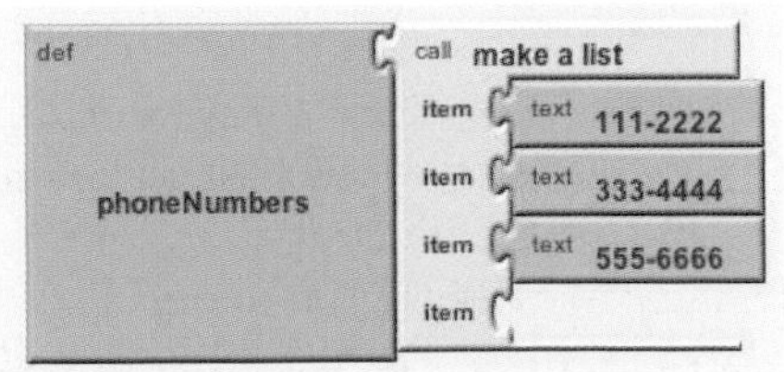

Figure 19-4. As each item is added to the list, a new slot opens up

You can plug any type of data into an "item" slot, but in this case, the items should be text objects, not numbers, because phone numbers have dashes and other formatting symbols that you can't put in a number object, and you won't be performing any calculations on the numbers (in which case, you would want number objects instead).

The blocks in Figure 19-4 define a variable named phoneNumbers. Any variables you define are created when the app launches, so memory slots like the ones in Table 19-1 will be created and filled when the app starts. Once you have a variable list, it's time to start working with the data in that list.

Selecting an Item in a List

Your app can access particular items of a list with the **select list item** block and by specifying an *index* in the list. The index indicates the position of an item within a list. So, if a list has three items, you can access the items with indices 1, 2, and 3. Figure 19-5 shows the blocks that select the second item of a list.

Figure 19-5. Selecting the second item of a list

With **select list item**, you plug in the list you want in the first slot, and the index you want in the second slot. The blocks in Figure 19-5 tell the app to select the second element of the list phoneNumbers. If you were selecting from the phoneNumbers list defined in Table 19-1, the result would be "333–4444."

Selecting an item in a list is just the first step—once you've selected the item, you can do a variety of things with it. We'll look at some examples next.

Using an Index to Traverse a List

In many apps, you'll define a list of data and then allow the user to step through (or *traverse*) it. The Presidents Quiz in Chapter 8 provides a good example of this: in that app, when the user clicks a Next button, the next item is selected from a list of questions and displayed.

But how do you select the next item in a list? Our example in Figure 19-5 selected item 2 from phoneNumbers. When you traverse a list, the item number you're selecting changes each time; it's relative to your current position in the list. Therefore, you need to define a variable to represent that current position. index is the common name for such a variable, and it is usually initialized to 1 (the first position in the list), as shown in Figure 19-6.

Figure 19-6. Initializing the variable index to 1

When the user does something to move to the next item, you *increment* the index variable by adding a value of 1 to it, and then select from the list using that incremented value. Figure 19-7 shows the blocks for doing this.

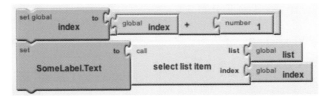

Figure 19-7. Incrementing the index value and using the incremented value to select the next list item

Example: Traversing a List of Paint Colors

Let's look at an example app that lets the user peruse each potential paint color for his house by clicking a button. Each time he clicks, the button's color changes. When the user makes it through all of the possible colors, the app takes him back to the first one.

For this example, we'll use some basic colors. However, you could customize the code blocks to iterate through any set of colors. For more information on colors, see the App Inventor documentation at *http://appinventor.googlelabs.com/learn/reference/blocks/colors.html*.

Our first step is to define a list variable for the colors list and initialize it with some paint colors as items, as depicted in Figure 19-8.

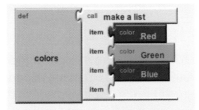

Figure 19-8. Initializing the list colors with a list of paint colors

Next, define an index variable that tracks the current position in the list. It should start at 1. You could give the variable a descriptive name like currentColorIndex, but if you aren't dealing with multiple indexes in your app, you can just name it index, as shown in Figure 19-9.

Figure 19-9. Using the index variable, which is initialized to 1, to track the current position in a list

The user traverses to the next item (color) in the list by clicking the ColorButton. When he clicks, the index should be incremented and the BackgroundColor of the button should change to the currently selected item, as shown in Figure 19-10.

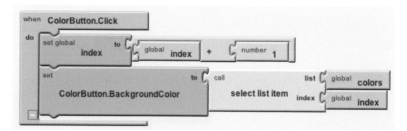

Figure 19-10. Letting the user traverse the color list by clicking a button—changing the button color with each click

Let's assume the button's background is initially set to Red in the Component Designer. The first time the button is clicked, index will change from its initial value of 1 to 2, and the button's background color will change to the second item in the list, Green. The second time the user clicks, the index will change from 2 to 3, and the background color will switch to Blue.

But what do you think will happen on the next click?

If you said there would be an error, you're right! index will become 4 and the app will try to select the fourth item in the list, but the list only has three items. The app will *force close*, or quit, and the user will see an error message like the one in Figure 19-11.

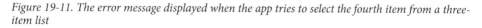

Figure 19-11. The error message displayed when the app tries to select the fourth item from a three-item list

Obviously, that message is not something you want your app's users to see. To avoid that problem, add an **if** block to check whether the last color in the list has been reached. If it has, the index can be changed back to 1 so that the first color is again displayed, as shown in Figure 19-12.

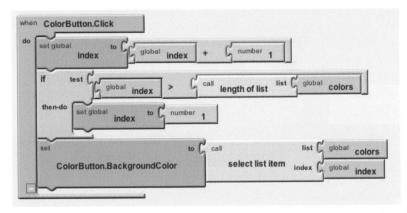

Figure 19-12. Using the if test to check for whether the index value is larger than the length of the list, and reset it to 1 if the test returns true

When the user clicks the button, the index is incremented and then checked to see if its value is too large. The index is compared to **length of list**, not 3, so your app will work even if you add items to the list. By checking if the index is greater than your list length (versus checking if it is greater than the specific number 3), you've eliminated a *code dependency* in your app. A code dependency is a programming term for instances when you program aspects of your app *too* specifically, such that if you change something in one place (e.g., the items in your list), you'll have to hunt down all the places in your app where you use that list and change those blocks as well.

As you can imagine, these kinds of dependencies could get messy very quickly, and they generally lead to many more bugs for you to chase down as well. In fact, the design for our House Paint Color app contains another code dependency as we currently have it programmed—can you figure out what it is?

If you changed the first color in your list from Red to some other color, the app won't work correctly unless you also remembered to change the initial Button .BackgroundColor you set in the Component Designer. The way to eliminate this code dependency is to set the initial **ColorButton.BackgroundColor** to the first color in the list rather than to a specific color. Since this change involves behavior that happens when your app first opens, you do this in the **Screen.Initialize** event handler that is invoked when an app is launched, as illustrated in Figure 19-13.

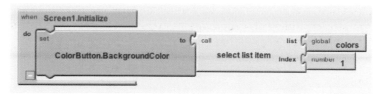

Figure 19-13. Setting the BackgroundColor of the button to the first color in the list when the app is launched

Creating Input Forms and Dynamic Lists

The previous House Paint Color app involved a *static* list: one whose elements are defined by the programmer (you) and whose items don't change unless you change the blocks themselves. More often, however, apps deal with *dynamic* lists: lists that change based on the end user entering new items, or new items being loaded in from a database or web information source. In this section, we'll discuss an example Note Taker app, one in which the user enters notes in a form and can view all of her previous notes.

Defining a Dynamic List

Just as with a static list, you define a dynamic list with the **make a list** block. But with a dynamic list, you don't add any predefined items in the list definition. For example, consider a Note Taker app. You would define the dynamic list of notes with the definition in Figure 19-14.

Figure 19-14. The blocks to define a dynamic list don't contain any predefined items

Adding an Item

The first time someone launches the app, the notes list is empty. But when the user enters some data in a form and clicks Submit, new notes will be added to the list. The form might be as simple as the one shown in Figure 19-15.

Note Taker

| enter a note | Submit |

Figure 19-15. Using a form to add new items to the notes list

When the user enters a note and clicks the Submit button, the app calls the **add items to list** function to add the newly entered item to the list, as shown in Figure 19-16.

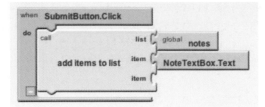

Figure 19-16. Calling add items to list to add the new note when the user clicks the SubmitButton

The **add item to list block** appends the item to the end of the list. Each time the user clicks the SubmitButton, a new note is added.

You'll find the **add item to list** block in the List drawer. Be careful: there is also an **append to list** block, but that one is a fairly rare block for appending one list to another.

Displaying a List

The contents of list variables like notes are not visible to the user; you'll recall that a variable is a way for the app to remember information that is not necessarily shown to the user. The blocks in Figure 19-16 will add items to the list on each button click submit, but the user will not see any feedback that it is happening until you program more blocks to actually display the contents of the list.

The simplest way to display a list in your app's user interface is to use the same method you use for displaying numbers and text: put the list in the Text property of a Label component, as illustrated in Figure 19-17.

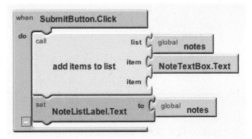

Figure 19-17. Displaying the list to the user within the Text property of the NotesListLabel

Unfortunately, this simple method of displaying a list isn't very elegant; it puts the list within parentheses, with each item separated by a space and not necessarily on the same line. For instance, if the user entered, "Will I ever finish this book?" as the first note, and "I forget what my son looks like!" as the second, the app would display the notes list as shown in Figure 19-18.

If you've already completed the "Amazon at the Bookstore" app (Chapter 13), this problem will be familiar. In Chapter 20, you'll learn how to display a list in a more sophisticated fashion.

Figure 19-18. The defult list display is not very elegant

Removing an Item from a List

You can remove an item from a list with the **remove list item** block, shown in Figure 19-19.

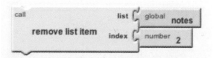

Figure 19-19. Removing an item from a list

The blocks in Figure 19-19 remove the second item from the list named notes. Generally, however, you won't want to remove a fixed item (e.g., 2), but instead will allow the user to choose the item to remove.

ListPicker is a user interface component that can be used for removing items. List Picker comes with an associated button. When the button is clicked, the ListPicker displays the items of a list and allows the user to choose one. When the user chooses an item, the app can remove it.

ListPicker is easy to program if you understand its two key events, **BeforePicking** and **AfterPicking**, and its two key properties, Elements and Selection, as listed in Table 19-2.

Table 19-2. Two key events of the ListPicker component and their properties

Event	Property
BeforePicking: Triggered when button is clicked.	`Elements`: The list of choices.
AfterPicking: Triggered when user makes a choice.	`Selection`: The user's choice.

The **ListPicker.BeforePicking** event is triggered when the user clicks the `ListPicker`'s associated button but before the choices are listed. In the **ListPicker .BeforePicking** event handler, you'll set the **ListPicker.Elements** property to a list variable. For the Note Taker app, you'd set `Elements` to the `notes` variable that contains your list of notes, as shown in Figure 19-20.

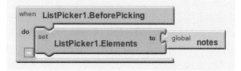

Figure 19-20. The Elements property of ListPicker1 is set to the list contained in notes

With these blocks, the items of the list `notes` will appear in the `ListPicker`. If there were two notes, it would appear as shown in Figure 19-21.

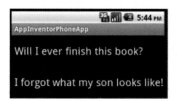

Figure 19-21. The list of notes appears in the ListPicker

When the user chooses an item in the list, the **ListPicker.AfterSelection** event is triggered. In this event handler, you can access the user's selection in the `ListPicker .Selection` property.

Recall, however, that the **remove item from list** block expects an index (list position), not an item. Unfortunately, the `Selection` property of the `ListPicker` is the actual data (the note item), not the index, and the `ListPicker` component doesn't provide direct access to the index of the list (this will certainly be added in later versions of App Inventor).

The workaround is to take advantage of another block in the list drawer, **position in list**. Given some text, this function will return the position of the first match to that text in a list. Using **position in list**, the **ListPicker1.AfterPicking** event handler can remove the selected item, as the blocks in Figure 19-22 show.

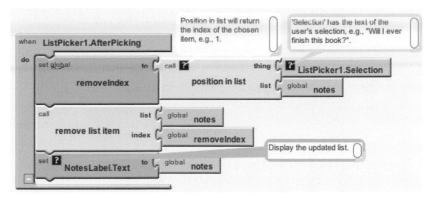

Figure 19-22. Using the position in list block to find the index of the item to remove

When **AfterPicking** is triggered, **ListPicker1.Selection** contains the text of the user's choice (e.g., "Will I ever finish this book?"). The goal is to find the index of that selection in the list notes in order to remove it, so **position in list** is called. If the user's selection was "Will I ever finish this book?", **position in list** will return 1 because it's the first item. This number is put into the variable removeIndex, which is then used as the index in the call to **remove list item**.

Here's a question to chew on before reading further: do you think this scheme will work in all cases?

The answer is that the scheme works fine *unless* there is duplicate data in the list. Say the user has entered, "I'm having a great day" as both his second and tenth notes. If he clicks the remove (ListPicker) button and chooses the tenth item, the second will be removed instead of the tenth. **position in list** only returns the index for the selected item and stops there, so you never find out that the tenth item is the same and should be removed from the list as well. You'd have to include some conditional checks (see Chapter 18) to loop through the list to see if there were any other entries that also matched the selected item, and then remove those as well.

Lists of Lists

The items of a list can be numbers, text, colors, or Boolean values (true/false). But the items of a list can also be lists. You'll commonly see such complex data structures. For example, a list of lists could be used to convert the Presidents Quiz from Chapter 8 into a multiple-choice quiz. Let's look again at the Presidents Quiz's basic structure, which is a list of questions and a list of answers, as shown in Figure 19-23.

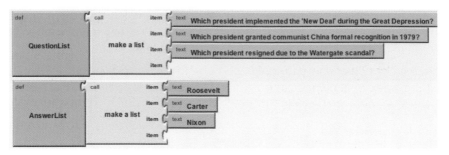

Figure 19-23. A list of questions and a list of answers

Each time the user answers a question, the app checks to see if it is correct by com-
paring the answer to the current item in the AnswerList.

To make the quiz multiple choice, you'd need to keep a list of choices for each answer
to each question. The multiple-choice list is represented as a variable list of lists,
defined by placing three **make a list** blocks within an outer **make a list** block, as
demonstrated in Figure 19-24.

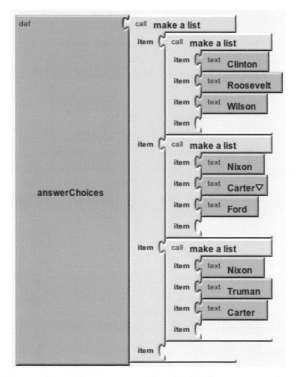

*Figure 19-24. A list of lists is formed by inserting make a list blocks as items within an outer make a
list block*

Each item in the variable answerChoices is itself a list containing three items. If you select an item from answerChoices, the result is a list. Now that you've populated your multiple-choice answers as lists, how would you display that to the user?

As with the Note Taker app, you could use a ListPicker to present the choices to the user. If the index were named currentQuestionIndex, the **ListPicker.BeforePicking** event would appear as shown in Figure 19-25.

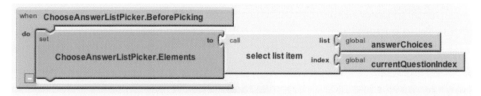

Figure 19-25. Using the List Picker to present the list of choices to the user

These blocks would take the current sublist of answerChoices and let the user choose from it. So, if currentQuestionIndex were 1, the ListPicker would show a list like the one in Figure 19-26.

![Screenshot showing the AppInventorPhoneApp with answer choices: Clinton, Roosevelt, Wilson]

Figure 19-26. The answer choices presented to the user for the second question

When the user chooses, you check the answer with the blocks shown in Figure 19-27.

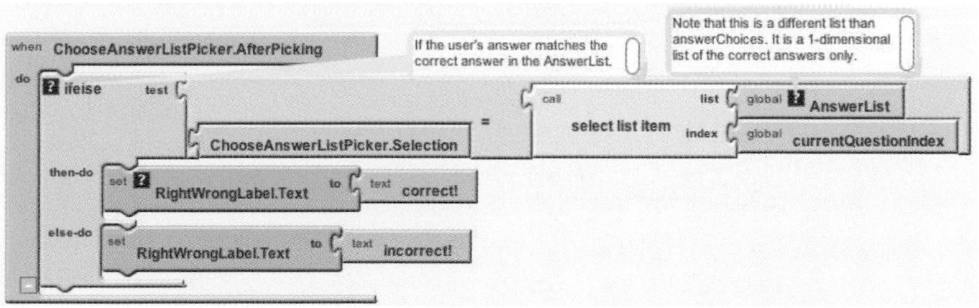

![Blocks diagram for ChooseAnswerListPicker.AfterPicking checking whether the user's answer matches the correct answer]

Figure 19-27. Checking whether the user chose the correct answer.

In these blocks, the user's selection from the `ListPicker` is compared to the correct answer, which is stored in a different list, `AnswerList` (since `answerChoices` provides only the choices and does not denote the correct answer).

Summary

Lists are used in almost every app you can think of. Understanding how they work is fundamental to programming. In this chapter, we explored one of the most common programming patterns: using an index variable that begins at the front of the list and is incremented until each list item is processed. If you can understand and customize this pattern, you are indeed a programmer!

We then covered some of the other mechanisms for list manipulation, including typical forms for letting the user add and remove items. Such programming requires yet another level of abstraction, as you have to envision the data—after all, your lists are empty until the user puts something in them. If you can understand this, you might even think of quitting your day job!

We concluded the chapter by introducing a complex data structure, a list of lists. This is definitely a difficult concept, but we explored it using fixed data: the answer choices for a multiple-choice quiz. If you mastered that and the rest of the chapter, your final test is this: create an app that uses of a list of lists, but with dynamic data! One example would be an app that allows people to create their own multiple-choice quizzes, extending even further the MakeQuiz app in Chapter 10. Good luck!

While you think about how you'll tackle that, understand that our exploration of lists isn't done. In the next chapter, we'll continue the discussion and focus on list iteration with a twist: applying functions to each item in a list.

CHAPTER 20

Repeating Blocks: Iteration

One thing computers are good at is repeating operations—like little children, they never tire of repetition. They are also very fast and can do things like process your entire list of Facebook friends in a microsecond.

In this chapter, you'll learn how to program repetition with just a few blocks instead of copying and pasting the same blocks over and over. You'll learn how to do things like send an SMS text to every phone number in a list and sort list items. You'll also learn that repeat blocks can significantly simplify an app.

Controlling an App's Execution: Branching and Looping

In previous chapters, you learned that you define an app's behavior with a set of event handlers: events and the functions that should be executed in response. You also learned that the response to an event is often not a linear sequence of functions and can contain blocks that are performed only under certain conditions.

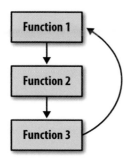

Figure 20-1. Repeat blocks cause a program to loop

Repeat blocks are the other way in which an app behaves nonlinearly. Just as **if** and **ifelse** blocks allow a program to branch, repeat blocks allow a program to *loop*; that is, to perform some set of functions and then jump back up in the code and do it again, as illustrated in Figure 20-1.

When an app executes, a *program counter* working beneath the hood of the app keeps track of the next operation to be performed. So far, you've examined apps in which the program counter starts at the top of an event handler and (conditionally) performs operations top to bottom. With repeat blocks, the program counter loops back up in the blocks, continuously repeating functions.

In App Inventor, there are two types of repeat blocks: **foreach** and **while.foreach** is used to specify functions that should be performed on each item of a list. So, if you have a list of phone numbers, you can specify that a text should be sent to each number in the list.

The **while** block is more general than the **foreach**. With it, you can program blocks that continually repeat until some arbitrary condition changes. **while** blocks can be used to compute mathematical formulas such as adding the first *n* numbers or computing the factorial of *n*. You can also use **while** when you need to process two lists simultaneously; **foreach** processes only a single list at a time.

Repeating Functions on a List Using foreach

In Chapter 18, we discussed a Random Call app. Randomly calling one friend might work out sometimes, but if you have friends like mine, they don't always answer. A different strategy would be to send a "Missing you" text to *all* of your friends and see who responds first (or more charmingly!).

With such an app, clicking a button sends a text to more than one friend. One way to implement this would be to simply copy the blocks for texting a single number, and then copy and paste them for each friend you want to text, as shown in Figure 20-2.

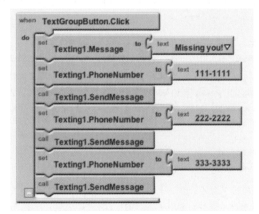

Figure 20-2. Copying and pasting the blocks for each phone number to be texted

This "brute force" copy-paste method is fine if you have just a few blocks to repeat. But data lists, such as the list of your friends, tend to change. You won't want to have to modify your app with the copy-paste method each time you add or remove a phone number from your list.

The **foreach** block provides a better solution. You define a phoneNumbers list variable with all the numbers and then wrap a **foreach** block around a single copy of the blocks you want to perform. Figure 20-3 shows the **foreach** solution for texting a group.

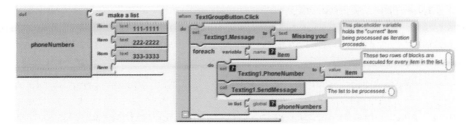

Figure 20-3. Using the foreach block to perform the same blocks for each item in the list

This code can be read as:

For each item (phone number) in the list phoneNumbers, *set the* Texting *object's phone number to the item and send out the text message.*

When you drag out a **foreach** block, you must specify the list to process by plugging a reference into the "in list" parameter at the bottom of the block. In this case, the **global phoneNumbers** block was dragged out of the My Definitions palette and plugged in to provide the list of phone numbers to text.

At the top of the **foreach** block, you also provide a name for a *placeholder* variable that comes with the **foreach**. By default, this placeholder is named "var." You can leave it that way or rename it. One common name for it is "item," as it represents the current item being processed in the list.

The blocks within the **foreach** are repeated for each item in the list, with the place-holder variable (in this example, item) always holding the item currently being processed. If a list has three items, the inner blocks will be executed three times. The inner blocks are said to be subordinate to, or within, the **foreach** block. We say that the program counter "loops" back up when it reaches the bottom block within the **foreach**.

A Closer Look at Looping

Let's examine the mechanics of the **foreach** blocks in detail, because understanding loops is fundamental to programming. When the TextGroupButton is clicked and the event handler invoked, the first operation executed is the **set Texting1.Message to** block, which sets the message to "Missing you." This block is only executed once.

The **foreach** block then begins. Before the inner blocks of a **foreach** are executed, the placeholder variable item is set to the first number in the phoneNumbers list (111–1111). This happens automatically; the **foreach** relieves you of having to manu-ally call **select list item**. After the first item is selected into the variable item, the blocks within the **foreach** are executed for the first time. The Texting1.PhoneNumber property is set to the value of item (111–1111), and the message is sent.

After reaching the last block within a **foreach** (the **Texting.SendMessage** block), the app "loops" back up to the top of the **foreach** and automatically puts the next item in the list (222–2222) into the variable item. The two operations within the **foreach** are then repeated, sending the "Missing you" text to 222–2222. The app then loops back up again and sets item to the last item in the list (333–3333). The operations are repeated a third time, sending the third text.

Because the final item in the list—in this case, the third—has been processed, the **foreach** looping stops at this point. We say that control "pops" out of the loop, which means that the program counter moves on to deal with the blocks below the **foreach**. In this example, there are no blocks below it, so the event handler ends.

Writing Maintainable Code

To the end user, the **foreach** solution just described behaves exactly the same as the "brute force" method of copying and then pasting the texting blocks. From a programmer's perspective, however, the **foreach** solution is more *maintainable* and can be used even if the data (the phone list) is entered dynamically.

Maintainable software is software that can be changed easily without introducing bugs. With the **foreach** solution, you can change the list of friends who are sent texts by modifying *only* the list variable—you don't need to change the logic of your program (the event handler) at all. Contrast this with the brute force method, which requires you to add new blocks in the event handler when a new friend is added. Anytime you modify a program's logic, you risk introducing bugs.

Even more important, the **foreach** solution would work even if the phone list was dynamic—that is, one in which the end user, not just the programmer, could add numbers to the list. Unlike our sample, which has three particular phone numbers listed in the code, most apps work with dynamic data that comes from the end user or some other source. If you redesigned this app so that the end user could enter the phone numbers, you would *have* to use a **foreach** solution, because when you write the program, you don't know what numbers to put in the brute force solution.

A Second foreach Example: Displaying a List

When you want to display the items of a list on the phone, you can plug the list into the Text property of a Label, as shown in Figure 20-4.

Figure 20-4. The simple way to display a list is to plug it directly into a label

When you plug a list directly into a Text property of a Label, the list items are displayed in the label as a single row of text separated by spaces and contained in parentheses:

(111–1111 222–2222 333–3333)

The numbers may or may not span more than one line, depending on how many there are. The user can see the data and perhaps comprehend that it's a list of phone numbers, but it's not very elegant. List items are more commonly displayed on separate lines or with commas separating them.

To display a list properly, you need blocks that transform each list item into a single text value with the formatting you want. Text objects generally consist of letters, digits, and punctuation marks. But text can also store special *control* characters, which don't map to a character you can see. A tab, for instance, is denoted by \t. (To learn more about control characters, check out the Unicode standard for text representation at *http://www.unicode.org/standard/standard.html*.)

In our phone number list, we want a newline character, which is denoted by \n. When \n appears in a text block, it means "go down to the next line before you display the next thing." So the text object "111–1111\n222–2222\n333–3333" would appear as:

111–1111
222–2222
333–3333

To build such a text object, we use a **foreach** block and "process" each item by adding it and a newline character to the PhoneNumberLabel.Text property, as shown in Figure 20-5.

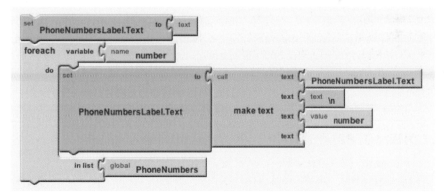

Figure 20-5. Using the foreach block to process the list and put a newline character before each item

Let's trace the blocks to see how they work. As discussed in Chapter 15, tracing shows how each variable or property changes as the blocks are executed. With a **foreach**, we consider the values after each *iteration*; that is, each time the program goes through the **foreach** loop.

Before the **foreach**, the PhoneNumbersLabel is initialized to the empty text. When the **foreach** begins, the app automatically places the first item of the list (111–1111) into the placeholder variable **number**. The blocks in the **foreach** then **make text** with **PhoneNumbersLabel.Text** (the empty text), \n, and **number**, and set the result into **PhoneNumbersLabel.Text**. Thus, after the first iteration of the **foreach**, the pertinent variables store the values shown in Table 20-1.

Table 20-1. The values of the variables after the first iteration of foreach

number	PhoneNumbersLabel.Text
111–1111	\n111–1111

Since the bottom of the **foreach** has been reached, control loops back up and the next item of the list (222–2222) is put into the variable **number**. When the inner blocks are repeated, **make text** concatenates the value of **PhoneNumbersLabel .Text** (\n111–1111) with \n, and then with **number**, which is now 222–2222. After this second iteration, the variables store the values shown in Table 20-2.

Table 20-2. The variable values after the second iteration of foreach

number	PhoneNumbersLabel.Text
222–2222	\n111–1111\n222–2222

The third item of the list is then placed in **number**, and the inner block is repeated a third time. The final value of the variables, after this last iteration, is shown in Table 20-3.

Table 20-3. The variable values after the final iteration

number	PhoneNumbersLabel.Text
333–3333	\n111–1111\n222–2222\n333–3333

So, after each iteration, the label becomes larger and holds one more phone number (and one more newline). By the end of the **foreach**, PhoneNumbersLabel.Text is set so that the numbers will appear as:

    111–1111
    222–2222
    333–3333

Repeating Blocks with while

The **while** block is a bit more complicated to use than **foreach**. The advantage of the **while** block lies in its generality: **foreach** repeats over a list, but **while** can repeat *while any arbitrary condition is true*. As a trivial example, suppose you wanted to text every *other* person in your phone list. You couldn't do it with **foreach**, but with **while**, you could just increment the index by two instead of one each time.

As you learned in Chapter 18, a condition tests something and returns a value of either true or false. **while-do** blocks include a conditional test, just like **if** blocks. If the test of a **while** evaluates to true, the app executes the inner blocks, and then loops back up and rechecks the test. As long as the test evaluates to true, the inner blocks are repeated. When the test evaluates to false, the app "pops" out of the loop (like we saw with the **foreach** block) and continues with the blocks below the **while**.

Using while to Synchronously Process Two Lists

A more instructive example of **while** and its generality involves situations in which you need to process two lists in a synchronous fashion. For example, in the MakeQuiz app (Chapter 10), you keep separate lists of the quiz questions and answers, along with an index variable to keep track of the current question number. To display each question-answer pair together, you need to iterate through the two lists in a synchronous fashion, grabbing the index*th* item of each. **foreach** only allows for traversing a single list, but with a **while** loop, you can use the index to grab an item from each list. Figure 20-6 illustrates using a **while** block to display the question-answer pairs on separate lines.

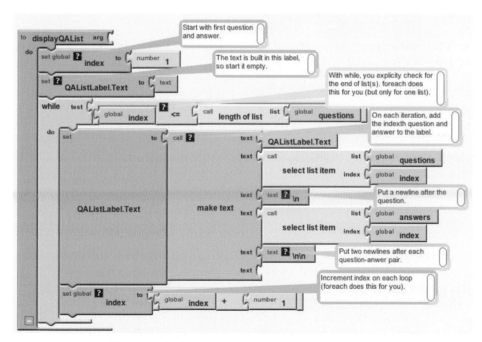

Figure 20-6. Using a while loop to display the question-answer pairs on separate lines

Because a **while** is used instead of a **foreach**, the blocks explicitly initialize the index, check for the end of the list, select the items in each loop, and increment the index.

Using while to Compute a Formula

Here's another example of **while** that repeats operations but has nothing to do with a list. What do you think the blocks in Figure 20-7 do, at a high level? One way to figure this out is to trace each block (see Chapter 15 for more on tracing), tracking the value of each variable as you go.

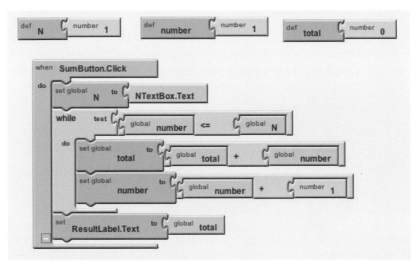

Figure 20-7. Can you figure out what these blocks are doing?

The blocks within the **while** loop will be repeated *while the variable number is less than or equal to the variable* N. For this app, N is set to a number that the end user enters in a text box (NTextBox). Say the user entered a 3. The variables of the app would look like Table 20-4 when the **while** block is reached.

Table 20-4. This is how the variables look when the while block is reached

N	number	total
3	1	0

The **while** block first asks: is number less than or equal to (<=) N? The first time this question is asked, the test is true, so execution proceeds within the **while** block. total is set to itself (0) plus number (1), and number is incremented. After the first iteration of the blocks within the **while**, the variable values are as listed in Table 20-5.

Table 20-5. The variable values after the first iteration of the blocks within the while block

N	number	total
3	2	1

On second iteration, the test "number<=N" is still true (2<=3), so the inner blocks are executed again. total is set to itself (1) plus number (2). number is incremented. When this second iteration completes, the variables are as listed in Table 20-6.

Table 20-6. The variable values after the second iteration

N	number	total
3	3	3

The app loops back up again and tests the condition. Once again, it is true (3<=3), so the blocks are executed a third time. Now total is set to itself (3) plus number (3), so it becomes 6. number is incremented to 4, as shown in Table 20-7.

Table 20-7. The values after the third iteration

N	number	total
3	4	6

After this third iteration, control loops back one more time. Now the test "number<=N", or 4<=3, evaluates to false. Thus, the inner blocks of the **while** are not executed again, and the event handler completes.

So what did these blocks do? They performed one of the most fundamental mathematical operations: counting numbers. Whatever number the user enters, the app will report the sum of the numbers 1..N, where N is the number entered. In this example, we assumed the user had entered 3, so the app came up with a total of 6. If the user had entered 4, the app would have calculated 10.

Summary

Computers are good at repeating the same function over and over. Think of all the bank accounts that are processed to accrue interest, all the grades processed to compute students' grade point averages, and countless other everyday examples where computers use repetition to perform a task.

App Inventor provides two blocks for repeating operations. The **foreach** block applies a set of functions to each element of a list. By using it, you can design processing code that works on an abstract list instead of concrete data. Such code is more maintainable, and it's required if the data is dynamic.

Compared to **foreach**, **while** is more general: you can use it to process a list, but you can also use it to synchronously process two lists or compute a formula. With **while**, the inner blocks are performed continuously while a certain condition is true. After the blocks within the **while** are executed, control loops back up and the test condition is tried again. Only when the test evaluates to false does the **while** block complete.

CHAPTER 21

Defining Procedures: Reusing Blocks

Programming languages like App Inventor provide a base set of built-in functionality—in App Inventor's case, a base set of blocks. Programming languages also provide a way to extend that functionality by adding new functions (blocks) to the language. In App Inventor, you do this by defining procedures—named sequences of blocks—that your app can call just as it calls App Inventor's predefined blocks. As you'll see in this chapter, being able to create such abstractions is very important for solving complex problems, which is the cornerstone of building truly compelling apps.

When parents tell their child, "Go brush your teeth before bed," they really mean "take your toothbrush and toothpaste from the cabinet, squeeze out some toothpaste onto the brush, swivel the brush on each tooth for 10 seconds (ha!)," and so on. "Brush your teeth" is an *abstraction*: a recognizable name for a sequence of lower-level instructions. In this case, the parents are asking the child to perform the instructions that they've all agreed mean "brush your teeth."

In programming, you can create such named sequences of instructions. Some programming languages call them *functions* or *subprograms*. In App Inventor, they're called *procedures*. A procedure is a named sequence of blocks that can be called from *any place in an app.*

Figure 21-1 is an example of a procedure whose job is to find the distance, in miles, between two GPS coordinates you send to it.

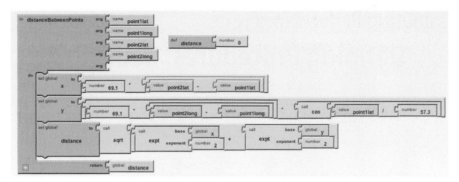

Figure 21-1. Procedure for computing the distance between points

Don't worry about the internals of this procedure too much just yet; just realize that procedures like this let you extend the language by which you design and build programs. If every parent had to explain the steps of "brush your teeth" to his or her child each night, that kid might not make it to the fifth grade. It's much more efficient to just say, "Brush your teeth," and everyone can move on with getting to bed at a reasonable hour.

Similarly, once you define the procedure distanceBetweenPoints, you can ignore the details of how it works and simply refer to the procedure's name (or *call* it) when designing or coding a larger app. This type of *abstraction* is key to solving large problems and lets us break down a large software project into more manageable chunks of code.

Procedures also help reduce errors because they eliminate *redundancy* in your code. With procedures, you can put a chunk of code in one place and then call it from various places in your app. So, if you're building an app that needs to know the minimum distance between your current location and 10 other spots, you don't need to have 10 copies of the blocks shown in Figure 21-1. Instead, you just define the procedure and then call it whenever you need it. The alternative—copying and pasting blocks—is much more error-prone because when you make a change, you have to find all the other copies of those blocks and change each one in the same way. Imagine trying to find the 5–10 places where you pasted a particular chunk of code in an app with 1,000 lines or blocks! Instead of forcing you to copy and paste, a procedure lets you *encapsulate* blocks in one place.

Procedures also help you build up a library of code that can be reused in many apps. Even when building an app for a very specific purpose, experienced programmers are always thinking of ways to reuse parts in other apps should the need arise. Some programmers never even create apps, but instead focus solely on building reusable code libraries for other programmers to use in their apps!

Eliminating Redundancy

Take a look at the code blocks in Figure 21-2. See if you can you identify the redundant ones.

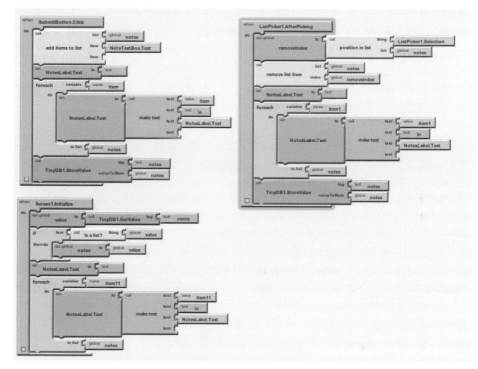

Figure 21-2. A Note Taker app with redundant code

The redundant blocks are the ones involving a **foreach** block (actually the **foreach** and the **set NotesLabel.Text to** above it). In all three **foreach** instances, the block's job is to display the notes list. In this app, this behavior needs to take place when a new item is added, when an item is removed, and when the list is loaded from the database at application launch.

When experienced programmers see such redundancy, a bell goes off in their heads, probably even before they've copied and pasted the blocks in the first place. They know that it's best to encapsulate such redundancy into a procedure, both to make the program more understandable and so that changes will be much easier later.

So an experienced programmer would create a procedure, move the redundant blocks into it, and then call the procedure from the three places containing the redundant blocks. The app will not behave any differently, but it will be easier to maintain and easier for other programmers to work with. Such code (block) reorganization is called *refactoring*.

Defining a Procedure

Let's build a procedure to do the job of the redundant code blocks from Figure 21-2. In App Inventor, you define a procedure in a manner similar to how you define variables. From the Definition drawer, drag out either a **to procedure** block or a **to procedure with result** block. Use the latter if your procedure should calculate some value and return it (we'll discuss this approach a bit later in the chapter).

After dragging out a **to procedure** block, you can change its name from the default "procedure" by clicking the word "procedure" and typing the new name. The redundant blocks we're refactoring performed the job of displaying a list, so we'll name the procedure displayList, shown in Figure 21-3.

Figure 21-3. Giving the procedure a name

The next step is to add the blocks within the procedure. In this case, we're using blocks that already exist, so we'll drag one of the original redundant blocks out of its event handler and place it within the **to displayList** block, as shown in Figure 21-4.

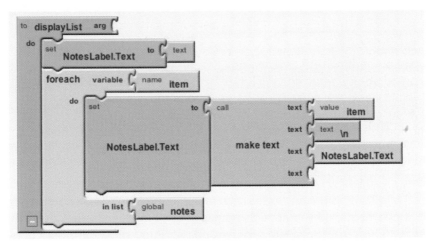

Figure 21-4. The displayList procedure encapsulates the redundant code

We can now display the notes list using a procedure that you can easily call from elsewhere in your app!

Calling a Procedure

Procedures, like displayList and "brush your teeth," are entities with the *potential* to perform a task. However, they'll only perform that task if they are called upon to do so. Thus far, we've created a procedure but haven't *called* it. To call a procedure means to *invoke* it, or to make it happen.

In App Inventor, you call a procedure by dragging out a **call** block from the My Definitions drawer. Recall that the My Definitions drawer is empty when you first begin an app. Each time you define something, new blocks appear in it. When you define a variable, blocks to set and access the variable's value are added. When you define a procedure, a call block is added, as shown in Figure 21-5.

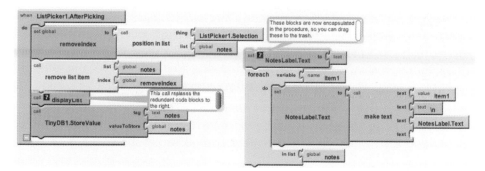

Figure 21-5. A call block appears in "My Definitions" when you define a procedure

You use **call** blocks all the time to call App Inventor's predefined functions, like **Ball.MoveTo** and **Texting.SendMessage**. When you define a procedure, you have in essence created your own block; you've extended the App Inventor language. The new **call** block lets you invoke your creation.

For the Note Taker app sample, you'd drag out three **call displayList** blocks and use them to replace the redundant code in the three event handlers. For instance, the **ListPicker1.AfterPicking** event handler (for deleting a note) should be modified as shown in Figure 21-6.

Figure 21-6. Using the displayList call to invoke the blocks now in the procedure

The Program Counter

To understand how the **call** block works, think of an app as having a pointer that steps through the blocks performing functions. In computer science, this pointer is called the *program counter*.

When the program counter is performing the blocks within an event handler and it reaches a **call** block, it jumps over to the procedure and executes the blocks in it. When the procedure completes, the program counter jumps back to its previous location (the **call** block) and proceeds from there. So, for the Note Taker example, the **remove list item** block is performed; then the program counter jumps to the displayList procedure and performs its blocks (setting the **NotesLabel.Text** to the empty text, and the **foreach**); and finally the program counter returns to perform the **TinyDB1.StoreValue** block.

Adding Parameters to Your Procedure

The displayList procedure allows redundant code to be refactored into a single place. The app is easier to understand because you can read the event handlers at a high level and generally ignore the details of how a list is displayed. It is also helpful because you may decide to modify how you display the list, and the procedure allows you to make such a modification in a single place (instead of three).

The displayList procedure has limits in terms of its *general* usefulness, however. The procedure works for a specific list (notes) and displays that list in a specific label (NotesLabel). You couldn't use it to display a different data list—say, a list of the app's users—because it is defined too specifically.

App Inventor and other languages provide a mechanism called *parameters* for making procedures more general. Parameters comprise the information a procedure needs to do its job—the specifics of how the procedure should be performed. In our bedtime tooth-brushing example, you might define "toothpaste type" and "brushing time" as parameters of the procedure "brush your teeth."

You define parameters for a procedure by dragging out a **name** block from the Definition drawer and plugging it into a procedure slot labeled "arg." For the display List procedure, we would define a parameter named "list," as shown in Figure 21-7.

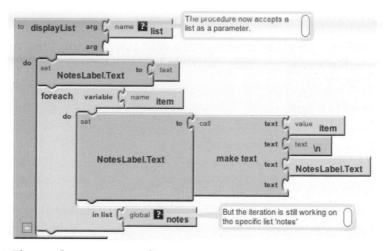

Figure 21-7. The procedure now accepts a list as a parameter

Even with the parameter defined, the blocks still refer directly to the specific list notes (it's plugged into the "in list" slot of the **foreach**). Because we want the procedure to use the list we send in as a parameter, we replace the reference to **global notes** with a reference to **value list**, as demonstrated in Figure 21-8.

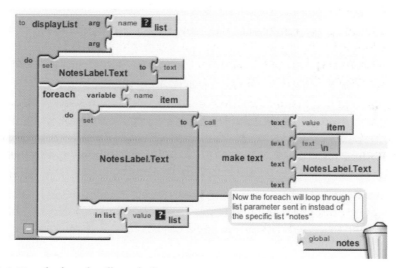

Figure 21-8. Now the foreach will use the list sent in

The new version of the procedure is more generic: whatever calls displayList can now send it any list, and displayList will display it. When you add a parameter to a procedure, App Inventor automatically puts a corresponding slot in the **call** block. So, when the parameter list is added to displayList, the call blocks to displayList look like Figure 21-9.

Figure 21-9. Calling displayList now requires you to specify which list to display

The **name list** within the procedure definition is called a *formal parameter*. The corresponding slot within the call block is called an *actual parameter*. When you call a procedure from somewhere in the app, you must supply an actual parameter for each formal parameter of the procedure.

For the Note Taker app, you'd add a reference to the notes list as the actual parameter. Figure 21-10 shows how **ListPicker.AfterSelection** should be modified.

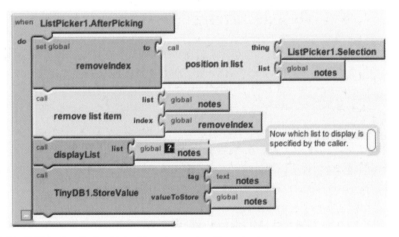

Figure 21-10. Calling the displayList with notes sent as the actual parameter

Now when displayList is called, the list notes is sent over to the procedure and placed in the parameter list. The program counter proceeds to execute the blocks in the procedure, referring to the parameter list but really working with the variable notes.

Because of the parameter, the procedure displayList can now be used with any list, not just notes. For example, if the Note Taker app was shared among a list of users and you wanted to display the list, you could call displayList and send it the user List, as shown in Figure 21-11.

Figure 21-11. The displayList procedure can now be used to display any list, not just notes

Returning Values from a Procedure

There is still one issue with the displayList procedure in terms of its reusability—can you figure out what it is? As it's currently written, it can display any list of data, but it will always display that data in the label NotesLabel. What if you wanted the list to be displayed in a different user interface object (e.g., you had a different label for displaying the userList)?

One solution is to reconceptualize the procedure—to change its job from displaying a list in a particular label to simply returning a text object that can be displayed anywhere. To do this, you'll use a **procedureWithResult** block, shown in Figure 21-12, instead of the **procedure** block.

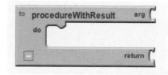

Figure 21-12. The procedureWithResult block

You'll notice that, when compared to the **procedure** block, the **procedureWithResult** block has an extra slot at the bottom. You place a variable in this slot and it's returned to the caller. So, just as the caller can send data to a procedure with a parameter, a procedure can send data back with a return value.

Figure 21-13 shows the reworked version of the preceding procedure, now using a **procedureWithResult** block. Note that because the procedure is now doing a different job, its name is changed from displayList to convertListToText.

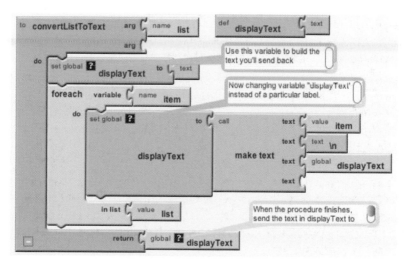

Figure 21-13. convertListToText returns a text object that the caller can place in any label

In the blocks shown in Figure 21-13, a variable displayText is defined to hold the text as the procedure iterates through each item of the list. This text variable replaces the overly specific NotesLabel component that was previously being used. When the **foreach** completes, the variable displayText contains the list items, with each item separated by a newline character, \n (e.g., "item1\nitem2\item3"). This displayText variable is then plugged into the return value slot.

When a **procedureWithResult** is defined, its corresponding call blocks look different than those for a procedure. Compare the call to convertListToText with the call to the displayList in Figure 21-14.

Figure 21-14. The call on the right returns a value and so must be plugged into something

The difference is that the **call convertListToText** has a plug on the left. This is because when the call is executed, the procedure will run through its task and then return a value to the **call** block. That return value must be plugged into something.

In this case, the callers to displayList can plug that return value into any label they want. For the notes example, the three event handlers that need to display a list will call the procedure as shown in Figure 21-15.

Figure 21-15. Converting the list notes into text and displaying it in NotesLabel

The important point here is that, because the procedure is completely generic and doesn't refer to any lists or labels specifically, another part of the app could use convertListToText to display any list in any label, as exemplified in Figure 21-16.

Figure 21-16. The procedure is no longer tied to a particular Label component

Reusing Blocks Among Apps

Reusing code blocks through procedures need not be restricted to a single app. There are many procedures, like `convertListToText`, that could be used in just about any app you create. In practice, organizations and programming communities build up code libraries of procedures for their domains of interest—for example, a code library of animation procedures.

Typically, programming languages provide an "import" utility that allows for including library code in any app. App Inventor doesn't yet have such a utility, but one is being developed. In the meantime, you can create procedures in a special "library app" and begin new app development by saving a new copy of that app and working from it.

A Second Example: distanceBetweenPoints

With the `displayList` (`convertListToText`) example, we characterized procedure definition as a way to eliminate redundant code: you start writing code, find redundancies as you go along, and refactor your code to eliminate them. Generally, however, a software developer or team will design an app from the beginning with procedures and reusable parts in mind. This sort of planning can save you significant time as the project progresses.

Consider an app to determine the local hospital closest to one's current location, something that would come in very handy in case of an emergency. Here's a high-level design description of the app:

> When the app launches, find the distance, in miles, between the current location and the first hospital. Then find it for the second hospital, and so on. When you have the distances, determine the minimum distance and display the address (and/or a map) to that location.

From this description, can you determine the procedures this app needs?

Often, the verbs in such a description hint at the procedures you'll need. Repetition in your description, as indicated with the "so on," is another clue. In this case, *finding the distance between two points* and *determining the minimum of some distances* are two necessary procedures.

Let's think about the design of the `distanceBetweenPoints` procedure. When designing a procedure, you need to determine its inputs and outputs: the parameters the caller will send to the procedure for it to do its job, and the result value the procedure will send back to the caller. In this case, the caller needs to send the latitude and longitude of both points to the procedure shown in Figure 21-17. The procedure's job is to return the distance, in miles.

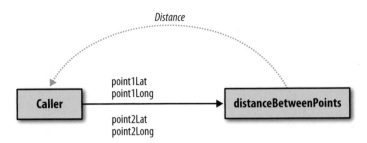

Figure 21-17. The caller sends four input parameters and receives a distance

Figure 21-18 shows the procedure we encountered at the start of the chapter, using a formula for approximating the mileage between two GPS coordinates.

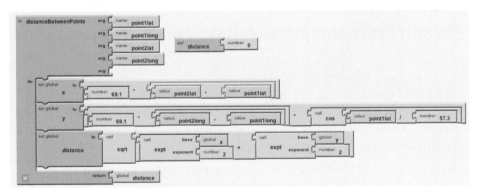

Figure 21-18. distanceBetweenPoints procedure

Figure 21-19 shows blocks that make two calls to the procedure, each of which finds the distance from the current location to a particular hospital.

For the first call, the actual parameters for point1 are the GPS coordinates for St. Mary's Hospital, while point2 uses the current readings from the LocationSensor. The result value is placed in the variable distanceStMarys. The second call is similar, but instead uses the data for CPMC Hospital for point1.

The app goes on to compare the two distances returned to determine which hospital is closest. But if there were more hospitals involved, you'd really need to compare a list of distances to find the minimum. From what you've learned, can you create a procedure called findMinimum that accepts a list of numbers as a parameter and returns the index of the minimum?

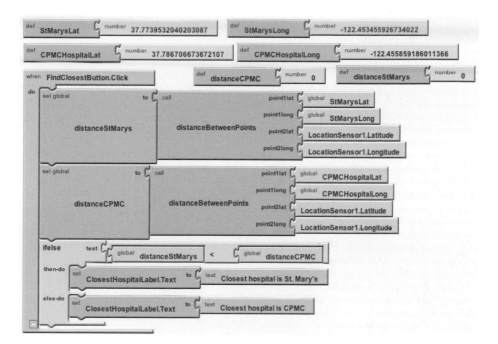

Figure 21-19. Two calls to the distanceBetweenPoints procedure

Summary

Programming languages like App Inventor provide a base set of built-in functionality. Procedures let app inventors extend that language with new abstractions. App Inventor doesn't provide a block for displaying a list, so you build one. Need a block for computing the distance between GPS coordinates? You can create your own.

The ability to define higher-level procedure blocks is the key to engineering large, maintainable software and solving complex problems without being constantly overwhelmed by all of the details. Procedures let you encapsulate code blocks and give those blocks a name. While you program the procedure, you focus solely on the details of those blocks. But in programming the rest of the app, you now have an abstraction—a name—that you can refer to at a high level.

CHAPTER 22

Working with Databases

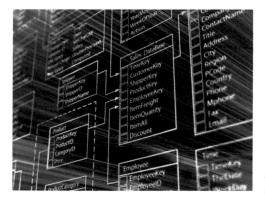

Facebook has a database of every member's account information, friends list, and posts. Amazon has a database of just about everything you can buy. Google has a database of information about every page in the World Wide Web. Though not to this scale, almost every nontrivial app you can create will have a database component.

In most programming environments, building an app that communicates with a database is an advanced programming technique: you have to set up a server with database software like Oracle or MySQL and then write code that interfaces with that database. In universities, such programming is generally not taught until an upper-level software engineering or database course.

App Inventor does the heavy lifting for you when it comes to databases (and lots of other useful things!). The language provides components that reduce database communication to simple store and get operations. You can create apps that store data directly on the Android device, and with some setup, you can create apps that share data with other devices and people by storing it in a centralized web database.

The data in variables and component properties is *short-term*: if the user enters some information in a form and then closes the app, that information will be gone when the app is reopened. To store information persistently, you must store it in a database. The information in databases is said to be *persistent* because even when you close the app and reopen it, the data is still available.

As an example, consider Chapter 4's No Texting While Driving app, which sends an autoresponse to texts that come in when the user is busy. This app lets the user enter a custom message to be sent in response to incoming texts. If the user changes the custom message to "I'm sleeping; stop bugging me" and then closes the app, the message should still be "I'm sleeping; stop bugging me" when the app is reopened. Thus, the custom message must be stored in a database, and every time the app is opened, that message must be retrieved from the database back into the app.

Storing Persistent Data in TinyDB

App Inventor provides two components to facilitate database activity: TinyDB and TinyWebDB. TinyDB is used to store persistent data directly on the Android device; this is useful for highly personalized apps where the user won't need to share her data with another device or person, as in No Texting While Driving. TinyWebDB, on the other hand, is used to store data in a *web* database that can be shared among devices. Being able to access data from a web database is essential for multiuser games and apps where users can enter and share information (like the MakeQuiz app in Chapter 10).

The database components are similar, but TinyDB is a bit simpler, so we'll explore it first. With TinyDB, you don't need to set up a database at all; the data is stored in a database directly on the device and associated with your app.

You transfer data to long-term memory with the **TinyDB.StoreValue** block, as shown in Figure 22-1, which comes from the No Texting While Driving app.

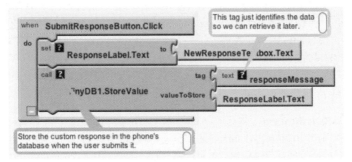

Figure 22-1. The TinyDB.StoreValue block stores data to the device's long-term memory

A tag-value scheme is used for database storage. In Figure 22-1, the data is tagged with the text "responseMessage." The value is some text the user has entered for the new custom response—say, "I'm sleeping; stop bugging me."

The tag gives the data you're storing in the database a name —a way to reference the information—while the value is the data itself. You can think of the tag as a key that you'll use later when you want to retrieve the data from the database.

Likewise, you can think of an App Inventor TinyDB database as a table of tag-value pairs. After the **TinyDB1.StoreValue** in Figure 22-1 is executed, the device's database will have the value listed in Table 22-1.

Table 22-1. The value stored in the databases

Tag	Value
responseMessage	I'm sleeping; stop bugging me

An app might store many tag-value pairs for the various data items you wish to be persistent. The tag is always text, while the value can be either a single piece of information (a text or number) or a list. Each tag has only one value; every time you store to a tag, it overwrites the existing value.

Retrieving Data from TinyDB

You retrieve data from the database with the **TinyDB.GetValue** block. When you call **GetValue**, you request particular data by providing a tag. For the No Texting While Driving app, you can request the custom response using the same tag as we used in the **StoreValue**, "responseMessage." The call to **GetValue** returns the data, so you must plug it into a variable.

Often, you'll retrieve data from the database when the app opens. App Inventor provides a special event handler, **Screen.Initialize**, which is triggered when the app starts up. The general pattern is to call **GetValue**, put the returned data into a variable, and then check to see if the database indeed returned some information. This check is important, because generally the first time you run the app, there is no database data yet (e.g., the first time No Texting While Driving runs, the user hasn't yet entered a custom response).

The blocks in Figure 22-2, for the **Screen.Initialize** of No Texting While Driving, are indicative of how many apps will load data on initialization.

The blocks put the data returned from **GetValue** into the variable response and then check if response has a length greater than 0. If it does, then the database *did* return a nonempty custom response, and it should be put in the ResponseLabel. If the length of the value returned is 0, it means no data with a tag of "responseMessage" has been stored, so no action is necessary.

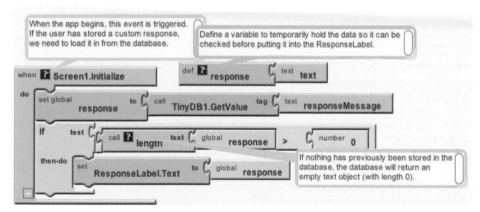

Figure 22-2. A template for loading database data when the app launches

Storing and Sharing Data with TinyWebDB

The TinyDB component stores data in a database located directly on the Android device. This is appropriate for personal-use apps that don't need to share data among users. For instance, many people might download the No Texting While Driving app, but there's no need for the various people using the app to share their custom responses with others.

Of course, many apps do share data: think of Facebook, Twitter, and popular multiuser games such as Words with Friends. For such data-sharing apps, the database must live on the Web, not the device. The MakeQuiz/TakeQuiz apps from Chapter 10 provide another example: a person on one phone creates a quiz and stores it in a web database so that a person on another phone can load the quiz and take it.

TinyWebDB is the web counterpart to TinyDB. It allows you to write apps that store data on the Web, using a StoreValue/GetValue protocol similar to that of TinyDB.

By default, the TinyWebDB component stores data using a web database set up by the App Inventor team and accessible at *http://appinvtinywebdb.appspot.com*. That website contains a database and "serves" (responds to) web requests for storing and retrieving data. The site also provides a human-readable web interface that a database administrator (you) can use to examine the data stored there.

To explore the web database, open a browser to *http://appinvtinywebdb.appspot.com* and check out some of the tag-value data stored there.

This default database is for development only; it is limited in size and accessible to all App Inventor programmers. Because any App Inventor app can store data there, you have no assurance that another app won't overwrite your data!

If you're just exploring App Inventor or in early the stages of a project, the default web database is fine. But if you're creating an app for real deployment, at some point you'll need to set up your own web database. Since we're just exploring right now, we'll use the default web database. Later in the chapter, you'll learn how to create your own web database and configure TinyWebDB to use it instead.

In this section, we'll build a voting app (depicted in Figure 22-3) to illustrate how TinyWebDB works. The app will have the following features:

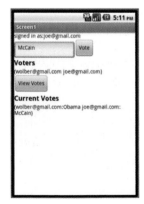

- Users are prompted to enter their email address each time the app loads. That account name will be used to tag the user's vote in the database.

- Users can submit a new vote at any time. In this case, their old vote will be overwritten.

- Users can view the votes from everyone in the group.

Figure 22-3. A Voting app that stores votes to TinyWebDB

- For the sake of simplicity, the issue being voted on is determined outside the app, such as in a classroom setting in which the teacher announces the issue and asks everyone to vote electronically. (Note that this example could be extended to allow users to prompt votes by posting issues to vote on from within the app.)

Storing Data with TinyWebDB

The **TinyWebDB.StoreValue** block works the same as **TinyDB.StoreValue**, only the data is stored on the Web. For our voting sample, assume the user can enter a vote in a text box named VoteTextBox and click a button named VoteButton to submit the vote. To store the vote to the web database so others can see it, we'll code the **VoteButton.Click** event handler like the example in Figure 22-4.

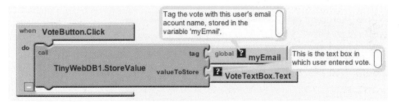

Figure 22-4. Using the VoteButton.Click event handler to store a vote to the database

The tag used to identify the data is the user's email, which has previously been stored in the variable myEmail (we'll see this later). The value is whatever the user entered in VoteTextBox. So, if the user email was *wolber@gmail.com* and his vote was "Obama," the entry would be stored in the database as shown in Table 22-2.

Table 22-2. The tag and value for the vote are recorded in the database

tag	value
wolber@gmail.com	Obama

The **TinyWebDB.StoreValue** block sends the tag-value pair over the Web to the database server at *http://appinvtinywebdb.appspot.com*. Because it's the default service, it shows lots of data from various apps, so you may or may not see your app's data in the initial window that appears. If you don't see your data, there is a /getValue link that allows you to search for data with a particular tag.

 Test your app. *As you program with* TinyWebDB, *use the web interface of the database server to test that data is being stored as you expect.*

Requesting and Processing Data with TinyWebDB

Retrieving data with TinyWebDB is more complicated than with TinyDB. With TinyDB, the **GetValue** operation immediately returns a value because your app is communicating with a database directly on the Android device. With TinyWebDB, the app is requesting data over the Web, so Android requires a two-step scheme for handling it.

With TinyWebDB, you request the data with **GetValue** and then process it later in a **TinyWebDB.GotValue** event handler. **TinyWebDB.GetValue** should really be called "RequestValue" because it just makes the request to the web database and doesn't actually "get" a value from it right away. To see this more clearly, check out the difference between the **TinyDB.GetValue** block (Figure 22-5) and the **TinyWebDB. GetValue** block (Figure 22-6).

Figure 22-5. The TinyDB.GetValue block

Figure 22-6. The TinyWebDB.GetValue block

The **TinyDB.GetValue** block returns a value right away, and thus a plug appears on its left side so that the returned value can be placed into a variable or property. The **TinyWebDB.GetValue** block does not return a value immediately, so there is no plug on its left side.

Instead, when the web database fulfills the request and the data arrives back at the device, a **TinyWebDB.GotValue** event is triggered. So you'll call **TinyWebDB.GetValue** in one place of your app, and then you'll program the **TinyWebDB.GotValue** event handler to specify how to handle the data when it actually arrives. An event handler like **TinyWebDB.GotValue** is sometimes called a *callback procedure*, because some external entity (the web database) is in effect calling your app back after processing your request. It's like ordering at a busy coffee shop: you place your order and then wait for the barista to call your name to actually go pick up your drink. In the meantime, she's been taking orders from everyone else in line too (and those people are all waiting for their names to be called as well).

GetValue-GotValue in Action

For our sample app, we need to store and retrieve a list of the voters who have the app, as the ultimate goal is to show the votes of all users.

The simplest scheme for retrieving list data is to request the data when the app launches, in the **Screen.Initialize** event, as shown in Figure 22-7. (In this example, we'll just call the database with the tag for "voterlist.")

Figure 22-7. Requesting data in the Screen1.Initialize event

When the list of voters arrives from the web database, the **TinyWebDB1.GotValue** event handler will be triggered. Figure 22-8 shows some blocks for processing the returned list.

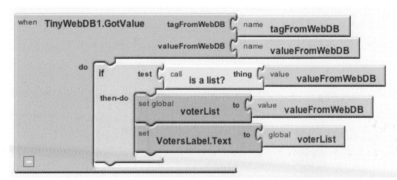

Figure 22-8. Using the GotValue event handler to process the returned list

The valueFromWebDB *argument* of **GotValue** holds the data returned from the database request. Event arguments like valueFromWebDB have meaning only within the event handler that invokes them (they are considered *local* to the event handler), so you can't reference them in other event handlers.

It may seem a bit counterintuitive, but once you get used to the idea of arguments holding local data, you're probably already thinking about something that can handle data more *globally* (anywhere in an app): variables. Given that, it makes sense that **GotValue**'s key job is to transfer the data returned in valueFromWebDB into a variable. In this case, the data is transferred into the variable voterList, which you'll use in another event handler.

The **if** block in the event handler is also often used in conjunction with **GotValue**, the reason being that the database returns an empty text ("") in valueFromWebDB if there is no data for the requested tag—most commonly, when it's the first time the app has been used. By asking if the valueFromWebDB is a list, you're making sure there is some data actually returned. If the valueFromWebDB is the empty text (the **if** test is false), you don't put it into voterList.

Note that *get data*, *check data*, *set data* (into a variable) is the same pattern you used in the preceding TinyDB example, but here you are expecting a list, so you use a slightly different test.

A More Complex GetValue/GotValue Example

The blocks in Figure 22-8 are a good model for retrieving data in a fairly simplistic app. In our voting example, however, we need more complicated logic. Specifically:

- The app should prompt the user to enter his email address when the program starts. We can use a Notifier component for this, which pops up a window. (You can find the Notifier in the "Other stuff" palette in the Designer.) When the user enters his email, we'll store it in a variable.

- Only after determining the user's email should we call **GetValue** to retrieve the voter list. Can you figure out why?

Figure 22-9 shows the blocks for this more complicated scheme for requesting the database data.

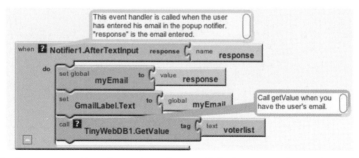

Figure 22-9. In this more complex scheme, GetValue is called after getting the user's email

On startup (**Screen1.Initialize**), a Notifier component prompts the user to enter his email. When the user enters it (**Notifier.AfterTextInput**), his entry is put into a variable and label, and then **GetValue** is called to get the list of voters. Note that **GetValue** isn't called directly in **Screen.Initialize** because we need the user's email to be set first.

So, with these blocks, when the app initializes, it prompts the user for his email and then calls **GetValue** with a tag of "voterlist." When the list arrives from the Web, **GotValue** will be triggered. Here's what we want to happen:

- **GotValue** should check if the data that arrives is nonempty (someone has used the app and initiated the voter list). If there is data (a voter list), we should check if our particular user's email is already in the voter list. If it's not, it should be added to the list, and the updated list should be stored back to the database.

- If there isn't yet a voter list in the database, we should create one with the user's email as the only item.

Figure 22-10 shows the blocks for this behavior.

The blocks first ask if a nonempty voter list came back from the database by calling **is a list?**. If so, the data is put into the variable voterList. Remember, voterList will have emails for everyone who has used this app. But we don't know if this particular user is in the list yet, so we have to check. If the user is not yet in the list, he is added with **add item to list**, and the updated list is stored to the web database.

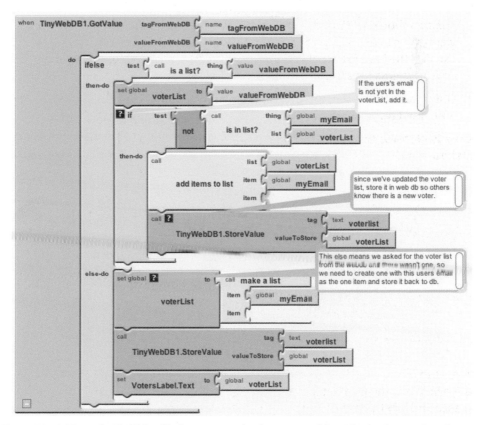

Figure 22-10. Using the GotValue blocks to process the data returned from the database and perform different actions based on what is returned

The "else-do" part of the **ifelse** block is invoked if a list wasn't returned from the web database; this happens if nobody has used the app yet. In this case, a new voterList is created with the current user's email as the first item. This one-item voter list is then stored to the web database (with the hope that others will join as well!).

Requesting Data with Various Tags

The voting app thus far manages a list of an app's users. Each person can see the emails of all the other users, but we haven't yet created blocks for retrieving and displaying each user's vote.

Recall that the VoteButton allowed the user to submit a vote with a tag-value pair of the form "email: vote." If two people had used the app and voted, the pertinent database entries would look something like Table 22-3.

Table 22-3. The tag-value pairs stored in the database

tag	value
voterlist	[wolber@gmail.com, joe@gmail.com]
wolber@gmail.com	Obama
joe@gmail.com	McCain

When the user clicks on the ViewVotes button, the app should retrieve all votes from the database and display them. Supposing the voter list has already been retrieved into the variable voterList, we can use a **foreach** to request the vote of each person in the list, as shown in Figure 22-11.

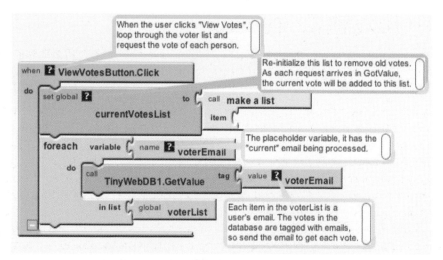

Figure 22-11. Using a foreach block to request the vote of each person in the list

Here we initialize a variable, currentVotesList, to an empty list, as our goal is to add the up-to-date votes from the database into this list. We then use **foreach** to call **TinyWebDB1.GetValue** for every email in the list, sending the email (voterEmail) as the tag in the request. Note that the votes won't actually be added to current-VotesList until they arrive via a series of **GotValue** events.

Processing Multiple Tags in TinyWebDB.GotValue

Now that we want to display the votes in our app, things get a bit more complicated yet again. With the requests from ViewVotesButton, **TinyWebDB.GotValue** will now be returning data related to all the email tags, as well as the "voterlist" tag used to retrieve the list of user emails. When your app requests more than one item from the database with different tags, you need to code **TinyWebDB.GotValue** to handle all possible requests. (You might think that you could try to code multiple **GotValue** event handlers, one for each database request—can you figure out why this won't work?)

To handle this complexity, the **GotValue** event handler has a tagFromWebDB argument that tells you which request has just arrived. In this case, if the tag is "voterlist," we should continue to process the request as we did previously. If the tag is something else, we can assume it's the email of someone in the user list, stemming from the requests triggered in the **ViewVotesButton.Click** event handler. When those requests come in, we want to add the data—the voter and vote—to the currentVotesList so we can display it to the user.

Figure 22-12 shows the entire **TinyWebDB.GotValue** event handler.

Setting Up a Web Database

As we mentioned earlier in the chapter, the default web database at *http://appinvtiny webdb.appspot.com* is intended for prototyping and testing purposes only. Before you deploy an app with real users, you need to create a database specifically for your app.

You can create a web database using the instructions at *http://appinventorapi.com/ program-an-api-python/*. This site was set up by one of the authors (Wolber) and contains sample code and instructions for setting up App Inventor web databases and APIs. The instructions point you to some code that you can download and use with only a minor modification to a configuration file. The code you'll download is the same as that used for the default web database set up by App Inventor. It runs on Google's App Engine, a cloud computing service that will host your web database on Google's servers for free. By following the instructions, you can have your own private web database (that is compliant with App Inventor's protocols) up and running within minutes and begin creating web-enabled mobile apps that use it.

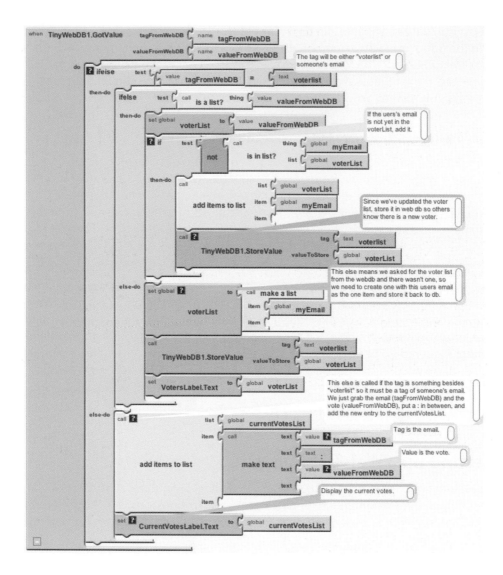

Figure 22-12. The TinyWebDB.GotValue event handler

Once you create and deploy your own custom web database (at which point, you'll know the URL for it), you can create apps that use it. For an app to use your custom database, you'll need to change a property in the TinyWebDB component, ServiceURL, so the component knows to store and retrieve data from your new custom database. Figure 22-13 illustrates how to do this.

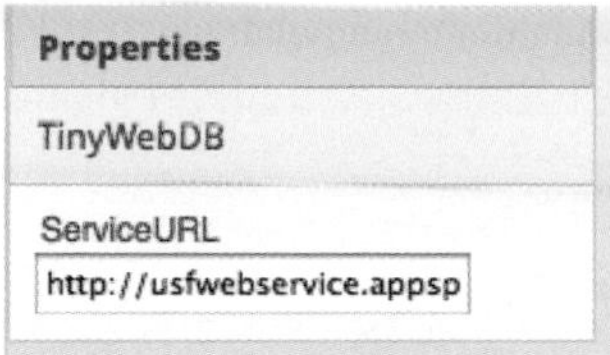

Figure 22-13. Changing the
ServiceURL property to the URL
of your custom database

In this example, the ServiceURL is set to *http://usfweb service.appspot.com*, a web database that one of the authors set up for his students' apps (the end of "appspot.com" is cut off in the text box in Figure 22-13). Once the ServiceURL is set, all **TinyWebDB. StoreValue** and **TinyWebDB.GetValue** calls will be sent to the specified URL.

Summary

App Inventor makes it easy to store data persistently through its TinyDB and TinyWebDB components. Data is always stored as a tag-value pair, with the tag identifying the data for later retrieval. Use TinyDB when it is appropriate to store data directly on the device. When data needs to be shared across phones (e.g., for a multiplayer game or a voting app), you'll need to use TinyWebDB instead. TinyWebDB is more complicated because you need to set up a callback procedure (the **GotValue** event handler), as well as a web database service.

Once you get the hang of working with databases—especially the key *get data*, *check data*, *set data* pattern—you'll be building more complex apps in no time!

CHAPTER 23

Reading and Responding to Sensors

Point your phone at the sky, and Google Sky Map tells you which stars you're looking at. Tilt your phone, and you can control the game you're playing. Take your phone on your daily walk, and a breadcrumb app records your route. All of these apps are possible because the mobile devices we carry have high-tech sensors for detecting our location, orientation, and acceleration.

In this chapter, you'll revisit the App Inventor components LocationSensor, OrientationSensor, *and* AccelerometerSensor. *Along the way, you'll learn about the global positioning system (GPS); orientation measures like pitch, roll, and yaw; and some math for processing accelerometer readings.*

Creating Location-Aware Apps

Until the popularization of the smartphone, computing was on desktop lockdown. Yes, laptops are mobile, but not in the same sense as the tiny devices we now carry around in our pockets. Computing has left the lab and the office, and is now taking place out in the world.

One significant effect of carrying our computing with us is a new, very interesting piece of data for every app: a current location. Knowing where people are as they move about the world has far-reaching implications and the potential to help us greatly in our lives. It also has the potential to invade our privacy and be a detriment to humanity.

The "Android, Where's My Car?" app (Chapter 7) is an example of a *location-aware* app that provides a personal benefit. It lets you remember a previous location so you can get back to it at a later time. That app is private—your location information is stored only in your phone's database.

The same idea can be applied to groups. For instance, a group of hikers might want to keep track of one another's whereabouts in the wilderness, or a group of business associates might want to find one another at a large conference. Such apps are starting to appear in the marketplace, with two of the most popular being Google's Latitude (*www.google.com/latitude*), and Facebook's Places (*www.facebook.com/places*). Due to the public's privacy concerns, these apps faced criticism on their launch.

Another type of location-aware app uses *augmented-reality* tools. These apps use your location and the phone's orientation to provide overlay information that augments the natural setting. So you might point a phone at a building and see its price on the real-estate market, or you might walk near an exotic plant in a botanical garden and have an app tell you its species. Early players in this genre include Wikitude, Layar, and Google Sky Map.

Wikitude even allows users to add data to the *mobile cloud* through its website, *http://wikitude.me*. At the site, you pull up a map to *geotag* the information you post. Later, when you or someone else uses Wikitude's mobile app at that location, your information appears.

GPS

To create a location-aware app, you first need to understand how the *global positioning system* (GPS) works. GPS data comes from a satellite system maintained by the US government. As long as you have an unobstructed sight line to at least three satellites in the system, your phone can get a reading. A GPS reading consists of your latitude, longitude, and altitude. Latitude is how far north or south you are of the equator, with values for north being positive and south being negative. The range is –90 to 90. Figure 23-1 shows a Google map of a spot near Quito, Ecuador. The latitude shown on the map is –0.01—just barely south of the equator!

Figure 23-1. Quito, Ecuador, is on the equator

Longitude is how far east or west you are of the Prime Meridian; east coordinates have positive values and west coordinates are negative. The most well-known place it runs through is Greenwich, a town near London that is the home of the Royal Observatory. The map in Figure 23-2 shows Greenwich and its longitude of 0.0.

Figure 23-2. The Royal Observatory in Greenwich shoots a beam of light along the Prime Meridian

Longitude values range from −180 to 180. Figure 23-3 shows a spot in Russia, very close to Alaska, that has a 180.0 longitude. You might say that a location like this is halfway around the world from Greenwich (0.0 longitude).

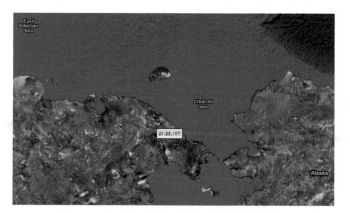

Figure 23-3. A point near the Russian–Alaskan border has longitude 180

Sensing Location with App Inventor

App Inventor provides the LocationSensor component for accessing GPS informa-tion. The component has properties for Latitude, Longitude, and Altitude. It also communicates with Google Maps, so you can get a reading for your current street address.

LocationSensor.LocationChanged, pictured in Figure 23-4, is the key event handler for the `LocationSensor`.

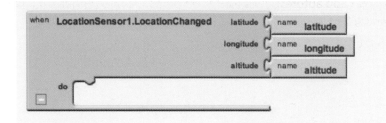

Figure 23-4. The LocationSensor1.LocationChanged event handler

This event is triggered the first time the sensor gets a reading and each subsequent time the phone is moved enough so that new data is read. There's often a delay of quite a few seconds before an app's first reading, and sometimes the device can't get a reading at all. For instance, if you're indoors and not connected to WiFi, the device might not get a reading. Your phone also has settings that allow you to turn GPS reading off to save battery life; this is another potential reason the component can't get a reading. For these reasons, you shouldn't assume that the `LocationSensor` properties have a valid setting until the **LocationSensor.LocationChanged** event occurs.

One way to deal with the unknowns in location sensing is to create a variable `lastKnownLocation`, initialize it to "unknown,"and then have the **LocationSensor .LocationChanged** event handler change the value of that variable, as shown in Figure 23-5.

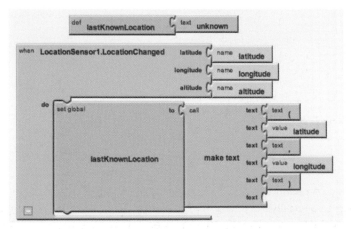

Figure 23-5. The value of the lastKnownLocation variable changes whenever the location changes

By programming the **LocationSensor.LocationChanged** event handler in this way, you can always display the current location or record it in a database, with "unknown" appearing until the first reading. This strategy is used in No Texting While Driving (Chapter 4); that app autoresponds to SMS texts and includes either "unknown" or the last reading taken in the response.

You can also ask explicitly whether the sensor has a reading using the **LocationSensor.HasLongitudeLatitude** block pictured in Figure 23-6.

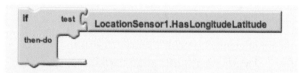

Figure 23-6. Testing whether the sensor has a reading with the HasLongitudeLatitude block

Checking Boundaries

One common use of the **LocationChanged** event is to check whether the device is within a *boundary*, or a set area. For example, consider the code in Figure 23-7, which vibrates the phone each time a new reading shows that a person has moved farther than 0.1 longitude from the Prime Meridian.

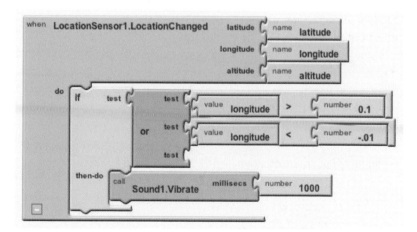

Figure 23-7. If a reading isn't close to the Prime Meridian, the phone vibrates

Such boundary checking has numerous applications; for example, warning parolees if they're nearing a legally specified distance from their home, or alerting parents or teachers if a child leaves the playground area. If you'd like to see a slightly more complex example, see Chapter 18's discussion of conditional blocks.

Location Information Providers: GPS, WiFi, and Cell ID

An Android device can determine its own location in a number of ways. The most accurate method—within a few meters—is through the satellites that make up the GPS maintained by the US government. You won't get a reading, however, if you're inside and there are skyscrapers or other objects in the way; you need a clear path to at least three satellites in the system.

If GPS isn't available or the user has disabled it, the device can obtain its position through a wireless network. You have to be near a WiFi router, of course, and the position reading you'll get is the latitude/longitude of that WiFi station.

A third way a device can determine positioning is through Cell ID. Cell ID provides a location for the phone based on the strength of signals from nearby cell phone towers. It is generally not very accurate unless you have numerous cell towers near you. However, it does use the least amount of battery power compared to GPS or WiFi connectivity.

Using the Orientation Sensor

The OrientationSensor is used for game-like apps in which the user controls the action by tilting the device. It can also be used as a compass to find out which direction (north/south, east/west) the phone is pointing.

The OrientationSensor has five properties, all of which are unfamiliar to most people other than aeronautical engineers:

Roll *(Left–Right)*
> Roll is 0 degrees when the device is level, increases to 90 degrees as the device is tilted up onto its left side, and decreases to −90 degrees when the device is tilted up onto its right side.

Pitch *(Up–Back)*
> Pitch is 0 degrees when the device is level, increases to 90 degrees as the device is tilted so its top is pointing down, and increases further to 180 degrees as it is turned over. Similarly, as the device is tilted so its bottom points down, Pitch decreases to −90 degrees and then down to −180 degrees as it is turned all the way over.

Yaw *(Compass)*
> Yaw is 0 degrees when the top of the device is pointing north, 90 degrees when it is pointing east, 180 degrees when it is pointing south, and 270 degrees when it is pointing west.

Magnitude *(Speed of a rolling ball)*
> Magnitude returns a number between 0 and 1 that indicates how much the device is tilted. Its value indicates the force exerted by a ball rolling on the surface of the device.

Angle *(Angle of a rolling ball)*

Angle returns the direction in which the device is tiled. That is, it tells the direction of the force that would be exerted by a ball rolling on the surface of the device.

The OrientationSensor also provides the **OrientationChanged** event, which is triggered every time the orientation changes. To explore these properties further, write an app that illustrates how the properties change as the user tilts the device. Just add five heading labels, and five other labels to show the current values of the properties in the preceding list. Then add the blocks shown in Figure 23-8.

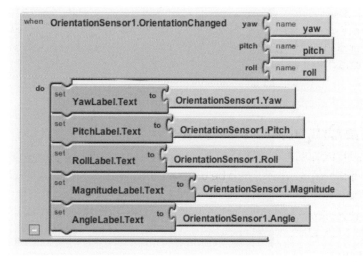

Figure 23-8. Blocks to display the OrientationSensor data

Figure 23-9. A user interface for exploring how "roll" can be used to move an image

Using the Roll Parameter

Now let's try to move an image left or right on the screen based on the user tilting the device, like you might do in a shooting or driving game. Drag out a Canvas and set the Width to "Fill parent" and the Height to 200 pixels. Then add an ImageSprite or Ball within the Canvas, and add a Label named RollLabel under it to display a property value, as shown in Figure 23-9.

The OrientationSensor's Roll property will tell you if the phone is tilted left or right (i.e., if you hold the phone upright and tilt it slightly to the left, you'll get a positive reading for the roll; if you tilt it slightly right, you'll get a negative reading). Therefore, you can let the user move an object with an event handler like the one shown in Figure 23-10.

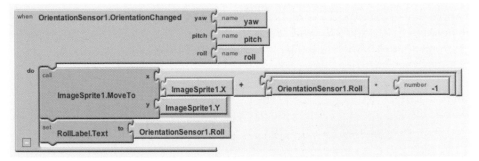

Figure 23-10. Responding to changes in the Roll property with the OrientationChanged event

The blocks multiply the roll by –1, as tilting left gives a positive roll and should move the object left (thereby making the *x* coordinate smaller). For a review of how the coordinate system works in animated apps, see Chapter 17.

Note that this app works only when the device is in portrait mode (upright), not in landscape mode. As is, if you tilt the phone too far, the screen will autorotate into landscape mode and the image will stay marooned on the left side of the screen. The reason is that if the device is on its side, it is tilted left and thus will always get a positive reading for the roll. A positive roll reading, as shown in the blocks in Figure 23-10, will always make the *x* coordinate smaller.

If App Inventor provided the capability, you could either (1) lock the phone so it didn't autorotate for this app, or (2) find out the phone's mode and modify your formula for moving the object based on that setting. Such capabilities will certainly be added to the system, but you should instruct your users on how the app works currently.

Moving Any Direction with Heading and Magnitude

The example in the previous section moves the image left or right. If you want to allow for movement in any direction, you can use the Angle and Magnitude properties of the OrientationSensor. These are the properties used to move the ladybug in the game described in Chapter 5.

In Figure 23-11, you can see the blocks for a test app that lets the user tilt the device to move a character in any direction (you need two labels and an image sprite for this example).

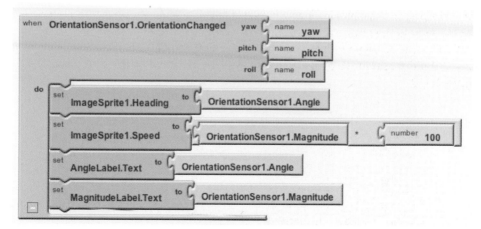

Figure 23-11. Moving a character using angle and magnitude

Try this one out. The Magnitude property, a value between 0 and 1, denotes how much the device is tilted. In this test app, the image moves faster as the magnitude gets bigger.

Using the Phone As a Compass

Compass apps and apps like Google Sky Map need to know the phone's orientation in the world, east/west and north/south. Sky Map uses the information to overlay information about the constellations at which the phone is pointing.

The Yaw reading is useful for this type of orientation. Yaw is always between 0 and 360 degrees, with 0 being north; 90, east; 180, south; and 270, west. So a reading of 45 means the phone is pointing northeast, 135 means southeast, 225 means southwest, and 315 means northwest.

The blocks in Figure 23-12 are for a simple compass that displays in text which direction the phone is pointing (e.g., Northwest).

As you may have noticed, the blocks show only one of four possibilities: Northwest, Northeast, Southwest, and Southeast. As a challenge, see if you can modify it to show just a single direction (North, South, East, or West) if the reading specifies that you are pointing within a few degrees of it.

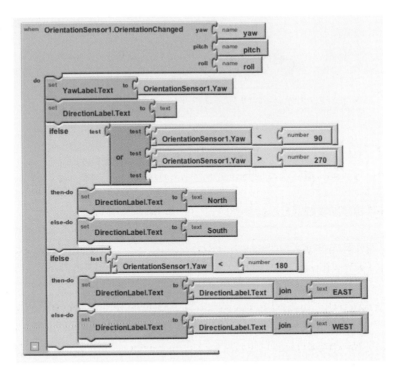

Figure 23-12. Programming a simple compass

Using the Accelerometer

Acceleration is the rate of change of velocity over time. If you press your foot to the gas pedal of your car, the car accelerates—its velocity increases at a particular rate.

An accelerometer—like the one in your Android device—measures acceleration, but its frame of reference is not the device at rest, but rather the device in free fall: if you drop the phone, it will register an acceleration reading of 0. Simply put, the readings take gravity into account.

If you want to know more about the physics of the matter, you'll have to consult your Einstein-related books. But in this section, we'll explore the accelerometer enough to get you started. We'll even examine an app that could help save lives!

Responding to the Device Shaking

If you've been going through the chapters and completed the app in Chapter 1 (HelloPurr), you've already used the AccelerometerSensor. In that app, you used the **Accelerometer.Shaking** event to make the kitty meow when the phone was shaken, as shown in Figure 23-13.

Figure 23-13. Playing a sound when the phone is shaken

Using the AccelerometerSensor's Readings

Like the other sensors, the accelerometer has an event for when the readings change, **AccelerometerSensor.AccelerationChanged**. That event has three arguments corresponding to the acceleration in three dimensions:

xAccel
> Positive when the device is tilted to the right (that is, its left side is raised), and negative when the device is tilted to the left (its right size is raised).

yAccel
> Positive when the device's bottom is raised, and negative when its top is raised.

zAccel
> Positive when the device display is facing up, and negative when the display is facing down.

Detecting Free Fall

We know that if all the acceleration readings are near 0, the device is free-falling to the ground. With this in mind, we can mimic a free-fall event by checking the readings in the **AccelerometerSensor.AccelerationChanged** event. Such blocks, with lots of testing, could be used to detect when an elderly person has fallen and automatically send an SMS message out in response.

Figure 23-14 shows the blocks for an app that simply reports that a free fall has occurred (and lets the user click a Reset button to check again).

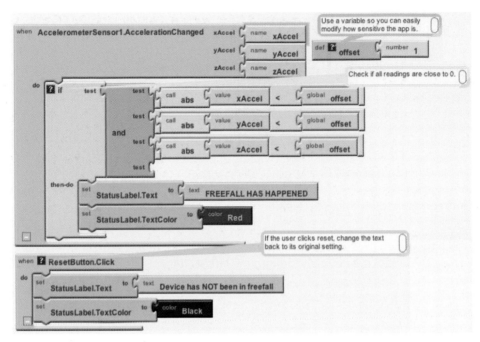

Figure 23-14. Reporting when a free fall has occurred

Each time the sensor gets a reading, the blocks check the *x*, *y*, and *z* dimensions to see if they're near 0 (if their absolute value is less than 1). If all three are near 0, the app changes a status label to denote that the phone is in free fall. When the user clicks the ResetButton, the status label is reset to its original state ("Device has NOT been in free fall").

If you'd like to try this app, you can download it at *http://examples.oreilly.com/ 0636920016632*.

Detecting Acceleration Using Calibrated Values

The AcclerometerSensor's readings are calibrated to the free-fall state. If you want to instead measure the acceleration relative to its value when the phone is lying inert on a table, you need to calibrate the readings to that standard. To *calibrate* means to check, adjust, or determine by comparison with a standard; in this case, the standard you want is the readings when the device is lying flat.

To do this, you need the user to help you by laying the device flat on a table and then clicking a Calibrate button. When the user clicks the button, the app records the readings for the flat surface. Those readings can then be used later, in **AccelerationChanged** events, to offset the new readings and tell you if the device is moved rapidly in some dimension.

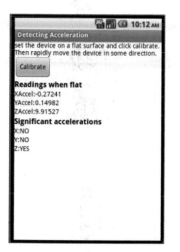

Figure 23-15. Calibrating the acceleration readings

Figure 23-15 shows a sample app that lets the user calibrate the readings and then detects acceleration.

You can download and install this app from *http://examples.oreilly.com/0636920016632/*. Run it, set the phone on a table, and click Calibrate. The readings will appear in the "Readings when flat" area. If you raise the phone slowly, the readings in the "Significant accelerations" area won't change. But if you raise the phone rapidly, the "No" reading for Z will change to "Yes," as shown in Figure 23-15. Similarly, if you move the phone rapidly across the table, you'll get a significant acceleration for X or Y. Figure 23-16 shows the blocks for getting the initial calibration.

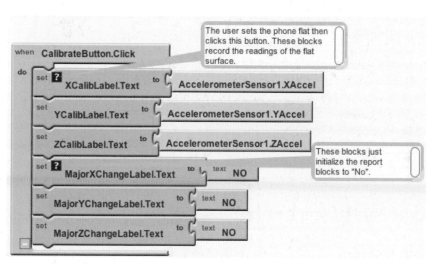

Figure 23-16. Getting the initial calibration

These blocks take the readings and place them in three labels: XCalibLabel, YCalibLabel, and ZCalibLabel. The blocks also initialize the labels that will be used to report accelerations later, after this calibration step.

The accelerometer should get a reading of zAccel around 9.8 when the phone is flat, and xAccel and yAccel readings of around 0. But the calibration step tells us exactly how the accelerometer is working. Once the calibration readings are set, your app can detect changes in the *x*, *y*, or *z* dimensions by measuring new readings offset from the old (similar to the boundary-checking app covered in Chapter 18). Figure 23-17 provides the blocks for detecting acceleration using the calibrated readings.

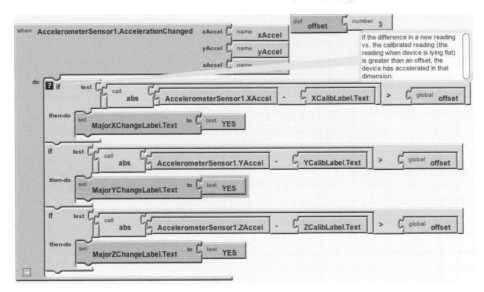

Figure 23-17. Detecting acceleration using the calibrated readings

These blocks will be triggered if the device is moved. They check the new accelerometer readings to see if they are significantly different (within 3) of those taken when the phone was lying flat. Suppose that our calibration step had put a 9.0 in ZCalibText. If you slowly lift the phone, the new readings will remain close to 9, and no change will be reported. But if you rapidly lift the phone, the reading will become significantly higher, and the blocks will report a change.

Summary

Sensors are of great interest in mobile apps because they allow your users to truly interact with their environments. By taking computing mobile, you are opening up (almost literally) a whole world of opportunities in user experiences and app development. However, you'll need to think carefully about how, where, and when you use sensors in your apps. Many people have privacy concerns, and they might not use your app if they're worried about what you're doing with their sensor data. But with all the options in games, social networking, travel, and more, the possibilities for positive implementations are nearly endless.

CHAPTER 24

Communicating with Web APIs

Mobile technology and the ubiquitous nature of the Web have changed the world we live in. You can now sit in the park and do your banking, search Amazon.com to find reviews of the book you're reading, and check Twitter to see what people in every other park in the world are thinking about. Mobile phones have moved well past just calling and texting— now you have instant access to the world's data, too.

You can use your phone's browser to reach the Web, but often the small screen and limited speed of a mobile device can make this problematic. Custom apps, specially designed to pull in small chunks of particularly suitable information from the Web, can provide a more attractive alternative to the mobile browser.

In this chapter, we'll take a broader look at apps that source information from the Web. You'll start by creating an app that asks a website to generate a bar chart (image) of a game player's scores for display. Then we'll discuss how TinyWebDB *can be used to access any type of data (not just images) from the Web, and we'll provide a sample that accesses stock data from Yahoo! Finance. Finally, we'll discuss how you can create your own web information sources that can be used by App Inventor apps.*

Creativity is about remixing the world, combining (*mashing*) old ideas and content in interesting new ways. Eminem popularized the music *mashup* when he set his Slim Shady vocal over AC/DC and Vanilla Ice tracks. This kind of "sampling" is now common, and numerous artists—including Girl Talk and Negativland—focus primarily on creating new tracks from mashing old content.

The web and mobile world are no different: websites and apps remix content from various data sources, and most sites are now designed with such *interoperability* in mind. An illustrative example of a web mashup is Housing Maps (http://*www. housingmaps.com*), pictured in Figure 24-1, which takes apartment rental information from Craigslist (*http://www.craigslist.org*) and mashes it with the Google Maps API.

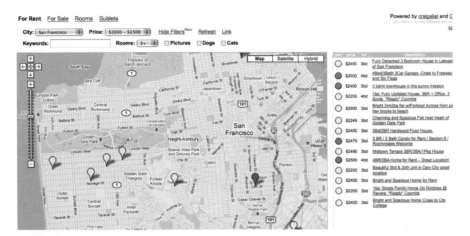

Figure 24-1. Housing Maps mashes information from Craigslist and Google Maps

Mashups like Housing Maps are possible because services like Google Maps provide both a website and a corresponding *web service API*. We humans visit *http://maps .google.com/* in a browser, but apps like Housing Maps communicate *machine to machine* with the Google Maps API. Mashups process the data, combine it with data from other sites (e.g., Craigslist), and then present it in new and interesting ways.

Just about every popular website now provides this alternative, machine-to-machine access. The program providing the data is called a *web service*, and the protocol for how a *client* app should communicate with the service is called an *application pro-grammer interface*, or *API*. In practice, the term *API* is used to refer to the web service as well.

The Amazon Web Service (AWS) was one of the first web services, as Amazon realized that opening its data for use by third-party entities would eventually lead to more books being sold. When Facebook launched its API in 2007, many people raised their eyebrows. Facebook's data isn't book advertisements, so why should it let other apps "steal" that data and potentially draw many users away from the Facebook site (and its advertisements!). But its openness led Facebook toward becoming a *platform* instead of just a site—meaning that other programs, like FarmVille, could build on and tap into Facebook's functionality—and no one can argue with its success today. By the time Twitter launched in 2009, API access was an expectation, not a novelty, and Twitter acted accordingly. Now, as shown in Figure 24-2, most websites offer both an API and a human interface.

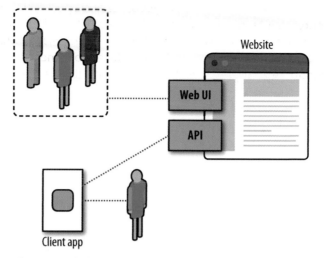

Figure 24-2. Most websites provide both a human interface and an API for client apps

So the Web is one thing to us average humans—a collection of sites to visit. To programmers, it is the world's largest and most diverse database of information. Machine-to-machine communication is now poised to outpace human–machine communication on the Web!

Talking to Web APIs That Generate Images

As we saw in Chapter 13 ("Amazon at the Bookstore"), most APIs accept requests in the form of a URL and return data (typically in standard formats like XML, or Extensible Markup Language; and JSON, JavaScript Object Notation). For these APIs, you use the TinyWebDB component to communicate, a topic we'll discuss in greater detail later in the chapter.

Some APIs, however, don't return data; they return a picture. In this section, we'll discuss how you can communicate with these image-generating APIs in order to extend App Inventor's user interface capabilities.

The Google Chart API is such a service. Your app can send it some data within a URL, and it will send back a chart that you can display in your app. The service creates many types of charts, including bar charts, pie charts, maps, and Venn diagrams. The Chart API is a great example of an interoperable web service whose purpose is to enhance the capabilities of other sites. Since App Inventor doesn't provide much in terms of visualization components, the ability to leverage a service like the Chart API is crucial.

The first thing to do is to understand the format of the URL you should send to the API. If you go to the Google Chart API site (*http://code.google.com/apis/chart*), you will see the overview shown in Figure 24-3.

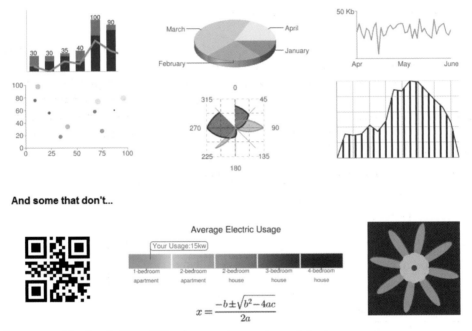

What is the Google Chart API?

The Google Chart API lets you dynamically generate charts with a URL string. You can embed these charts on your web page, or download the image for local or offline use.

What Kind of Charts Can I Make?

You can make a lot of things with the Google Chart API:

Some things that look like charts...

And some that don't...

Average Electric Usage

$$x = \frac{-b \pm \sqrt{b^2 - 4ac}}{2a}$$

Figure 24-3. The Google Chart API generates numerous types of charts

The site includes complete documentation and a wizard to interactively create charts and explore how to build the URLs. The wizard is especially helpful, because you can use a form to specify the kind of chart you want and then examine the URL that the wizard generates to reverse-engineer what you want to send it for your specific data.

Go ahead and play around with the website and the wizard and build some charts, and then take a look at the details of the URLs used to build them. For example, if you enter the following URL in a browser:

```
http://chart.apis.google.com/chart?cht=bvg&chxt=y&chbh=a&chs=300x225&chco=
A2C180&chtt=Vertical+bar+chart&chd=t:10,50,60,80,40,60,30
```

you'll get the chart shown in Figure 24-4.

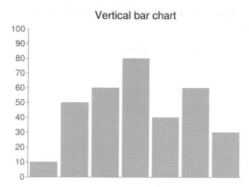

Figure 24-4. Google's Chart API generates this chart from the URL

To understand the rather complicated-looking URL specified previously, you need to understand how URLs work. In your browsing experience, you've probably noticed URLs with question marks (?) and ampersands (&). The ? character specifies that the first parameter of the URL request is coming. The & character then separates each succeeding parameter. Each parameter has a name, an equals sign, and a value. So the sample URL is calling the Chart API (*http://chart.apis.google.com/chart*) with the parameters listed in Table 24-1.

Table 24-1. The Chart API utilizes a URL with these parameters

Parameter	Value	Meaning
cht	bvg	The chart type is bar, vertical, grouped.
chxt	y	Show the numbers on the y-axis.
chbh	a	Width/spacing is automatic.
chs	300x225	The size of the chart in pixels.
chco	A2C180	The bar colors in hexadecimal notation.
chd	t:10,50,60,80,40,60,30	The data of the chart, with basic text format (t)
chtt	Vertical+bar+chart	The chart title; a + character indicates a space.

By modifying the parameters, you can generate various graphs. For more information on the types of graphs you can create, check out the API documentation at *http:// code.google.com/apis/chart/index.html*.

Setting the Image.Picture Property to a Chart API

Now you know how to type the sample Chart API URL into a web browser to see the chart that is generated. To get a chart to appear in an app, you'll need to set the `Picture` property of an `Image` component to that same URL. To explore this, do the following:

1. Create a new app with a screen title of "Sample Chart App".

2. Add an Image component with a Width of "Fill parent" and Height of 300.

3. Set the Image.Picture property to the sample URL (*http://chart.apis.google. com/chart?cht=bvg&chxt=y&chbh=a&chs=300x225&chco=A2C180&chtt=Vert ical+bar+chart&chd=t:10,50,60,80,40,60,30*). You can't set the property in the Component Designer, as it only allows you to upload a file. But you can set it in the Blocks Editor, as shown in Figure 24-5, so add a **Screen.Initialize** event handler and set the Image.Picture property there (note that you can't copy and paste on some machines, so you'll have to type out the full URL).

Figure 24-5. When the app starts, it sets the picture to a chart returned from the Chart API URL

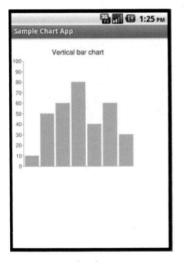

Figure 24-6. The chart in an app

You should see the image in Figure 24-6 on your phone or emulator.

Building a Chart API URL Dynamically

The preceding example shows how you can get a generated chart in your app, but it uses a URL with fixed data (10,50,60,80,40,60,30). Generally, you'll show *dynamic* data in your chart—that is, data stored in your variables. For example, in a game app, you might show the user's previous scores, which are stored in a variable Scores.

To create such a dynamic chart, you must *build* the URL for the Chart API and load your variable data into it. In the sample URL, the data for the chart is fixed and specified in the parameter chd (chd stands for chart data):

chd=t:10,50,60,80,40,60,30

To build your scores chart dynamically, you'll start with the fixed part, chd=t:, and then step through the Scores list, concatenating each score to the text (along with a comma). Figure 24-7 shows a complete solution.

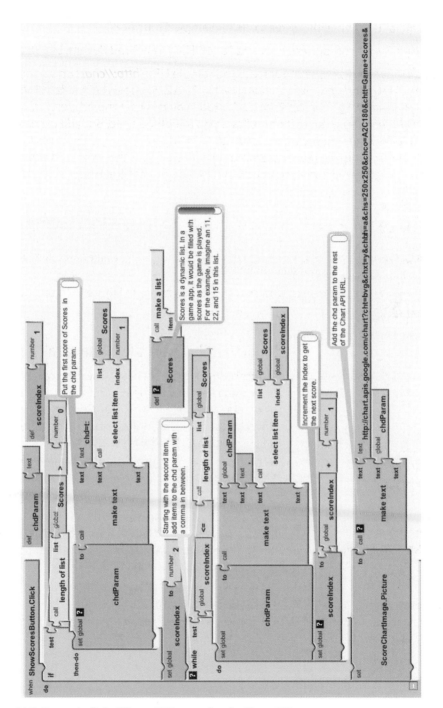

Figure 24-7. Dynamically building a URL to send to the Chart API

Let's examine the blocks more closely, because there's a lot going on in here, much of which we've covered in previous chapters. To understand such code, it's important to envision some real data. So let's assume the user has played three games in this app and that the variable Scores has three items: 11, 22, and 15.

The blocks in Figure 24-8 define a variable chdParam to store the part of the URL that will contain the chd data. The first row of blocks initializes the text of the chdParam from the list of Scores.

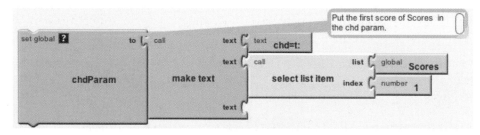

Figure 24-8. Beginning the chd parameter with "chd=t:" and the first score

After these blocks are performed, chdParam will contain chd=t:11, as 11 is the first value of the Scores list.

The next set of blocks, shown in Figure 24-9, adds the rest of the scores to the chdParam.

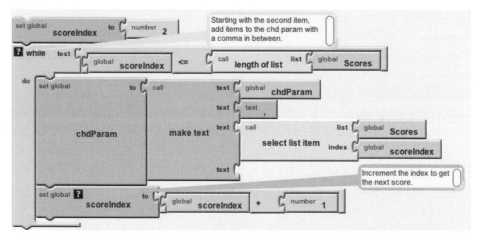

Figure 24-9. Adding the successive scores to the chdParam variable

We use a **while** block in this example instead of a **foreach** because **foreach** only allows you to do the same thing to each item. Here, we want to insert commas before the second item and any items that come after it (but not the first). With **while**, we can put the first item in (Figure 24-8) and then loop starting from the second item, always inserting a comma *before* the item (make sure not to put a space afterward). For more information on **while** and **foreach**, see Chapter 20.

An index is used to keep track of where we are in the Scores list. On each iteration, **make text** adds a comma and the next item in Scores. After these blocks are performed, the chdParam will contain chd=t:11,22,15. We have built the chd parameter dynamically! (And we've also built it so that if more scores are added beyond these first three, it will still work.)

The blocks' last job is to concatenate the chd parameter with the rest of the Chart API URL, as shown in Figure 24-10.

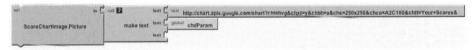

Figure 24-10. Setting the picture to the full URL, including the chd parameter just built

The blocks set the ScoreChartImage.Picture property to this full URL: *http://chart .apis.google.com/chart?cht=bvg&chxt=y&chbh=a&chs=300x225&chco=A2C180&chtt= Game+Scores&chd=t:11,22,15*. Your users will see something similar to what is shown in Figure 24-11.

You could add such a display to any game or app by adding blocks similar to this example. You could also talk to other APIs that generate images and bring those into your app as well. The key is that App Inventor provides a useful connection to the Web through the Image component.

Talking to Web Data APIs

The Google Chart API is a web API that responds to requests by returning a picture. More commonly, APIs will return data that an app can process and use however it wants. The "Amazon at the Bookstore" app in Chapter 13, for instance, returns data in the form of a list of books, with each book including a title, current lowest price, and ISBN.

Figure 24-11. The dynamically generated chart

To talk to an API from an App Inventor app, you don't need to build a URL, as we did with the Chart API example. Instead, you query the API much like you would a web database (Chapter 22): just send your request as the tag to the **TinyWebDB. GetValue** block. The TinyWebDB component takes care of actually generating the URL that you send to the API.

TinyWebDB does not provide access to all APIs, even those that return a standard data format such as RSS. TinyWebDB can only talk to web services for which an App Inventor "wrapper" service, with a particular protocol, has been created. Fortunately, a number of these services have been created already, and more will soon follow. You can find some of these at *http://appinventorapi.com*.

Exploring the Web Interface of an API

In this section, you'll learn how to use TinyWebDB to bring in stock price data from the App Inventor–compliant API at *http://yahoostocks.appspot.com*. If you go to the site, you'll see the web (human) interface of the service pictured in Figure 24-12.

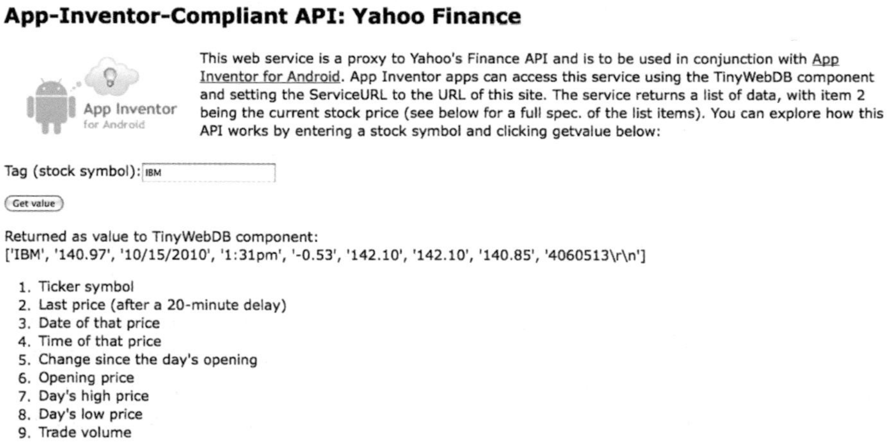

App-Inventor-Compliant API: Yahoo Finance

App Inventor
for Android

This web service is a proxy to Yahoo's Finance API and is to be used in conjunction with App Inventor for Android. App Inventor apps can access this service using the TinyWebDB component and setting the ServiceURL to the URL of this site. The service returns a list of data, with item 2 being the current stock price (see below for a full spec. of the list items). You can explore how this API works by entering a stock symbol and clicking getvalue below:

Tag (stock symbol): IBM

(Get value)

Returned as value to TinyWebDB component:
['IBM', '140.97', '10/15/2010', '1:31pm', '-0.53', '142.10', '142.10', '140.85', '4060513\r\n']

1. Ticker symbol
2. Last price (after a 20-minute delay)
3. Date of that price
4. Time of that price
5. Change since the day's opening
6. Opening price
7. Day's high price
8. Day's low price
9. Trade volume

Figure 24-12. The web interface of the App Inventor–compliant Yahoo! Finance API

Try entering "IBM" or some other stock symbol into the Tag input box. The web page returns current stock information as a list, with each item representing a different piece of information, as described in the numerical listing further down the page.

Note that this web interface isn't meant as a new or interesting way to find stock information; its sole purpose is to allow *programmers* to explore the API for communicating with the underlying machine-to-machine web service.

Accessing the API Through TinyWebDB

The first step in creating an app that talks to the preceding web service is to drag a TinyWebDB component into the Component Designer. There is only one property associated with TinyWebDB, its ServiceURL, shown in Figure 24-13. By default, it is set to a default web database, *http://appinvtinywebdb.appspot.com*. Since we want to instead access the Yahoo! Stocks API, set this property to *http://yahoostocks.appspot .com*, the same URL you entered at the browser address bar earlier to see the web page interface.

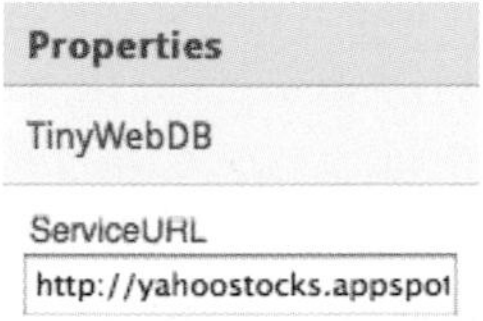

Properties

TinyWebDB

ServiceURL
http://yahoostocks.appspot

Figure 24-13. The ServiceURL is set to http:// yahoostocks.appspot.com

The next step is to make a **TinyWebDB.GetValue** call to request data from the site. You might do this in response to the user entering a stock symbol and clicking a Submit button in your app's UI, or you might do it in the **Screen .Initialize** event to bring in information about a particular stock right when the app is opened. In any case, when you call **GetValue**, you should set the tag to a stock symbol, as illustrated in Figure 24-14, just as you did at the *http:// yahoostocks.appspot.com* website.

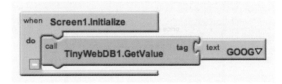

Figure 24-14. Requesting stock information

As we covered in Chapter 10's MakeQuiz app and in Chapter 22's discussion of databases, the TinyWebDB communication is *asynchronous*: your app requests the data with **TinyWebDB.GetValue** and then goes about its business. You must provide a separate event handler, **TinyWebDB.GotValue**, to program the steps the app should take when the data actually comes back from the web service. From our examination of the human interface of *http://yahoostocks.appspot.com*, we learned that the data returned from **GetValue** is a list, with particular list items representing different data about the stock (e.g., item 2 is the latest price).

A client app can use some or all of the data the service provides. For example, if you just wanted to display the current stock price and its change since the day's opening, you might configure blocks as shown in Figure 24-15.

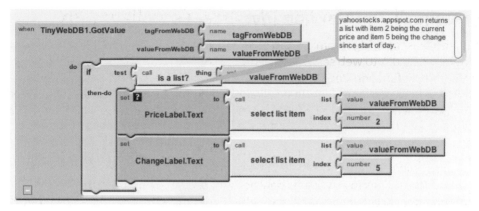

Figure 24-15. Using the GotValue event to process the data that arrives from Yahoo!

If you check the API specification at *http://yahoostocks.appspot.com*, you'll see that the second item in the returned list is indeed the current price, and the fifth item is the change since stocks began trading that day. This app simply extracts those items from what is returned by the API, and shows them in the labels `PriceLabel` and `ChangeLabel`. Figure 24-16 provides a snapshot of the app in action.

Figure 24-16. The Stocks App in action

Creating Your Own App Inventor–Compliant APIs

TinyWebDB is the bridge from an App Inventor app to the Web. It lets App Inventor programmers talk to web services with the simple tag-value protocol inherent in the GetValue function. You send a particular tag as the parameter, and a list or text object is returned as the value. In this way, the App Inventor programmer is shielded from the difficult programming required to *parse* (understand and extract data from) standard data formats like XML or JSON.

The tradeoff is that App Inventor apps can talk only to web services that follow TinyWebDB's expected protocol—it expects data to be returned in a very specific way, and the API has to provide its data accordingly. App Inventor doesn't have a component for accessing an arbitrary web service that returns standard data formats such as XML or JSON. If there isn't an App Inventor–compliant API already available, someone with the ability to write a web program must create it.

In the past, building APIs was difficult because you not only needed to understand the programming and web protocols, but you also needed to set up a server to host your web service, and a database to store the data. Now it's much easier, as you can leverage cloud-computing tools like Google's App Engine and Amazon's Elastic Compute Cloud to immediately deploy the service you create. These platforms will not only host your web service, but they'll also let thousands of users access it before charging you a single dime. As you can imagine, these sites are a great boon to innovation.

Customizing Template Code

Writing your own API may seem daunting, but the good news is that you don't need to start from scratch. You can leverage some provided template code that makes it especially easy to create App Inventor–compliant APIs. The code is written in the Python programming language and uses Google's App Engine. The template provides boilerplate code for getting the data into the form that App Inventor needs, and a function, get_value, that you can customize.

You can download the template code and instructions for deploying it on Google's App Engine servers at *http://appinventorapi.com/using-tinywebdb-to-talk-to-an-api/*. You might notice that the link takes you to the same *appinventorapi.com* site that was used in Chapter 21 to create a custom web database. Building an API is similar, only instead of just storing and retrieving data, you'll call some other service to access the data you need.

To create your own web API, you'll download the template, modify a few key places in the code, and then upload it to App Engine. Within minutes, you will have your own API that can be called using TinyWebDB in an App Inventor app.

Here's the particular code from the template that you'll need to customize (don't worry about the text that comes after the # symbol; like the comments in App Inventor, it just describes what the code following it is doing):

```
def get_value(self, tag):
    #For this simple example, we just return hello:tag, where tag is sent in by client
    value="hello:"+tag
    value = "\""+value+"\""    # add quotes if the value is has multiple words
    if self.request.get('fmt') == "html":
        WriteToWeb(self,tag,value )
    else:
        WriteToPhone(self,tag,value)
```

This code is for a *function* (same as a *procedure* in App Inventor) called get_value, and it's indeed the code that is invoked when your app calls an API with the **TinyWebDB.GetValue** function. tag is a *parameter* of the function and corresponds to the tag you send in the **GetValue** call.

The bolded code is the part you'll change. By default, it simply takes the tag sent in with the request and sends back "hello tag." (In other words, if you call this code with the tag "joe," it returns "hello joe"). It does this by setting the variable value, which is then sent to the function WriteToWeb if the request came from the Web, or WriteToPhone if the request came from a phone.

Note. *Even if you've never looked at Python or other programming code, you may find the sample above somewhat readable from your experience with App Inventor. The "def get_value…" line defines a procedure, the "value=…" lines are setting the variable "value" to something, and the "if.." statements should look familiar. The fundamental concepts are the same, its just text instead of blocks.*

To customize the template, you replace the bold code with any computation you want, as long as that code places something in the variable value. Often, your API will make a call to another API (this is called "wrapping" a call—more specifically, your get_value function will make the call to some other API).

Many APIs are complicated, with hundreds of functions and complex user authorization schemes. Others, however, are quite simple, and you can even find sample code for accessing them on the Web, as you'll see in the next section.

Wrapping the Yahoo! Finance API

The Yahoo! Stocks API for App Inventor used in this chapter was created by modifying the template code above with code found through a simple web search. As the goal was wrapping the Yahoo! Stocks API for use by App Inventor, the developer (Wolber) did a web search for "Python Yahoo Stocks API". From the site http://www.gummy-stuff.org/Yahoo-data.htm, he found that a URL in the form:

http://download.finance.yahoo.com/d/quotes.csv?f=sl1d1t1c1ohgv&e=.cs v&s=IBM

would return a text file with a single comma-separated string of data. The preceding URL returns this text string:

```
"IBM",140.85,"10/15/2010","3:00pm",-0.65,142.10,142.10,140.60,4974553
```

He then found some Python code for accessing the Yahoo! Stocks API at http://www.goldb.org/ystockquote.html. With some quick cutting and pasting and a bit of editing, the App Inventor wrapper API was created by modifying the template in the following manner:

```
def get_value(self, tag):
    # Need to generate a string or list and send it to WriteToPhone/ WriteToWeb
    # Multi-word strings should have quotes in front and back
    # e.g.,
    #    value = "\""+value+"\""
    # call the Yahoo Finance API and get a handle to the file that is returned
    quoteFile=urllib.urlopen("http://download.finance.yahoo.com/d/quotes.csv?f=
    sl1d1t1c1ohgv&e=.csv&s="+tag)
    line = quoteFile.readline()  # there's only one line
    splitlist = line.split(",")  # split the data into a list
    # the data has quotes around the items, so eliminate them
    i=0
    while i<len(splitlist):
        item=splitlist[i]
        splitlist[i]=item.strip('"') # remove " around strings
        i=i+1
    value=splitlist
    if self.request.get('fmt') == "html":
        WriteToWeb(self,tag,value )
    else:
        WriteToPhone(self,tag,value)
```

The bolded code calls the Yahoo! API within the urllib.urlopen function call (this is one way to call APIs from the Python language). The URL has a parameter, f, that specifies the type of stock data you want (this parameter is something like the cryptic parameters required by the Google Chart API). The data returned from Yahoo! is then put into the variable line. The rest of the code splits up the items into a list, removes the quotation marks around each item, and sends the result to the requester (either the web interface or an App Inventor app).

Summary

Most websites and many mobile apps are not standalone entities; they rely on the interoperability of other sites to do their jobs. With App Inventor, you can build games, quizzes, and other standalone apps, but soon enough, you'll encounter issues related to web access. Can I write an app that tells me when the next bus will arrive at my usual stop? Can I write an app that texts a special subset of my Facebook friends? Can I write an app that sends tweets? App Inventor provides two hooks to the Web: (1) you can set the `Image.Picture` property to a URL to bring in a (generated) image, and (2) you can use `TinyWebDB` to access data in a specially designed web API.

App Inventor does not provide arbitrary access to APIs. Instead, the system relies on programmers to create "wrapper" APIs that follow a particular protocol. Once created, these APIs are available to App Inventor app programmers using the same **TinyWebDB.GetValue** scheme they use to access databases. Actually writing APIs is certainly a bigger hurdle than writing apps in App Inventor, but if you're interested in learning how, be sure to check out some Python books and courses (O'Reilly has a few of those!), and you'll be on your way.

Index

About the Authors

David Wolber is a professor of Computer Science at the University of San Francisco and has taught App Inventor since the initial Google pilot program of 2009. The apps created by his students—mostly humanities and business majors with no programming experience—have been chronicled by the *New York Times*, *San Francisco Chronicle*, *Tech Crunch*, *Fortune.CNN.com*, and *Wired* Magazine. Wolber is the author of the advanced tutorials now appearing on the App Inventor site as well as an O'Reilly Breakdown video series on App Inventor.

Harold (Hal) Abelson, a professor of Electrical Engineering and Computer Science at MIT, has a long-standing interest in using computation as a conceptual framework in teaching. He has played a key role in fostering the MIT institutional educational technology initiative and is a founding director of Creative Commons and Public Knowledge. Hal's book, *Turtle Geometry*, written with Andrea diSessa in 1981, presented a computational approach to geometry that has been cited as "the first step in a revolutionary change in the entire teaching/learning process."

Ellen Spertus is an Associate Professor of Computer Science at Mills College—where she has taught with App Inventor—and a Senior Research Scientist at Google, where she was one of the App Inventor developers. She and her work have been written about in *Wired*, *USA Today* (which described her as "a geek with principles"), and the *New York Times* (as one of three "women who might change the face of the computer industry"). In addition to her many technical publications, her writings have appeared in the book *She's Such a Geek: Women Write about Science, Technology, and Other Nerdy Stuff* and in the magazines *Technology Review*, *Chronicle of Higher Education*, *Odyssey: Adventures in Science*, and *Glamour*.

Liz Looney is a senior software engineer at Google, where she helped develop App Inventor and is a member of the Robotics Task Force. She has over 20 years of experience in creating programming tools and holds a bachelor's degree in Computer Science from the University of New Hampshire.

Colophon

Dan Fauxsmith provided quality control for *App Inventor*. Jasmine Perez provided production assistance. The book was composited in Adobe InDesign CS4 by Nancy Kotary.

The heading and text font is Myriad Pro, the code font is TheSansMonoCondensed, and the cover font is Gravur Condensed.